Where There's Smoke

Where There's Smoke

The Environmental Science,
Public Policy, and
Politics of Marijuana

Edited by Char Miller

Foreword by Jared Huffman

University Press of Kansas

Published by the University Press of Kansas (Lawrence, Kansas 66045), which
was organized by the Kansas Board of Regents and is operated and funded by
Emporia State University, Fort Hays State University, Kansas State University,
Pittsburg State University, the University of Kansas, and Wichita State
University.

Library of Congress Cataloging-in-Publication Data

Names: Miller, Char, 1951– editor.
Title: Where there's smoke : the environmental science, public policy, and
politics of marijuana / edited by Char Miller ; foreword by Jared Huffman.
Description: Lawrence, Kansas : University Press of Kansas, [2018] |
Includes bibliographical references and index.
Identifiers: LCCN 2017052561
ISBN 9780700625222 (cloth : alk. paper)
ISBN 9780700625239 (ebook)
Subjects: LCSH: Cannabis—United States. | Marijuana—Government
policy—United States. | Agriculture—Environmental aspects—United States. |
Public lands—Environmental aspects—United States.
Classification: LCC HV5822.C3 W494 2018 | DDC 362.29/50973—dc23
LC record available at https://lccn.loc.gov/2017052561.

British Library Cataloguing-in-Publication Data is available.

Printed in the United States of America

10 9 8 7 6 5 4 3 2 1

The paper used in this publication is recycled and contains 30 percent
postconsumer waste. It is acid free and meets the minimum requirements of
the American National Standard for Permanence of Paper for Printed Library
Materials Z39.48-1992.

Contents

Foreword

Jared Huffman

Not every member of Congress gets to wear a "screamer suit" when conducting site visits in their home districts—though maybe more should. My chance to get buckled into the strangely comfortable, sling-like harness came in August 2014 at the end of a long day witnessing the aftermath of a bust of a significant trespass marijuana growing operation. I was on French Creek in the Shasta-Trinity National Forest, in the Trinity Alps wilderness—one of the most remote corners of the district I represent in Congress, and more than 200 miles north of the San Francisco Bay Area. The day had started out with another unusual experience for a then first-term member of Congress: an early morning departure from Moffett Field aboard a Blackhawk helicopter that carried me those many miles north to a landing zone near the trespass grow, followed by a 2-mile bushwhacking "hike" down rugged, steep terrain.

I arrived a couple hours after the initial raid, as evidence was being gathered and an environmental assessment was getting underway. But even without a formal assessment you could see the damage that this relatively small trespass grow of a few thousand plants had inflicted. To feed an elaborate irrigation system, two springs had been tapped and completely diverted—dewatering small creeks that lead into protected rivers. Many trees had been leveled to open up the canopy so that the rows of marijuana plants could thrive in the warm California sun; fertilizer and rodenticide was spread all over the place. The "camp" was essentially a garbage dump that looked like well over a dozen people had lived there, though only three were seen running away when law enforcement arrived.

This operation was one of many that summer, each the result of a broad collaboration between interested parties, from the California National Guard, to law enforcement and fish and wildlife agencies at all levels, to scientists from UC Davis. In my district, these efforts have also operated in conjunction with the tribal officials and agencies who call the region home: in the case of the raid I witnessed

Figure F.1. *From left*: Mark Higley, Lieutenant (Retired) R. P. Gaske, Warden Tim Bola,
Congressman Jared Huffman, Dr. Mourad Gabriel, and Dr. Greta Wengert.
Courtesy of the Integral Ecology Research Center

it was the Hoopa Valley Tribe who participated. The next year, Operation Yurok
targeted multiple trespass marijuana sites in and around the Yurok Reservation.

Yet each of these successful operations still only addresses a small fraction of
the larger problem. Although shutting down trespass grow sites in these coordi-
nated raids can stop the harm, there aren't dedicated funds to fully clean up and
remediate the affected areas, meaning that wilderness, wildlife, and everything
downstream continue to feel the effects. Just how devastating these sites can be
is captured in the following data about what federal, state, and local authorities
hauled out of only seven sites in Trinity and Humboldt Counties in one season:

- 8,188 pounds of fertilizer
- 104 pounds of rodenticide
- 560 gallons of insecticide
- 68 ounces of concentrated Carbofuran (reconstituting 60–70 gallons)
- 205 bags (50 gallons) of garbage
- 8.5 miles of irrigation line

The diversion and irrigation infrastructure installed at these sites is sophisticated, and they would be impressive engineering achievements if they weren't drawing down scarce water and jeopardizing fish and wildlife, including the salmon and steelhead that have been painstakingly restored to these watersheds. In those seven sites alone, 67.5 million gallons of water were diverted per grow season. That comes to a little more than 200 acre-feet—the unit of measurement that professional water managers use to calculate the amount of water needed to cover an acre of ground to a depth of a foot—across just a few sites, making this very literally a drop in the bucket in the overall picture of illegal grow operations in California.

Although there is a range of estimates of how many plants are grown and harvested in trespass sites like these across the state, it is clear that law enforcement has only discovered a small fraction of these illegal grows that make public and private forests unsafe for working and recreation. Combined, these operations have resulted in threats to public safety, major illegal water diversions, the rampant use of toxic chemicals, the cutting down of trees, the poisoning of endangered wildlife, and the drying-up of streams and the fisheries they support, an accounting that is detailed throughout *Where There's Smoke*.

This book's focus on the complex environmental—and political—impact of illegal and trespass marijuana operations is reflected as well in my deep concern for this issue. I represent California's second congressional district, which runs from the Golden Gate Bridge, just north of San Francisco, up the entire length of the state's magnificent north coast. That means I represent the so-called Emerald Triangle of Mendocino, Humboldt, and Trinity Counties. This is a predominantly rural, heavily forested region that covers about 10,000 square miles in the northwest corner of the state. The Emerald Triangle since the 1960s has been at the center of our nation's marijuana culture and the cannabis economy and is today the national epicenter of illegal marijuana trespass grows.

Like many of my constituents, I supported California's recreational marijuana 2016 ballot measure, Proposition 64, which I am hopeful will begin to shift state policy away from this underground economy. Until that transition is complete, the black- and gray-market industry will continue to do tremendous environmental damage. That's why I authored a bipartisan bill in early 2014 that directed the US Sentencing Commission to impose stiff penalties for people who cause environmental damage—whether clear-cutting trees, poisoning wildlife, or impairing watersheds—while cultivating marijuana on "trespass grows" on private timber- or forestlands or on federal public lands. Despite bipartisan support in the House and Senate, the leadership of the House of Representatives did not take up the bill for consideration, so we had to take another path. Fortunately, we were able to achieve our goals by working directly with the Sentencing Commission, which has now implemented new guidelines to increase the criminal penalties for trespass marijuana grow operations. Needless to say, it is already against the law to grow a controlled substance on federal property, but the Sentencing Commission concluded, in my view correctly, that these trespass operations deserve special attention, for they "interfere with the ability of others to safely access and use the area and also pose or risk a range of other harms, such as harms to the environment."

Because the commission now counts these trespass damages as separate or aggravating offenses, we have been able to give law enforcement and the criminal justice system a new tool to crack down on these destructive activities. Local law enforcement in California is already using the new guidelines to train officers to prioritize and accurately identify threats to the environment. It is not a complete solution by any means—among other things, law enforcement has to catch the perpetrators in the first place, who are often just the front-line laborers and not those calling the shots—but it is a step in the right direction.

However, the way the PLANT Act story played out points to one of the biggest threats to western forests and watersheds: the US Congress, especially under its current management. Even though experts across the West, including those in this very book, have documented the effects of trespass grows on landowners, park visitors, and fish and wildlife, and although we received a generally positive reception to our PLANT Act, we could not get so much as a hearing in the House of Representatives because our bipartisan legislation did not fit the preferred political narrative. Identifying and addressing complicated environmental problems, or even suggesting that fish and downstream users are harmed when the creeks upstream are illegally dewatered, does not fit neatly into the partisan argument that water shortages in the western United States are the fault of the Endangered Species Act.

Will legalization of marijuana change the political dynamics and the on-the-ground consequences of illegal marijuana grows? On the one hand, I've never toured any illegal trespass farms of soybeans or corn, so my inclination is to say legalization will certainly help. On the other, we'll need to move carefully, as suggested in the chapters in this volume on the successful legalization movements in Washington, Oregon, and Colorado. And my expectation is that legalization in California will be at least as complicated as in these bellwether states. There will be industry winners and losers in the transition, certainly, and we cannot just legalize marijuana and automatically expect to reap the environmental benefits.

Make no mistake, trespass marijuana farming is arguably the biggest environmental issue in my district and in many others across the country, bringing acute and watershed-specific impacts to water quality and quantity, jeopardizing important and rare plant and animal species, harming forest health, and endangering the general public and land managers. The more I have learned about these trespass grows' impact—including from the helicopter as I flew over the Shasta-Trinity National Forest, and from the "screamer suit" as I was lifted out—the more convinced I have become that this is a problem that needs a robust public policy response.

As you read *Where There's Smoke* you will understand the extent of my concern, and I hope you will also get a sense of what to watch for at the federal level in this new political era, as well as some of the positive steps we can take at state and local levels to address this growing problem.

Acknowledgments

This project has benefited most from the keen insights of, and occasional nudges from, Kim Hogeland at the University Press of Kansas. She had seen a piece I had written about marijuana's impact on the national forests and other public lands and thought that the subject required a longer and more detailed exploration: this anthology is a direct outgrowth of her initial idea. Ever since, she has been a wise critic and supportive voice—an ideal editor!

Equally ideal have been the many contributors to this project. Their fields of study range across the academic disciplines and also include policy makers, law enforcement officers, and activists: their varied perspectives have given this volume an energy and timeliness it otherwise would not have had. This dynamic array of voices and concerns captured the imagination of the anonymous readers who vetted the book proposal and then the final manuscript. In the process, they offered some telling suggestions, making the whole a more compelling contribution to the close analysis of marijuana's impact on the land and in politics. I am grateful to them all, gratitude that extends to artist Mike Flugennock and various organizations and entities who have given us permission to use images to illustrate the various chapters. As always, a shout-out to my remarkable colleagues at the Claremont Colleges Library and across the Claremont Consortium, who make this community such a stellar environment in which to teach, research, and write.

Introduction

The Sobreanes Fire, which blew up on July 22, 2016, was a monster. A wind-driven inferno, it roared across more than 70,000 acres of Garrapata State Park and the adjoining Los Padres National Forest on the Central Coast of California. Burning through redwood, pine, and chaparral, it killed one firefighter, destroyed dozens of homes, and forced the evacuation of more than 300 people living in remote canyons and rugged mountains. Among those fleeing for their lives were at least eleven men who had been managing an unknown number of trespass marijuana grows in rough backcountry. The county deputies who rescued these men could not arrest them because the fire had consumed the evidence; one crew of pot growers admitted that they had been tending 900 plants, with an estimated street value of $1 million. Neither firefighters nor law enforcement officers were surprised at the size of the operation or the number of people involved in its management. "We have them all over," said Sergeant Kathy Palazzolo of the Monterey County Sheriff's Department. They are located "all throughout the county, in the national forest, on private property, in riverbeds, we find them all over" (AP/CBS News 2016).

Beginning in late winter, these men—and those like them throughout the state and other major growing areas across the country—had hiked over isolated hills, up through ravines, and picked their way along boulder-strewn creek beds in search of relatively flat ground with access to even a thin trickle of water. Once they had selected a site, they would have dropped their bulky backpacks weighed down with tools, food, poison, plastic piping, and tents, and begun clearing the ground with hoes, shovels, and chainsaws. As they opened up the canopy, leaving just enough shade to camouflage their activities from aerial surveillance, they would have sprayed heavy amounts of herbicides to stop plants, shrubs, and trees from resprouting and to suppress invasive plants from gaining a toehold. Usually undocumented and toiling under the watchful eye of the drug cartels for whom they are often forced to work, these laborers would have laid out waterlines, built check dams, and prepared the soil before planting row upon row of cannabis seeds. Within weeks, as the earth and air warmed, the marijuana would have grown quickly.

The drug cartels running these illegal grows have been targeting the US public lands generally, but their special target has been the Golden State's 20 million acres of national forests. The cartels have targeted these forests, along with state, tribal, and county lands, in large part because they are often so remote. The combined impact that these illegal grows have had on these diverse terrains has been devastating, too. "Marijuana growing on public lands has been going on for 30-plus years, but they have just expanded dramatically," Daryl Rush, a special agent in the Forest Service's Law Enforcement and Investigations Unit, has pointed out. "Every forest is impacted, and the majority of our workload is on marijuana investigations on the forest" (Rush 2014).

The Los Padres National Forest has been among the most battered. In 2013 law enforcement teams discovered forty-seven trespass grows, uprooted 181,139 marijuana plants (the most in the state that year), and removed the following material:

- Infrastructure: 19,710 pounds
- Restricted poisons: 138 ounces
- Fertilizer: 4,595 pounds
- Common pesticides: 12 gallons
- Waterlines: 29,599 feet (5.6 miles)
- 20-pound propane bottles: 48
- 16-ounce propane bottles: 54
- Car batteries: 7
- Dams/reservoirs: 12

That same summer, strike forces were active in Southern California: in the Cleveland National Forest north and east of San Diego they eradicated nine grows, yielding 16,579 plants. In the Angeles National Forest, which includes most of the San Gabriel Mountains framing the northern skyline of Los Angeles, they spotted twenty-seven sites, blooming with a total of 76,400 plants. On twenty-one sites located in the San Bernardino Mountains, home to the eponymous national forest, they destroyed 114,095 plants. To the north, other hard-hit forests included the Sequoia (113,737 plants), Shasta-Trinity (158,261), Sierra (96,052), and Plumas (74,009).

The reality is much worse than the data suggests. Given the difficulty in detecting these illegal sites, hidden by foliage and accessible only by climbing up some of the nation's most difficult terrain, law enforcement officers can make but a small dent in growing operations statewide. Indeed, in 2012 the Forest Service reported that more than 83 percent of the 1,048,768 plants eradicated from the entire US National Forest system had been found in California, making it the national epicenter.

A stark reminder of that sobering reality, and its intractable nature, is captured in the daunting statistics that the California Department of Fish and Wildlife compiled in early August 2016 from the ninety-one missions its personnel conducted in the first seven months of that year (Nores 2016):

- 100 guns seized
- 453,000 marijuana plants eradicated
- 2,494 pounds of processed marijuana destroyed
- 87,185 pounds of grow-site trash/waste removed
- 260,640 feet (49 miles) of black irrigation water-diverting pipe pulled out
- 7,235 pounds of fertilizers removed
- 217 containers of pesticides removed
- 15 containers of banned toxic poisons removed as hazmat
- 68 dams and water diversions torn down and waterways restored

This mid-year data represented a 30 percent increase over August 2015 figures and was in good measure a result of the generous 2015–2016 winter rains that Northern California enjoyed after years of drought. Any effort to calculate the combined impact of the hazardous materials—all the canisters, boxes, bags, and bottles containing pesticides, herbicides, and rodenticides—must begin with this reflection: that Rachel Carson would be appalled by this wickedly toxic brew. In *Silent Spring* (1962), in language that is as lyrical as it is lacerating, she exposed the deleterious impact of toxins in watersheds and bloodstreams. She wondered how it came to be that these lethal substances were sprayed, dusted, and dumped into nature, only to work their way inevitably, irrevocably through water, air, and food into flora and fauna, including humans. "Who has made the decision that sets in motion these chains of poisonings, this ever-widening wave of death that spreads out, like ripples when a pebble is dropped into a still pond?" (Carson 1962, 127). Carson's chilling question came with another, every bit as unsettling: "Who has decided—who has the right to decide—for the countless legions of people who were not consulted that the supreme value is a world without insects, even though it is also a sterile world ungraced by the curving wing of a bird in flight?" (ibid.).

A half-century later, Carson's angered queries would be as blunt, knowing that for all the impact her book has had—and historians credit it with the banning of DDT in the United States and propelling such critical environmental legislation as the Clean Water Act into law—its dire warnings have not been fully heeded

(Souder 2013). Consider, for instance, the startling degree to which rodenticides, or rat poisons, have penetrated Northern California's biota. Marijuana growers are scattering rodenticide pellets by the shovelful around their clandestine plantations, laying it down like berms around the high-value cash crop itself, in thick lines paralleling irrigation infrastructure, and, as if a stout fence, mounding it around the lean-tos, tents, and shacks where the "farmers" rest their weary heads.

Consider, too, the growers' extensive use of Furadan and Metaphos. The former is an endrocrine disruptor and the latter is a cholinesterase inhibitor; each is highly toxic to insects, birds, and mammals (humans included) and for that reason the European Union and the United States have banned their use. But during a summer 2016 raid on a trespass grow in a state park located within the San Joaquin River watershed, a law enforcement team found ample evidence that growers had liberally deployed these toxins. Noting that these toxicants do not just kill "rodents, small game, and big game like bears, deer, [and] mountain lions," one officer on the scene told reporters that "pretty much anything that ingests it or even breathes it can die" (KTVU 2016). So lethal are Furadan and Metaphos that even fish and other marine life are known to have died when these poisons have leached into water sources.

Follow, then, the "elixirs of death," as Carson (1962, 15) styled them. Animals drawn to the rough camps in search of food or water can consume any number of these super toxins or eat other animals that have done so. Because the drug cartels are using second-generation rodenticides—upgrades that manufacturers developed precisely because some species have become resistant to earlier versions of the poison—this new anticoagulant is so powerful that if ingested at high enough levels it can lead to death by bleeding out. So prevalent has rodenticide use become that wildlife biologists have launched scientific investigations of its pathway through various ecosystems. Recently, researchers have identified high concentrations of these toxicants in more than twenty-five species, including falcons, owls, raccoons, and bobcats, and such endangered species as the San Joaquin kit fox and the Pacific fisher: there is "no grey area when it comes to this aspect of illegal marijuana grows," restoration experts have confirmed; "the wildlife is killed, plain and simple. Traps are set, deer, bear, and grey squirrels are poached, and mice are poisoned." Based on the tools that have been collected and the carcasses that have been identified, "the growers are engaged in a war with the natural world for the resources they require to continue their production of marijuana" (Central Valley California HIDTA 2010). The critical biodiversity that is sustained in the Los Padres National Forest, among others, as well as tribal lands, state parks, and county open spaces, are becoming lethal to the wildlife that call these landscapes home.

This lethality is heightened by the tremendous amount of water that these illegal grows consume. A 2015 study centered in northwestern California of the impact of "dewatering" at the watershed scale, made possible by aerial imagery and field-based research, concluded that the drawdown has had profound implications. Some of the study areas located in "smaller headwater tributaries" indicated that "marijuana cultivation may be completely dewatering streams, and for the larger fish-bearing streams downslope, the flow diversions are substantial and likely contribute to accelerated summer intermittence and higher stream temperatures." The larger implications of these intense demands for water in the Northern California region known as the Emerald Triangle are clear: "The existing level of marijuana cultivation in many northern California watersheds [is] unsustainable and [is] likely contributing to the decline of sensitive aquatic species in the region. Given the specter of climate change—[which] induced more severe and prolonged droughts and diminished summer stream flows in the region, continued diversions at a rate necessary to support the current scale of marijuana cultivation in northern California could be catastrophic for aquatic species" (Bauer et al. 2015, 20).

Less directly catastrophic perhaps, but no less real, are the threats that well-armed trespass growers pose to hikers and rangers. The number of weapons confiscated from the sites, including high-powered assault rifles, sawed-off shotguns, and semiautomatic pistols, along with anecdotes of gun-toting pot growers menacing hikers who stumble on the grows, has spiked in recent years. This dangerous situation is creating a chill factor, challenging rangers' ability to patrol and protect. As one land manager observed: "Visitor safety is our number-one priority, but I worry about our rangers," too, because on "99 percent of the grows I go into I find weapons" (quoted in Chapter 5 of this volume). One understandable strategy has been to limit people's access to the great outdoors, yet that necessarily undercuts one of these lands' key purposes: offering splendid recreational opportunities to millions of Americans each year.

That said, the important, if seemingly ad hoc, campaigns to root out illegal marijuana grows will not fully secure an increase in safety. There are simply too many illegal grows, and they are too difficult to locate, to ensure their complete eradication. Besides, the demand for marijuana and the cash to be made from it is so great that drug cartels have little incentive to alter their business model. It is unlikely that they will be deterred by the decision the US Sentencing Commission reached in 2014 to strengthen sentencing guidelines for those caught on these trespass grows; their charges may now include environmental damage, but those who pay the price for the despoliation are not those who profit the most from it.

To disrupt growers' impact on watersheds, hillsides, and woodlands may require either a massive infusion of fiscal and human resources to combat this problem or a political solution like Alaska, California, Colorado, Maine, Massachusetts, Nevada, Oregon, and Washington, along with the District of Columbia, reached when they legalized recreational use of marijuana. One ramification of their citizens' decision in support of legalization could be the regeneration of their national forests and other public land that in the past contained numerous illegal marijuana sites. For some law enforcement officials, the question about legalization's putative import may miss the point: "Whatever happens [with legalization]," one of them reported, "we've got a job to do. So legalization isn't a question for us. You're not allowed to grow corn or potatoes in national parks, so we would go after those grows too" (quoted in Chapter 5). Other officers, such as John Nores (see Chapter 6), are skeptical that legalization will alter the economics driving the drug cartels' operations to such an extent that they will pack up and move out of California.

Other dimensions of marijuana's impact on the land and in the political arena can be deciphered, and they serve as the framing devices for *Where There's Smoke: The Environmental Science, Public Policy, and Politics of Marijuana*. This interdisciplinary anthology, the first of its kind, draws on the insights of scientists, researchers, and activists, and it ranges across the humanities, natural sciences, and social sciences to explore the troubling environmental consequences of illegal marijuana production on public, private, and tribal lands. This array of topics is essential as well to any examination of the related emergence of a robust and nationwide legalization movement for medical and recreational use of marijuana. Part One: Growing Problems consists of five chapters that in different ways assess a series of environmental, social, and scientific concerns emanating from trespass grows like those the Sobreanes Fire torched in 2016. Anthony Silvaggio opens the discussion by probing the hitherto unexamined environmental consequences of the long-standing federal prohibition of marijuana, notably its classification as a Schedule 1 drug, the most restrictive level with the highest level of criminal punishment; for comparison, cocaine and methamphetamine are classified under the less restrictive Schedule 2. As such, marijuana has been a central focus of the so-called War on Drugs that began in the Nixon administration and escalated during the Regan administration. Silvaggio details the shifts in federal drug policy, demonstrates the influence enforcement funds have had on interdiction campaigns and the criminal-justice system, and establishes (as do other contributors) that one of the war's perverse outcomes has been to shift marijuana production from Mexico to the United States. To that end, Silvaggio is particularly interested in another unanticipated consequence of the federal government's punitive approach to marijuana. "Prohibition exacerbates environmental harms," he writes, by incentivizing "cannabis cultivators to set up environmentally damaging grow sites on public and private lands with little regard for the natural environment." That being the case, Silvaggio predicts that "state legalization efforts will have far less influence in reining in the ecologically unsustainable practices of cannabis agriculture than will putting an end to federal prohibition." It is too early to tell if his prediction will come true, but there is no question that the ecological damage these illegal grows are generating is substantial or that the Nixonian War on Drugs played a formative role in these damages. Tabulating some of the costs are three interrelated chapters drawn from the collaborative research team comprising Mourad Gabriel, J. Mark Higley, Craig Thompson, and Greta Wengert. They assess the broad spectrum of effects on land and water, flora, and fauna with Rachel Carson–like focus on landscape-scale depredations. Noting that "the diversity, spatial extent, and cumulative effects of marijuana cultivation on public lands have the potential to be monumental and formidable," and using the Pacific fisher as a marker of one such species that has borne the brunt of these effects, they locate these and other challenges as they are manifest on the Hoopa Reservation in Northern California. At stake is not just the health of the environment but also the millennia-long interactions among the tribe and the land and the resources that have long sustained them—physically and spiritually. Like the Hupa people, federal land managers are trying to figure out how to steward the resources under their care in a fraught context in which legal and illegal uses and users are interacting on the same landscape. To understand how some of these managers are responding to this tangled and often-dangerous state of affairs, Jeff Rose, Matthew T. J. Brownlee, and Kelly S. Bricker conducted a series of interviews with Bureau of Land Management and US Forest Service personnel about their experiences. Their interviewees offer a revealing perspective on inter- and intra-agency frustrations, the growing costs of eradication in terms of time and money, the concerns among federal employees that are magnified by knowing that the marijuana cartels outgun them in a literal and figurative sense, and the need to prevent resource degradation without access to all the tools or budget to do so. Illegal marijuana growing on public lands, many of the interviewees affirm, complicates an already very complicated job.

Adding complexity to these on-the-ground efforts is the thorny legal environment, which is the subject of Part Two: Downwind Consequences. It begins with John Nores Jr.'s eyewitness account of an interdiction he and his strike team from the California Department of Fish and Wildlife conducted in March 2012 near Morgan Hill in southern San Jose County. In addition to giving readers an up-close understanding of such an operation's logistics, tactics, and anxieties, not least the important role that K9 recon scouts play in tracking and apprehending growers, Nores identifies a critical element of the agency's mission. In addition to its traditional goals of "suspect apprehension and plant eradication" in 2012 the department added a third prong—"reclamation (the restoration of water quality and the rectification of environmental damages done throughout these cultivation sites)," an approach that other state and federal agencies have since adopted. What happens to the individuals that Nores and his colleagues arrest? Picking up that trail is Amos Irwin, whose chapter offers a focused reading of court records and draws from a series of interviews with attorneys, law enforcement officials, and incarcerated growers. Case studies of two such men and their experiences with the US court system illuminate the larger processes at work and the pressures in play. The cartels employ undocumented individuals because their illegal status makes them more vulnerable ("Marijuana Cultivation on US Public Lands" 2011). Their vulnerability makes it easier to lure them into this difficult work on false pretenses—and then compel them to live on site for the entire growing season, cutting down on the chances that law enforcement will detect them and the trespass grows they manage (and not incidentally making it hard for those arrested to offer much useful information to the police). These and other revelations, Irwin argues, indicate that those running these illegal grows are reacting to the increased law-enforcement crackdown by changing up their approach and thereby exacerbating "the social, environmental, and economic consequences of marijuana production." One of these ramifications is the spread of trespass grows into new areas. Although California and Oregon have long been at the heart of illegal production, beginning in the 1980s those southern states through which the Appalachians run have witnessed an uptick in illegal grows. Until the first decade of the twenty-first century, most of these were local operations; starting in 2007, law enforcement in Kentucky, Tennessee, Virginia, West Virginia, and North Carolina reported that they were apprehending Spanish-speaking laborers on trespass grows. Hawes Spencer and Char Miller examine this particular regional development, setting it within the wider context of the War on Drugs and establishing some of the implications this has had for the expansion of the clandestine industry, the hijacked labor essential to its operations, and the well-watered and remote high-country regions of the South.

It is not yet clear whether the legalization of marijuana will undercut the illegal industry that has grown up around the drug's production and distribution, and thus whether it will lessen the environmental damage associated with trespass grows. Anthony Silvaggio, for one, doubts that there will be a direct correlation as long as marijuana remains classified as a Schedule 1 drug; Amos Irwin and some of his interlocutors are more optimistic. Testing that hypothesis requires baseline data, and in this case, that data comes from those political jurisdictions that have legalized marijuana—for medical and/or recreational use. Setting that background are the chapters in Part Three: Regional Varieties, which examine the oft-rocky paths to legalization that the states of Colorado and Oregon, as well as the District of Columbia, have pursued. Each of the histories narrated here depends on local political conditions. So argues Courtenay Daum about Colorado's successful campaign and Anthony Johnson about Oregon's—their advocates built their coalitions, and the rhetoric that their proponents employed, in response to their state's distinct political cultures. The same was true of the District of

Columbia, note Karen August and Char Miller, for among the district's unique characteristics that doubles as a distinct disadvantage is the unchecked congressional oversight of its affairs, small and large. As for California, which legalized recreational marijuana use in November 2016, Amanda Reiman observes that while its pathbreaking 1998 medical marijuana initiative set off a round of similar campaign—and for reasons peculiar to the Golden State—it took marijuana advocates there eighteen years to secure voter approval of a proposition legalizing recreational use. In 2010 Proposition 19 lost, 53.5 percent to 46.5 percent, but the much-better-funded Proposition 64 on the November 2016 ballot reversed those percentages. Yet as different as are these jurisdictional politics, and as complicated as their individual routes to success have been, their initiatives were similar in some important respects. Each had to run multiple campaigns before it persuaded enough voters to support legalization; each did so by launching initial efforts to legalize medical marijuana and then subsequently attempted to secure sanction for recreational use. Each benefited from a slow but steady evolution in local and national public opinion in support for legalization. This lengthy process has had considerable backing from national marijuana reform organizations, among them the aptly named NORML (National Organization for the Reform of Marijuana Laws) and the Marijuana Policy Project. These entities have helped fund the various campaigns, provided staff and legal support, and served as clearinghouses for legalization reformers across the country seeking advice on how best to craft legislative language and develop winning political tactics, an indispensable contribution. In the end, though, it was up to the homegrown movement to determine the timing of a campaign, set its agenda, and do the necessary legwork to achieve victory: as they detail these exact processes, these chapters offer textbook examples of democracy in action.

Embedded in the Democratic Party's 2016 national platform is an example of how these homegrown state policies have come to define some national perspectives. Among the many planks that constitute this dense document is one devoted to the legalization of marijuana. The party's plank argues that marijuana should be removed from the list of Schedule 1 federally controlled substances so that it might be more appropriately regulated; the Democratic Party also committed itself to supporting "policies that will allow more research to be done on marijuana, as well as reforming our laws to allow legal marijuana businesses to exist without uncertainty" (Democratic Party Platform 2016, 16). As part of its rejection of the War on Drugs, the platform also included language that recognized that "our current marijuana laws have had an unacceptable disparate impact, with arrest rates for marijuana possession among African-Americans far outstripping arrest rates among whites despite similar usage rates." This link between the reforming of marijuana laws and the correcting of a social injustice was a key feature in the successful legalization campaigns in Washington state (Initiative 502: 2012; Jensen and Roussell 2016) and the District of Columbia (Initiative 71: 2014). Their success led the Democratic National Committee to acknowledge that the most innovative and far-reaching policy changes were coming from the local level, not from inside the Beltway. "We believe that the states should be laboratories of democracy on the issue of marijuana, and those states that want to decriminalize marijuana should be able to do so" (Democratic Party Platform 2016, 16). In adopting a federalist position—states' rights trumped federal law—the Democratic Party transformed cannabis, once reviled for its putative power to unleash "reefer madness" upon the nation, into a social good, a democratizing force.

WORKS CITED

AP/CBS News. 2016. "Firefighters Struggle to Get Upper Hand on Massive Calif. Wildfire." July 28. http://www.cbsnews.com/news/firefighters-struggle-to-get-upper-hand-on-massive-california-wildfire.

Bauer, S., J. Olson, A. Cockrill, M. van Hattem, L. Miller, M. Tauzer, et al. 2015. "Impacts of Surface Water Diversions for Marijuana Cultivation on Aquatic Habitat in Four Northwestern California Watersheds." *PLOS ONE* 10(3): e0120016. doi:10.1371/journal.pone.0120016.

Carson, R. 1962. *Silent Spring.* Boston: Houghton Mifflin.

Central Valley California HIDTA. 2010. "Marijuana Production: The Cause and Effect." December 10.

Democratic Party Platform. 2016. https://www.demconvention.com/platform.

Jensen, E. L., and A. Roussell. 2016. "Field Observations of the Developing Recreational Cannabis Economy in Washington State." *International Journal of Drug Policy* 33: 96–101. http://dx.doi.org/10.1016/j.drugpo.2016.02.023.

KTVU. 2016. "Investigators Target Toxic Poisons Used to Foster Illegal Marijuana Growth." May 20. http://www.ktvu.com/news/143494177-story.

"Marijuana Cultivation on US Public Lands." 2011. US Senate Caucus on International Narcotics Control, 112th Congress, First Session. December 7. https://www.hsdl.org/?view&did=695923.

Nores, John. 2016. Email communication to Char Miller. July 21. In author's possession.

Rush, D. 2014. Interview in "Marijuana Grows and Restoration," USDA Forest Service video. https://www.youtube.com/watch?v=IFNe_KZhPZw.

Souder, W. 2013. *On a Farther Shore: The Life and Legacy of Rachel Carson.* New York: Broadway Books.

PART ONE

Growing Problems

CHAPTER 1

Cannabis Agriculture in California

The Environmental Consequences of Prohibition

Anthony Silvaggio

For the past five decades the United States has led the global War on Drugs to stop the production, supply, and consumption of illicit substances. Drug policy scholars have noted that while hundreds of billions of dollars have been spent on this effort and hundreds of thousands of men and women have been incarcerated, drug production, distribution, and consumption have continued to rise (Miron 2010). Contradicting its intended effect, drug use and abuse have gone up, drug-related violence has increased, profits in illicit drug trade have risen, and drug trafficking organizations have continued to dominate the international landscape (Martin 2013). Although many of these "unintended" consequences associated with the prohibitionist drug war have been well studied, damage to the environment has not.

Since 2010 the environmental consequences of the War on Drugs have been felt most severely in the cannabis-producing region of Northern California known as the Emerald Triangle.[1] Whereas the presumed benefit of cannabis prohibition has been to deter production, domestic production has risen despite increased criminal penalties and eradication efforts, with unregulated production in California at an all-time high (Northern California High Intensity Drug Traffic Area Drug Market Analysis 2012). The first in the country to legalize medical cannabis (1996), California, particularly the northern part, is now the center of cannabis culture and agriculture, home to thousands of outdoor industrial cannabis farms and thousands more indoor enterprises. With estimates that range from $7 billion to $31 billion annually, cannabis agriculture dominates the landscape (Gettman 2006; Starrs and Goin 2010). Brought to the area by the countercultural "back to the land" movement in the late 1960s, the unregulated cannabis industry has grown to one that has significant ecological impacts on forests, wildlife, and water.

The environmental consequences of unregulated cannabis agriculture on this scale are extensive, with damages originating on private lands often times impacting public lands resources downstream.[2] These impacts include habitat loss and fragmentation from illegal logging and clearing of the land, illegal water diversions and dewatering of streams, and illegal road building and grading, as well as fertilizer, pesticide, fungicide, and fossil fuel runoff into waterways. The extraction of water for cannabis cultivation in some watersheds has had a lethal effect on federally listed salmon, steelhead trout, and salamander populations, virtually dewatering streams and collapsing aquatic ecosystems on both public and private lands (Bauer et al. 2015). In addition to these impacts, pesticide poisoning of terrestrial wildlife with rodenticides and illegal wildlife poaching are commonplace on trespass grows located on public lands and private timberlands (Gabriel et al. 2012).[3] Pollution from runoff and pesticide use more than often ends up in creeks, lakes, and rivers that supply water for rural and tribal communities. Most trespass grows also suffer from impacts of sustained human habitation, with months' worth of trash, human waste, and forest clearing. Miles of water lines, fertilizers, pesticides, fungicides, and other agricultural equipment are commonly left behind on public lands after harvest. Though some of these environmental impacts have been documented by federal, state, and county agencies, little is known about the extent to which they have impacted other fish and wildlife. With over 2 million plants eradicated in 2,000 outdoor cannabis grow sites in 2014 alone, illicit cannabis agriculture has become Northern California's primary environmental problem (DEA Domestic Cannabis Eradication/Suppression Statistics 2015).

To date, scholarly research on cannabis has largely been devoted to examining issues related to substance abuse (Keith et al. 2015), drug markets (Caulkins and Pacula 2016), public policy (Corva 2014), and public safety (Shepard and Blackley 2007), concentrating mostly on questions of consumption (Clements and Zhau 2009), public perceptions of cannabis legalization (Miron 2012; Nixon 2013), criminal sentencing (Austin 2005), and, more recently, medical cannabis (Chapkis and Webb 2008; Reiman 2009). Although natural resource managers have spearheaded recent efforts to document the specific impacts on wildlife (Gabriel et al. 2012), fish (Bauer et al. 2015), and the atmosphere (Mills 2012), there is little peer-reviewed research on the environmental impacts associated with cannabis cultivation.

In the following pages I analyze the federal government's attempts to alleviate California's ever-expanding cannabis problem, focusing on what heretofore has been neglected: the environmental consequences of the interaction between cannabis cultivators and the supply-side eradication efforts of the drug war. More specifically, I explore the role that cannabis prohibition and policing, as employed by state and federal authorities, has played in determining the range of agricultural practices available to cannabis growers.[4] Drawing on participant observation; ethnographic interviews with law enforcement, natural resource managers, environmentalists, cannabis cultivators, and legalization advocates; and secondary sources, this analysis focuses on understanding how structural changes in drug policy and enforcement—particularly around the policing of cannabis agriculture—have facilitated and rewarded poor environmental practices in the cannabis industry. Contrary to the claims of prohibitionist drug warriors, I argue that it is not simply unscrupulous cannabis growers but the drug war policies themselves that have exacerbated environmental devastation on public and private lands.

The first part of this chapter describes the sociohistorical context in which the cannabis industry emerged in northwestern California as it relates to cannabis prohibition and the evolution of cannabis cultivation practices. To develop my argument, I examine the impact of policy regimes on cannabis agriculture, using this analytic lens to help identify how shifts in drug policy and policing determined the choices available to cannabis cultivators, encouraging ecologically destructive practices on public, tribal, and private lands. I delineate four distinct policy regimes relevant to understanding the culture and practice of cannabis agriculture as it relates to the environment. These periods are: 1. Industry Emergence (1970–1983); 2. Militarization of Eradication (1983–1996); 3. The Gray Market (1996–2012); and 4. Legalization (2012–2016). The intensity of environmental impacts associated with each of these periods shows that the range of available environmentally sustainable agricultural practices diminished over time, a consequence of both criminalization and lack of meaningful environmental regulation. Throughout, I problematize these adverse environmental impacts not as inherent to cannabis agriculture but as the unintended consequences of prohibition. In the last section I examine the most recent changes in cannabis legislation and prohibition policing and what the ecological implications may be going forward.

INDUSTRY EMERGENCE (1970–1983)

Cannabis production in the Emerald Triangle began in the late 1960s and early 1970s during the countercultural revolution, when young, white, well-educated urbanites left mainstream society in pursuit of alternative ways of living (Anders 1990). They settled in the remote rural counties of Northern California where land, devastated by decades of industrial mining, logging, and fishing, was abundant and cheap. These new settlers brought with them an insatiable appetite for simplicity, freedom, community self-reliance, and closeness to nature. This rebellious subculture, with their distrust of authority and the mainstream concepts of "legality," also shared an affinity with cannabis and began planting it in their gardens. Cannabis cultivation at this time was primarily for personal consumption and viewed by these new immigrants as a form of political protest. The cultivation of this illicit plant was facilitated by the geographic isolation of the region, with its rugged, sparsely populated remote valleys, that made cultivation difficult to detect. This isolation, coupled with a culture that distrusted authority, made ideal conditions for a small cannabis cottage industry to develop in the region.

The domestic cannabis industry emerged at a time when the federal government's role in drug eradication efforts was expanding. In 1971 Republican president Richard Nixon officially declared the War on Drugs, dramatically increasing federal resources to control the production, distribution, and use of illicit drugs. Two years later he created the Drug Enforcement Administration to lead the national effort in fighting the drug war. In addition to successfully expanding the federal government's activities in drug eradication, Nixon led a successful effort to classify cannabis as a Schedule 1 narcotic, the most restrictive category of drugs, defined as having no accepted medical use and a high potential for abuse. At the time, there was little domestic production of cannabis—most of the cannabis consumed in the United States was of low quality and sourced from Mexico. To stem the flow of cannabis, Nixon spent hundreds of millions of dollars on massive interdiction efforts in Mexico. This increased the risk of arrest and detection by law enforcement interventions at the US-Mexico border and reduced the availability of imported cannabis in the consumer markets of the United States. As a result, production of cannabis was displaced, with the industry reorienting the supply chain to Colombia and other locations (Corva 2014). In an example of the "balloon effect," production was not eliminated but rather simply shifted to another region that expanded production to meet demand. Another eradication effort made by Nixon was the controversial paraquat program, a US-sponsored cannabis eradication program that involved spraying of the herbicide paraquat on cannabis fields in both Mexico and the United States (Jones 1985; Potter et al. 1990). Proponents of the prohibition-by-herbicide program went as far as launching a publicity campaign warning the public of the health risks associated with smoking "paraquat pot" (Riding 1978). The administration hoped that awareness of the herbicide program would deter cannabis consumption in the United States. In the end, Nixon achieved his goal of curtailing the supply of Mexican cannabis from coming into the country but failed to reduce consumption and overall production.

The increased cannabis policing in the 1970s and 1980s appears to have inadvertently prompted two adaptions in the cannabis industry domestically. First, domestic production was encouraged by these law enforcement interventions because the paraquat program acted as a type of farm aid for California, stimulating cannabis agriculture in places like the Emerald Triangle (Raphael 1985; Segal 1986). Domestic cannabis production became an adaptive and innovative strategy triggered by cannabis consumers who wanted paraquat-free cannabis. This growth in public awareness about the threat of herbicide contamination also helped to spur on innovations in cannabis horticulture, with cannabis pioneers from the Emerald Triangle traveling to places like Afghanistan and Southeast Asia to bring back new strains of cannabis. This helped to increase the plant diversity and potency of sinsemilla grown in California.[5] In the end, rather than restrict the supply of cannabis, the enforcement actions over the border helped to shift the production to California. Not surprisingly, prohibition policing also pushed the price of cannabis higher, increasing the economic incentive for growing it. As a result of the eradication efforts and new agricultural practices, the wholesale price of cannabis rose dramatically, to an estimated $2,000 a pound by 1980 (Corva 2014). This triggered the first "Green Rush," a slow migration of people to Northern California who came for the sole purpose of making money in the cannabis industry.[6]

Outside of government-sanctioned herbicide spraying, there were few unintended environmental consequences of prohibition policing during the early days of domestic cultivation. Cannabis policing during the 1970s was almost nonexistent, with few local and state resources devoted to cannabis eradication, posing little risk to cannabis homesteaders. Though some cannabis cultivation did take place on public lands and timberlands, trespass grows were small and had little environmental impact.[7] As a result, there were few documented environmental impacts from this emerging industry as the agricultural practices of these early settlers reflected their ecological values. With domestic eradication a low priority, growers were able to cultivate cannabis on their homesteads with little risk of arrest.

MILITARIZATION OF ERADICATION (1983–1996)

The policing practices of the 1970s that facilitated the rapid growth of cannabis agriculture in the Emerald Triangle and the horticultural innovations advanced by cultivators helped to establish a cottage industry in the region, and by the beginning of the 1980s cannabis became a leading export commodity in the region, fetching up to $2,000 a pound. The election of Ronald Reagan as president in 1980, however, signaled another powerful shift in prohibition policing and with it the intensification of cannabis agriculture in the region. Following the path of

Nixon, Reagan renewed the eradication effort, increasing funding for drug enforcement and pushing forward tougher new sentencing laws to punish drug offenders. His administration embraced a more punitive approach, implementing new mandatory minimum sentencing and forfeiture laws for drug offenses with the enactment of the Comprehensive Crime Control Act of 1984. Within five years, asset forfeitures for drug offenses increased from $27 million in 1984 to $644 million in 1989, more than a twenty-fold increase (Stahl 1992).

The creation of the Campaign Against Cannabis Planting (CAMP) in 1983 by the attorney general of California, John van de Kamp, ramped up the drug war and signaled a significant shift in cannabis policing in the Emerald Triangle. CAMP was a joint federal, state, and local law enforcement task force managed by the California Bureau of Narcotic Enforcement and organized expressly to eradicate illegal cannabis cultivation and trafficking in California. Utilizing helicopters as its primary method to detect cannabis gardens, and operating during the late summer months of August through October, when plants could be detected more easily from the air, the program concentrated its initial efforts on the back-to-the-land communities of the Emerald Triangle. The effect of this regional concentration of enforcement efforts led to geographical dispersion, with outdoor cultivation spreading to other counties throughout California and into public lands (Corva 2014). CAMP also forced growers to innovate their growing techniques in a variety of ways to conceal their activities from the air. To adapt to aerial surveillance, outdoor cultivators shifted from growing plants in large gardens in the full sun to planting shorter varieties of cannabis in multiple smaller gardens in the shade to avoid detection. The increased surveillance also led to another adaptation in cultivation—off-the-grid indoor growing with lights powered by large industrial diesel generators. This innovation allowed growers to conceal their plants under a roof, making it difficult for law enforcement to spot. This move from outdoor to indoor agriculture also provided growers with a layer of legal protection, as a search warrant, which was not necessary for outdoor grows spotted from the air, was needed to enter an enclosed structure. Growing "diesel dope" also offered the advantage of multiple harvests, enhancing the economic incentive to engage in this form of agriculture all year. By pushing outdoor cannabis growers indoors, the activities of CAMP produced a number of unintended environmental consequences for human and ecosystem health that were not present in traditional outdoor methods. Maintaining off-the-grid indoor cultivation year round required noisy carbon-polluting industrial generators powered by diesel and oil. To conceal the noise, generators were often placed close to streams and public waterways, gravity fed by 500- to 1,000-gallon diesel tanks located up stream. Unattended and poorly assembled, the fuel tanks and hoses oftentimes contaminated sites with oil and diesel fuel, impacting water supplies for both aquatic species and local communities. This method was yet another innovation to prohibition policing, and it became a more common practice for cannabis cultivators as the CAMP crusade continued through the 1990s.

To evade harsh criminal sentences and avoid costly land forfeiture threats, growers also responded by moving more of their operations onto public lands (CAMP Report 1983). In response to this adaptation, federal eradication campaigns began on public lands in the Emerald Triangle. In 1990 more than 200 armed federal agents, National Guard troops, and US Army soldiers were flown in on Blackhawk helicopters to eradicate cannabis gardens in the King Range National Conservation Area, about 200 miles north of San Francisco. This controversial campaign, named Operation Greensweep, marked the first time active-duty military personnel were used to combat cannabis growing in the United States (Bishop 1990). More than 1,400 cannabis plants were eradicated at twenty-eight grow sites, with 12 tons of growing equipment removed from these public lands (Mendel 1992). Overall plant eradications in the state rose from a low of 47,841 in 1983 to a high of 337,927 in 1996.[8]

Adaptations in cannabis cultivation practices were a direct response to the prohibition policing of the drug war, with each shift in eradication efforts leading to a new wave of innovations in cannabis agriculture. These innovations, however, came at an increasingly high cost to the environment and human health. With the Clinton administration upholding the nationwide ban on cannabis and escalating eradication efforts, and the price of cannabis fetching up to $4,000 a pound, producers moved into increasingly remote areas on public lands to avoid detection. These activities were carried out by locals as well as by foreign nationals arriving from cannabis-producing regions in Mexico and Eastern Europe.[9] Recognizing the opportunity to cash in on the cannabis economy, they brought their expertise to Northern California and set up clandestine farms in the remote wilderness. By the mid-1990s outdoors and off-the-grid diesel doping were the two dominant methods of cannabis agriculture. It would be the passage of medical cannabis legislation in California, and the subsequent regulatory discrepancies between state and federal drug laws to regulate it, however, that would help facilitate an upturn in environmental devastation on public and private lands.

THE GRAY MARKET (1996–2012)

In 1996, fed up with the federal policy on cannabis, California voters took to the polls to usher in a new era of cannabis regulation with the passage of Proposition 215, the California Compassionate Use Act.[10] This legislative victory, the first of its kind in the United States, was a groundbreaking event for advocates of legalization, dealing prohibition a huge blow and sending shock waves across state and federal law enforcement agencies. Though the new law provided no real guidance for growers or patients on how to carry out their activities, this shift in policy gave patients and growers an affirmative defense—a legal justification for possessing and cultivating "medical" cannabis within the state of California.[11] The passage of California's Senate bill 420 (SB 420) in 2003 marked another important policy shift that was advantageous to cannabis cultivators. The bill attempted to clarify the scope of Proposition 215 more clearly, allowing local municipalities the freedom to set their own limits on medical cannabis cultivators.[12] Humboldt County enacted the most liberal policy, allowing medical growers to cultivate up to 99 plants per card, one plant under the federal mandatory minimum (100 plants) for enforcement. Cannabis cultivators adapted to these provisions by creating grower cooperatives with multiple cards that provided legal protection for hundreds of plants to be grown at one location (Corva 2014). Proposition 215 began an era in which industrial cannabis cultivation became normalized in the region, leading to a surge in the number of grows and a migration of people to the county for the sole purpose of growing cannabis. Growers cultivated cannabis openly in the full sun as well as indoors, and as long as they stayed under the ninety-nine-plant limit they could be assured that the federal government was not going to prosecute them. With little risk of arrest and prosecution, mega-grows on private lands with thousands of plants became commonplace. Shielded by the protections of Proposition 215 and SB 420, people from all over the United States moved to the region to engage in cannabis agriculture in a second Green Rush, and by 2009 California was producing more outdoor cannabis than all of Mexico.[13] Spurred on by Proposition 215, the long-term trend away from small grows to larger-scale mega-grows on public and private lands clearly took root in the late 1990s and transformed cannabis culture in the region over the course of the next decade and a half. Eradication numbers doubled in years following medical legalization, from 2.5 million plants (1997–2000) to 6.4 million (2001–2004). Public lands eradications also doubled over the same period, from 646,943 (1997–2000) to 1.7 million (2001–2004) (Domestic Cannabis Cultivation Assessment 2009).

While CAMP continued its eradication efforts concentrating on public lands trespass grows and mega-grows on private lands, the Bush administration took a much harder line on cannabis than its predecessor, calling for an increase in federal enforcement efforts against medical cannabis users and those who facilitated cannabis access and cultivation. Physicians, garden supply stores, and even county officials were targeted. Bush escalated the war on cannabis when in 2007 his administration sent out letters to businesses and landlords in California informing them that they could be prosecuted and forfeit their property if they rented space to anyone engaged in the sale of cannabis. These new federal attacks on the cannabis industry helped to keep the price stable at around $3,000 per pound.

The expansion of cannabis agriculture was facilitated by the inability of the state and federal governments to come to an agreement on drug policy. Although California recognized cannabis as legal, this remained at odds with federal narcotics laws. Other than plant count limits, discrepancies between state and federal laws left the region a virtual Wild West for cannabis cultivators, who had no oversight regarding their cultivation practices. This fragmentation resulted in an approach to cannabis policy and policing that created the perfect conditions for environmental abuses to flourish. With policy gaps regulating cannabis agriculture, and lacking any significant state or federal oversight, cannabis cultivators were free to illegally log; grade roads; bury streams with sediment; dump nutrients, pesticides, and petroleum products into waterways; poison wildlife; and completely dewater sensitive aquatic habitats on both public and private lands. In addition to these impacts, cultivators began employing even more environmentally harmful practices, such as light deprivation, a forced flowering method that requires the construction of a cover over the plants to control the light and dark cycles. "Light dep" is a mix of indoor/outdoor techniques, where for a short time early in the season lights and heaters are used, usually powered by diesel generators. The purpose of this technique is twofold; it allows cultivators to plant and harvest more than one crop outdoors, and it allows an early harvest in order to beat the market glut during the high time of harvest season. This adaptation to increase production exacerbated environmental devastation in a number of ways, with cultivators diverting water from sensitive streams and clearing forests for greenhouse construction.

Although the Obama administration initially signaled a shift in relaxing the enforcement of cannabis laws, promising not to raid those in compliance with state law, in October 2011 the Justice Department arrested and prosecuted a number of state-compliant cannabis dispensaries and growers engaged in the medical cannabis industry (Riggs 2013). Perhaps the most notable action of his administration was on Mendocino County's 9.31 zip tie program, a local attempt to create a clear, legal, and regulated approach to medical cannabis agriculture. The first of its kind in the state, it created a licensing and monitoring system of cannabis growers to ensure the practices employed by cultivators were not harming the environment or human health. In 2012, with the federal government threating litigation and criminal action, the 9.31 program was shelved and with it one of the best models of regulating medical cannabis agriculture and protecting the environment. Some of the most compliant dispensaries and outdoor growers suffered federal raids despite statements by President Obama and the attorney general that no actions would be taken on compliant businesses. The fragmentation between the federal and state agencies led to a schizophrenic policy of enforcement that sent shock waves through the cannabis community. The crackdown on the most compliant cannabis actors also had the effect of alienating growers who were supportive of state oversight and regulation. Those who sought compliance were now out of the regulatory environment.

Perhaps the most painful example of how government policy impeded the implementation of environmental regulation in cannabis agriculture was its intimidation of those who were in the position to offer growers the best advice. County agricultural commissioners, university extension programs, and federal land managers were all forbidden to work with cannabis growers in any capacity. Growers who called into their offices seeking advice on pest control, water conservation, and other best management practices were turned away as a result of federal drug policy. Without access to adequate information, growers were left to fend for themselves, oftentimes treating their plants with alarmingly high levels of pesticides and fungicides intended for other purposes.

In 2009, the price of outdoor cannabis dropped almost by half, to around $1,500 per pound. The fall in cannabis price can be attributed to a number of factors, the first being the increase in supply of cannabis as a result of the Green Rush to the region. This glut of cannabis was also spurred by a generalized fear that cannabis cultivators had of impending legalization in California and other states. Growers ramped up production anytime cannabis legalization was on the ballot, regardless of where. For example, after Oregon passed medical cannabis legislation in 1998, eradications in California rose from 313,197 in 1998 to 831,193 plants a year later. Fearing the end of profitable cannabis agriculture as a result of legalization, both indoor and outdoor cultivators ramped up production to adjust for the drop in price. Eradication numbers in California rose steadily every year, from 1,109,066 plants in 2003 to a high of 7,204,355 in 2010.

As the priorities changed at the federal level in the fight against cannabis, so did the agricultural practices in the industry, with many cultivators moving onto public lands all over California. Cannabis eradication on public lands increased each year between 2004 and 2010, rising from 591,824 plants to an incredible 4,320,314, respectively.

LEGALIZATION (2012–2016)

As with the previous policy regimes, cannabis cultivation practices were a direct response to the prohibition policing of the drug war, with changes in eradication efforts leading growers to pursue more environmentally harmful forms of cannabis agriculture. From 2010 to 2014, California remained the largest domestic producer of cannabis in the United States, with an average of 3.8 million plants seized annually. Though eradication efforts concentrated on mega-grows on public and private lands, the raiding of above-the-board, state-compliant farms was commonplace. With the threat of being raided, and to make up for lost profits, some cultivators expanded their activities on public lands while others moved production indoors, creating additional environmental problems.[14]

In 2012 the expansion of cannabis agriculture in California was facilitated again by legalization efforts at the state level. The passage of Initiative 502 in Washington and Amendment 64 in Colorado legalized recreational cannabis and was a boom for cultivators who had seen the price of cannabis drop in recent years. Because both states struggled to meet the demand of recreational users and fine-tune the regulatory details of implementation, out-of-state buyers flocked to Northern California to purchase cannabis, helping to stabilize wholesale prices at around $1,800–$2,200 per pound.

Over the next two years, federal intransigence on the prohibition of cannabis continued to prevent the state from enacting any meaningful environmental regulations on cannabis cultivation. As a result, cannabis cultivation continued to expand with little oversight, overwhelming both law enforcement and natural resources managers. By 2012 outdoor mega-grows numbered in the thousands in most watersheds in the Emerald Triangle. With mature cannabis plants using up to 6 gallons of water a day during the driest part of the season, growers were dewatering creeks where endangered Coho salmon spawn. In one watershed in Humboldt County, greenhouse and outdoor cannabis cultivation combined to use over 18 million gallons of water, accounting for over 50 percent of the stream flow during low-flow periods. Fisheries biologists from the California Department of Fish and Wildlife estimated that demands for cannabis cultivation have exceeded stream flows by as much as 100 percent in some watersheds, completely dewatering streams and threatening the survival of federally listed salmon and steelhead populations (Bauer 2015).

In 2015, as California entered its fourth year of drought, law enforcement officials began citing increased environmental damage as justification for raids on large-scale cannabis grows. Left with few resources and absent any clear policy guidance, law enforcement and land managers had little success in eliminating or minimizing the overwhelming number of large-scale grows in the region. This increase in scale and frequency of environmental impacts became an important driver of efforts to craft regulations for cannabis cultivation. On October 9, 2015, the California legislature passed a series of bills that established the first statewide regulatory system for medical cannabis, with Governor Jerry Brown signing into law Assembly Bill 266, Assembly Bill 243, and Senate Bill 643. After nearly twenty years without oversight, the bills outlined key provisions of the Medical Cannabis Regulation and Safety Act (MCRSA). Each bill had a particular function, regulating the cultivation, processing, transportation, testing, and distribution of medical cannabis under the Department of Consumer Affairs and overseen by the Bureau of Medical Cannabis Regulation. Legislators crafted the bills with such specificity in hopes that robust regulations would satisfy the concerns of the federal government, allowing the state to operate without threats from the Department of Justice. Of MCRSA's three bills, AB 243 was the most germane to environmental issues, as it set out the guidelines on pesticides, water diversions and discharges, and health and safety guidelines. For the first time in twenty years medical cannabis growers on private lands would have to come into compliance with environmental regulations if they were to engage in cannabis cultivation.

In November 2016 California voters passed Proposition 64, legalizing marijuana for recreational use. This initiative allocates significant funding to environmental restoration of watersheds damaged by past cannabis cultivation and provides funding for law enforcement to ensure that cannabis growers are in compliance with state environmental regulations. Although the new legislation attempts to mitigate a range of environmental problems associated with cultivation and to bring cultivators into compliance with state law, with federal prohibition still in place, it is uncertain how successful state regulators will be in gaining the trust of cannabis communities in the region.

CONCLUSION

The reasons for environmental problems in cannabis agriculture and the solutions to them are not nearly as cut-and-dry as policy makers might lead us to believe. There is no doubt cannabis agriculture has negative environmental impacts on public and private lands, but it is increasingly clear that these environmental problems are linked directly to the regulatory vacuum that prohibition has created. More than forty years of federal intransigence concerning cannabis has forced state regulators and cannabis advocates to pursue a piecemeal approach to legalization and has done very little in the way of bringing growers into regulatory compliance, and even less at protecting the environment. Subsequently, it has only intensified the environmental destruction of California's ecosystems. If recreational legalization shows us anything, we will most likely see cultivation on public lands expand, as well as additional growth in outdoor, greenhouse, and light deprivation grows on private lands in order to satisfy the demand of expanding markets. Comprising the largest cannabis-producing region on the planet, California ecosystems will continue to bear the burden of supporting the nation's appetite for high-quality cannabis. Put simply, to effectively address the environmental problems generated by cannabis agriculture we must have an end to federal prohibition and the criminalization of cannabis. If cannabis production remains illegal at the federal level, one thing is clear: there will be continued expansion of cannabis agriculture on public and private lands in California, leading to an increase in environmental damages to ecosystems throughout the region. The use of GIS, Google Earth, and other technologies may help enhance the enforcement of environmental regulations contained in AB 243 and Proposition 64, but their deployment will simply force cultivators indoors, creating another set of environmental problems by adding tons of carbon dioxide into the atmosphere.[15]

The central argument of this chapter is that prohibition exacerbates environmental harms and incentivizes cannabis cultivators to set up environmentally damaging grow sites on public and private lands with little regard for the natural environment. In light of the past thirty or more years of cannabis agriculture in the region, it seems safe to assume that state legalization efforts will have far less influence in reining in the ecologically unsustainable practices of cannabis agriculture than will an end to federal prohibition. What is less clear, and merits further investigation, is the extent to which the federal government will go in maintaining a failed policy that generates a catalog of ecological harms in its wake.

WORKS CITED

Anders, Gentry. 1990. *Beyond Counterculture*. Pullman: Washington State University Press.

Austin, James. 2005. *Rethinking Consequences of Decriminalizing Marijuana*. Washington, DC: JFA Institute.

Bauer, Scott, Jennifer Olson, Adam Cockrill, Michael van Hattem, Linda Miller, Margaret Tauzer, and Gordon Leppig. 2015. "Impacts of Surface Water Diversions for Marijuana Cultivation on Aquatic Habitat in Four Northwestern California Watersheds." PLOS ONE 10, 9: e0137935. http://www.ncbi.nlm.nih.gov/pmc/articles/PMC4364984 (accessed October 11, 2015).

Bishop, Katherine. 1990. "Military Takes Part in Drug Sweep and Reaps Criticism and a Lawsuit." *New York Times*, August 10. http://www.nytimes.com/1990/08/10/us/military-takes-part-in-drug-sweep-and-reaps-criticism-and-a-lawsuit.html?pagewanted=all (accessed November 15, 2014).

Caulkins, Jonathan P., and Rosalie L. Pacula. 2006. "Marijuana Markets: Inferences from Reports by the Household Population." *Journal of Drug Issues* 36, 1: 173–220.

Central Valley High Intensity Drug Traffic Area Report. 2010. US Department of Justice National Drug Intelligence Center. http://www.justice.gov/archive/ndic/pubs40/40384/40384p.pdf (accessed January 10, 2015).

Chapkis, Wendy, and Richard J. Webb. 2008. *Dying to Get High: Marijuana as Medicine*. New York: New York University Press.

Clements, Kenneth W., and Xueyan Zhao. 2009. *Economics and Marijuana: Consumption, Pricing and Legalisation*. New York: Cambridge University Press.

Corva, Dominic. 2014. "Requiem for a CAMP: The Life and Death of a Domestic US Drug War Institution." *International Journal of Drug Policy* 25, 1: 71–80.

Domestic Cannabis Cultivation Assessment. 2009. US Department of Justice National Drug Intelligence Center. http://www.justice.gov/archive/ndic/pubs37/37035/public.htm.

Domestic Cannabis Eradication/Suppression Statistics. 2015. Drug Enforcement Administration. http://www.dea.gov/ops/cannabis.shtml (accessed October 12, 2015).

Gabriel, M. W., L. W. Woods, R. Poppenga, R. A. Sweitzer, C. Thompson, S. M. Matthews, J. M. Higley, S. M. Keller, K. Purcell, R. H. Barrett, G. M. Wengert, B. N. Sacks, and D. L. Clifford. 2012. "Anticoagulant Rodenticides on Our Public and Community Lands: Spatial Distribution of Exposure and Poisoning of a Rare Forest Carnivore." PLOS ONE 7, 7: e40163. http://www.iercecology.org/wp-content/uploads/2012/07/Gabriel_et_al_2012 (accessed June 10, 2015).

Gettman, Jon. 2006. "Marijuana Production in the United States." *Bulletin of Cannabis Reform*, December. http://www.drugscience.org/bcr/index.html (accessed October 12, 2014).

Jones, Roberta. 1985. "US Revives Plan to Kill Marijuana with Paraquat." *Los Angeles Times*, July 28. http://articles.latimes.com/1985-07-28/news/mn-5386_1_marijuana-eradication (accessed June 2, 2014).

Keith, D. R., C. L. Hart, M. P. McNeil, R. Silver, and R. D. Goodwin. 2015. "Frequent Marijuana Use, Binge Drinking and Mental Health Problems among Undergraduates." *American Journal on Addictions* 24: 499–506.

Lee, Martin. 2012. *Smoke Signals: A Social History of Marijuana—Medical, Recreational, and Scientific*. New York: Scribner.

Martin, William. 2013. "Cartels, Corruption, Carnage, and Cooperation." In *A War That Can't Be Won: Binational Perspectives on the War on Drugs*, ed. T. Payan, K. Staudt, and Z. A. Kruszewski, 33–64. Tucson: University of Arizona Press.

Mills, Evan. 2012. "The Carbon Footprint of Indoor Cannabis Production." *Energy Policy* 46: 58–67.

Miron, Jeffrey. 2010. "The Budgetary Implications of Drug Prohibition." Report funded by the Criminal Justice Policy Foundation, Harvard University, Boston. http://www.economics.harvard.edu/faculty/miron/files/budget%202010%20Final.pdf (accessed May 10, 2015).

Mozingo, Joe, 2012. "Roots of Pot Cultivation in National Forests Are Hard to Trace." *Los Angeles Times*, December 26. http://articles.latimes.com/2012/dec/26/local/la-me-mexican-marijuana-20121226 (accessed January 12, 2013).

Nixon, David. 2013. "Update to the Budgetary Implications of Marijuana Decriminalization and Legalization for Hawai`i." Drug Policy Action Group. https://acluhawaii.files.wordpress.com/2013/01/econreptmarijuana1_2013.pdf (accessed October 3, 2015).

Northern California High Intensity Drug Traffic Area Drug Market Analysis. 2012. US Department of Justice National Drug Intelligence Center. http://www.justice.gov/archive/ndic/dmas/Northern_CA_DMA-2011(U).pdf.

Potter, Gary W., Larry Gaines, and Beth Holbrook. 1990. "Blowing Smoke: An Evaluation of Kentucky's Marijuana Eradication Program." *American Journal of Police* 9, 1: 97 16.

Raphael, Ray. 1985. *Cash Crop: An American Dream*. Mendocino, CA: Ridgetop.

Reiman, Amanda. 2009. "Cannabis as a Substitute for Alcohol and Other Drugs." *Harm Reduction Journal* 6: 35.

Riding, Alan. 1978. "Mexico Won't Halt Marijuana Spraying." *Sarasota Herald Tribune*, May 23, 8A. https://news.google.com/newspapers?nid=1755&dat=19780523&id=akk0AA AAIBAJ&sjid=c2cEAAAAIBAJ&pg=6770,3068056&hl=en (accessed May 2, 2015).

Riggs, Mike. 2013. "Obama's War on Pot." Nation. https://www.thenation.com/article /obamas-war-pot (accessed February 3, 2016).

Segal, Bernard, ed. 1986. *Perspectives on Drug Use in the United States.* New York: Routledge.

Shepard, Edward M., and Paul R. Blackley. 2007. "The Impact of Marijuana Law Enforcement in an Economic Model of Crime." *Journal of Drug Issues* 37, 2: 403–424.

Starrs, Paul F., and Peter Goin. 2010. *Field Guide to California Agriculture.* Berkeley: University of California Press.

NOTES

1. Emerald Triangle refers to the three largest cannabis-producing counties in Northern California: Humboldt, Trinity, and Mendocino.

2. It is important to note that environmental damages from trespass grows have also impacted private lands downstream.

3. In 2012 the US Fish and Wildlife Service proposed granting Endangered Species Act protection to the Pacific fisher, a weasel-like forest dweller that has increasingly falling victim to rodenticides used in cannabis cultivation on public lands.

4. See Corva's (2014) examination of the economic "unintended consequences" of cannabis policing in Northern California.

5. Sinsemilla is the highly potent seedless flower produced by the female cannabis plant.

6. The new Green Rush migrants brought with them a new culture, and their agricultural practices reflected their economic motives. In addition to the "green rushers" Raphael (1985) reports that loggers, mill workers, and rural laborers engaged in cannabis agriculture at the time.

7. Most grows on public lands at the time took place in areas already devastated by the timber industry.

8. The eradication average statewide from 1983 to 1996 was 266,000 plants annually, with an average of 25,400 plants removed from public lands.

9. For well over twenty years, law enforcement agencies and politicians have racialized prohibition policing, blaming Mexican cartels for illegal grows on public lands. In 2012 Tommy Lanier, director of the National Cannabis Initiative, part of the Office of National Drug Control Policy, said there was no evidence that the cartels were operating on public lands. Lanier said law enforcement has long mislabeled cannabis grown on public land as "cartel grows" because Mexican nationals have been arrested in some cases, and the narrative of fighting "drug cartels" helps law enforcement agencies secure federal funding (see Mozingo 2012). Despite the evidence offered by Lanier, law enforcement and politicians continue to spread false information to the public concerning "cartel" involvement in public lands grows.

10. Medical cannabis advocates in San Francisco and Santa Cruz successfully passed a variety of resolutions supporting medical as early as 1991.

11. Despite the passage of Proposition 215, cannabis arrests rose both in California (57,677 in 1997) and in the United States (695,201) (Lee 2012).

12. SB 420 also established the California Medical Marijuana Program.

13. As there is no system or method that provides an accurate and reliable estimate of cannabis production in the United States, I use the number of plants eradicated by law enforcement as a measure of production. Plant eradication numbers in California swelled from 337,927 in 1996 to 831,193 in 1999. There were 7,519,580 total plants eradicated in 2009 (Central Valley High Intensity Drug Traffic Area Report 2010).

14. Nationwide, carbon dioxide pollution from indoor cannabis agriculture equals that of 3 million cars (Mills 2012).

15. This is already the dominant method of cultivation in Colorado, where surging electricity consumption is taxing electrical grids and sending carbon dioxide pollution into the atmosphere.

CHAPTER 2

Ecological Impacts across the Landscape

Trespass Marijuana Cultivation on Western Public Lands

Greta M. Wengert, Mourad W. Gabriel,
J. Mark Higley, and Craig Thompson

Marijuana cultivation in California: it is a phrase that conjures up images ranging from a back-to-the-earth movement that brought people closer to the land, to pot-smoking college students, to the influx of out-of-towners to small Northern California towns looking for a piece of the vast profits being generated in the drug trade. But only recently has this phrase also come to represent an even darker side to the industry, the less well-known drawbacks to an otherwise booming industry. This darker side is the broad assemblage of environmental impacts this industry has had and continues to have on the lands and natural resources of California and other western states. Water diversions, wildlife poisonings, and clearing of habitats are now understood to be common at cultivation sites throughout California. Going more unnoticed are the covert, less visible ecological disturbances unique to marijuana cultivation hidden within California's vast public lands. Though many of the same clear hazards exist both in the more evident quasi-legal grows occurring on private parcels as well as in the trespass grows littering the public landscape, there are stark differences in the nature, detectability, and expanse of impacts between the two. When considered at the regional scale across hundreds of trespass cultivation sites on California's public and tribal lands each year, the cumulative impacts could be substantial but are, as yet, largely unexplored. Furthermore, a large portion of sites that exist on public lands are not even discovered, so the vast majority are unremediated, leaving behind a legacy of environmental damage. This chapter's aim is to describe the landscape-scale impacts and consider the cumulative influences that direct as well as indirect and more covert environmental impacts might have across the California public landscape.

IDENTIFYING THE EXTENT AND DISTRIBUTION
OF TRESPASS GROW SITES ON PUBLIC LANDS

Law enforcement agencies estimate that each year between 500,000 and 1.5 million illegally grown marijuana plants are detected and eradicated on California's public lands. These numbers stem from roughly several hundred law enforcement–discovered sites per year. Moreover, there are hundreds of additional marijuana grow sites spread across much of California's public and tribal lands that go undetected. Newly established sites sprout up each year, such that cumulatively, there are many thousands of active, eradicated, and abandoned grow sites in California's national forests, national and state parks, national recreation areas, and state wildlife areas at the time of this writing (Figure 2.1). Though recent media suggests that the number of grow sites on public lands has already peaked and every year since 2011 has seen the discovery of fewer and fewer public-land sites, these observations must consider the ever-decreasing support that law enforcement agencies receive to conduct surveillance to even detect these sites. Lack of support and its resulting reduction in effort for detection of sites thus falsely portrays a decreasing trend in cultivation frequency and intensity on public lands. Most daunting is the estimate that law enforcement likely detects fewer than half of the active marijuana cultivation sites each year, and of those detected, fewer than 10 percent are reclaimed or restored to their natural state. With statistics such as this, it is surprising that this issue gets so little media attention in California, much less outside of the western United States, the region within which most of California's marijuana supply flows.

The uncertainty surrounding the true number and distribution of trespass marijuana grow sites on public lands in California makes it difficult to accurately describe the extent of environmental impacts and develop solutions to reverse the problem. Some efforts to model probable areas of marijuana cultivation based on environmental and/or anthropogenic variables have shown potential in predicting likely grow site locations and distribution. A study investigating the habitat and social correlates of trespass marijuana cultivation in national parks in the southern Sierra Nevada used locations of twelve and eighty-four known cultivation sites between 2000 and 2008 in Yosemite and Sequoia-Kings Canyon National Parks, respectively, to model areas that are most likely at risk for trespass marijuana cultivation (Partelow 2008). Though the model performed well, the study fell short

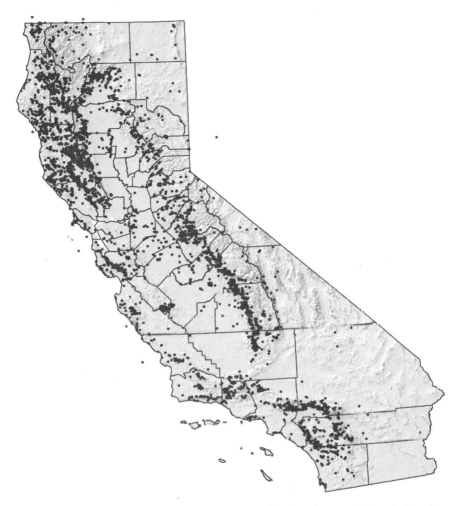

Figure 2.1. Distribution of trespass marijuana cultivation sites on public, tribal, and private industrial lands in California between 2004 and 2014.

of indicating which variables were more or less correlated with cultivation risk in the national parks. The study, however, highlighted the major concern about risks to natural and cultural resources from this illicit activity; this was the first published documentation of concern about the environmental risks from fertilizers and pesticides used in marijuana cultivation. Despite this publication, most of California's natural-resource managers and researchers are not aware of the depth and importance of this issue. Models predicting the distribution of cultivation sites used environmental and human-related variables to identify spatial risk in Mexico (Medel and Lu 2014), although no mention is made as to any detrimental impacts to the environment from these illegal cultivation sites or what land ownership these sites occupied. A modeling effort specifically focused on estimating cultivation site likelihood throughout the forested regions of California and southwestern Oregon and its overlap with habitat of sensitive wildlife species is still in the accuracy assessment phase, but preliminary results suggest that there is significant overlap between high-quality habitat for the fisher (*Pekania pennanti*), a candidate for the federal Endangered Species Act, and the federally threatened northern spotted owl (*Strix occidentalis caurina*) and regions with high likelihood of trespass cultivation (Wengert et al., unpublished data). Analyses are ongoing to assess overlap with other species of conservation concern, including the Humboldt marten (*Martes caurina humboldtensis*) and cold water refugia for impacted salmonid runs. This modeling project is the first assessment of landscape-scale marijuana cultivation risk and overlap with species of conservation concern and the habitats on which they depend.

ENVIRONMENTAL IMPACTS OF TRESPASS MARsIJUANA CULTIVATION ON PUBLIC LANDS

In the final chapter of John Nores's *War in the Woods*, a personal account of California's fight with trespass marijuana cultivation (which he updated in his chapter in this volume), Nores describes the environmental atrocities regularly seen at the cultivation sites that law enforcement eradicate. But he also laments the fact that so few are cleaned-up following interdiction (Nores and Swan 2010). Furthermore, the author cites water pollution, streambed alteration, littering, and poaching as significant problems needing to be addressed. Unfortunately, the presence and threat of these impacts were not generally known until recently, when independent researchers and some agency biologists began investigating anomalies in the wildlife populations they were actively monitoring (see Higley and Thompson chapters, this volume). Even then, it took several years to compile the anecdotal and evidence-based reports of wildlife mortality due to rodenticides at cultivation sites into a cumulative account of the landscape distribution of rodenticide impacts in California (Gabriel et al. 2012; Thompson et al. 2013; Gabriel et al. 2015). Since then, our understanding of the environmental impacts associated with this illicit activity has grown significantly due to focused investigations at cultivation sites and the areas surrounding them. The information that is available, however, consists of preliminary findings and anecdotal reports from which cumulative impacts can only be approximated.

A program collecting detailed information from trespass cultivation sites on public and tribal lands is in its infancy; it currently consists mainly of data from approximately fifty sites throughout California and southern Oregon, but all of these are primarily located in Northern California (Humboldt, Trinity, and Plumas Counties). In addition, researchers have collected a limited amount of information from sites within the southern Sierra Nevada, but these consist mainly of casual observations of the chemicals and fertilizers found during the reclamation process (Gabriel et al. 2013). For example, in the remediation of hundreds of cultivation sites throughout the foothills and mid-elevation slopes of the southern Sierra Nevada, Lead Reclamation Specialist Shane Krogen suggested there was seldom a site he encountered that did not have anticoagulant rodenticides (ARs) present. These hundreds of sites occurred in only two of California's national forests and excluded those occurring within the two adjacent national parks (the National Park Service generally conducts its own eradication and reclamation efforts). It is generally accepted, and law enforcement data supports, that all national forests in California whose climates and vegetation characteristics make the cultivation of marijuana feasible, experience comparable frequencies and densities of trespass cultivation sites.

Investigations and mapping of several cultivation sites from 2013 and 2015 have preliminary estimates of actual plant patch footprints at an average of over one acre. Based on anecdotal observations over the past several years, however, the spatial orientation and distribution of plant patches within the cultivation complexes appear to be shifting from a small number of large, expansive patches to networks of many small, disjunct patches scattered across a much larger overall footprint on the landscape. How this change will manifest in terms of impacts to wildlife, water, and other resources is unclear, but the notably larger footprint of rodenticide, pesticide, fertilizer, and water use likely equates to a greater cumulative, landscape-level impact, and certainly spreads its impacts to an area significantly greater than the acre of grow patch typically observed. Undoubtedly, plant patches scattered throughout a watershed have the ability to dewater multiple streams or springs, and the run-off from these more dispersed patches has greater potential and capacity to contaminate more of the watershed than a solitary larger patch on a single hillside.

Rodenticides (including ARss, neurotoxic rodenticides, and cholecalciferol compounds, which calcify the internal organs) are the cause of environmental impacts and likely have received the most scientific focus and media attention due to their causing mortality in a high-profile species being considered for listing under the federal Endangered Species Act (Gabriel et al. 2012; Gabriel et al. 2015; Thompson et al. 2013; see also Chapters 3 and 4 in this volume). These compounds are found at a majority of trespass marijuana cultivation sites investigated in California (Gabriel et al., unpublished data). With an average mass of 10 pounds per site, these toxicants are spread across all the plant patches and water cisterns associated with a trespass grow, along the irrigation lines feeding the site, and around the camps at which the growers live throughout the growing season (typically from April through September). Finally, many of these toxicants are housed in water-resistant containers, thus allowing long periods of time or the disturbance by an animal to compromise containers.

The cumulative effects of such unregulated and widespread use can be substantial. Animals either die directly from ingestion of the poisoned bait or die through secondary poisoning by consuming other animals that have ingested the baits. Rodents survive up to several days with the poisons in their systems, leave the cultivation areas, and therefore pose risks to carnivores and raptors well outside the footprints of the grow patches where the rodenticides are distributed. For instance, in our prey abundance sampling at grow and control sites in 2015, we inadvertently captured a mountain quail (*Oreortyx pictus*) in our control site (almost 2 km from the nearest known grow site) that tested positive for AR exposure. In addition, we know the residual impacts of ARs at grow sites can last many months after eradication because the majority of rodents captured at grow sites that were tested were positive for AR exposure 6–12 months after the site was eradicated and several months after the sites were remediated (Wengert et al., unpublished data). Furthermore, in a study of the fisher, a forest-obligate species, researchers found that 85 percent of all tested fishers were exposed to ARs in a northwestern California population and in two populations in the southern Sierra Nevada (Gabriel et al. 2015). Unfortunately, this percentage rose higher from an earlier study in which the researchers found no spatial pattern to the exposures, meaning AR exposure was ubiquitous throughout the fisher's range within the study areas (Gabriel et al. 2012).

Research investigating how these rodenticides impact the prey communities on which so many sensitive forest carnivore and raptors depend already suggests that prey diversity and populations are depressed at many of the sites (Wengert et al., unpublished data). Furthermore, there is evidence that ARs can bioaccumulate in invertebrates because they lack the clotting mechanisms upon which ARs act, making ARs nonlethal. It is unknown how quickly invertebrates metabolize these compounds, but they likely pose risks to countless other species that prey on ground-dwelling invertebrates for extended periods of time.

The pesticides placed throughout the plant patches and along irrigation lines also leach into the soil. Several types of ARs and carbofuran (a particularly hazardous pesticide notoriously used to kill lions in Africa as well as numerous other species worldwide [Richards 2011]) have been detected in soil within plant patches in several sites in Northern California (Gabriel and Wengert, unpublished data). Residual chemicals such as these remaining in the soil when the wet season arrives will get mobilized and washed into the watersheds. Consequently, pesticides used at grow sites have been detected by water sampling equipment placed in headwater streams just below grow sites (Gabriel and Wengert, unpublished data). One pesticide in particular, Diazinon, was found in stream water sampled just below three different grow sites in northwestern California (Gabriel and Wengert, unpublished data). This pesticide is acutely toxic to most insects so theoretically is impacting aquatic macroinvertebrate communities on which so many other aquatic species depend, but these potential impacts are just now starting to be investigated.

Aside from the vast direct and indirect effects of the illegal overuse of toxicants at nearly all trespass grow sites in California, growers also use all kinds of high-nutrient fertilizers in copious volumes, far exceeding the needs of the plants and soil area. The amounts of fertilizer we discovered at each trespass grow site during our investigations between 2012 and 2015 in Northern California and in the northern Sierra Nevada ranged from about 300 pounds to over 4,300 pounds of dry, soluble fertilizer distributed across single small patches or several large patches spanning hundreds of meters of creek drainage. In 2010, the US Forest Service conducted a massive eradication and cleanup effort on the Sequoia and Sierra National Forests, removing 5.4 tons of unused fertilizer from sixty-five trespass grow sites. This effort was conducted in August and September, after the growing season, meaning these 5.4 tons represented the *leftover* fertilizer (Thompson, unpublished data). Given that every site we've visited since 2012 has had vast amounts of fertilizer suggests that each of the thousands of sites strewn across California's public lands over the past decade have contributed to excessive nutrient loading to the ecosystem. One possible result of this nutrient excess is a multitude of fundamental changes to soil fertility across large swaths of the landscape. Preliminary results of nitrogen-fixing microbial diversity indicate significant differences between grow patches and nearby control patches (Siering and Wengert, unpublished data). Consider a short 25 km stretch of the South Fork of the Trinity River having at least twenty-six trespass grow sites within its tributaries (likely many more than that), with hundreds if not thousands of pounds of fertilizer at each. Much of this likely gets mobilized with early fall rains and ends up within the river. Concerns are that this immense influx of nutrients into the system might enhance growth of cyanobacteria, contributing to dangerous blue-green algae blooms that in turn can release microcystins posing risks to a wide array of taxa, yet another plausible threat to wildlife.

These direct threats to the forest and associated aquatic ecosystems are being investigated, and preliminary evidence is being generated to support their existence. However, there are a host of other ideas about how the activities at trespass marijuana cultivation sites might impact the forest communities in less direct ways. We have begun investigating how forest animals use the extensive network of trails that growers build within and between grow sites, in addition to the activity patterns of those animals frequenting the camps and dumps attracted by food and other olfactory attractants. Initial findings show frequent use of camps and dumps by many forest species, including black bears (*Ursus americanus*), bobcats (*Lynx rufus*), gray fox (*Urocyon cinereoargenteus*), coyotes (*Canis latrans*), ringtail (*Bassariscus astutus*), many species of rodents and hares, game species including black-tailed deer (*Odocoileus hemionus*), mountain quail and band-tailed pigeon *(Patagioenas fasciata)*, and certain high-profile species such as mountain lions (*Puma concolor*) and the fisher. Furthermore, the trails growers construct are commonly traveled by mountain lions, bobcats, coyotes, black-tailed deer, and the occasional fisher. Though seemingly benign, this encouraged use of trails by different species could lead to increased chances of interaction. If interactions are more frequent between fishers and their main predators (mountain lions and bobcats), we suspect predation rates on fishers will increase, and this is important because predation is the primary source of mortality for fishers throughout California (Wengert et al. 2014).

The depression of rodent and other small prey populations brought about by extensive use of rodenticides in and surrounding grow sites likely affects the survival and fitness of the carnivore species that depend on that prey. When prey resources decline precipitously, carnivore populations typically show a behavioral or numeric response, or both, by increased home range size, lower survival, and lower reproductive success (Pereira et al. 2006; Schmidt 2008; Ferreras et al. 2011). We know that the diversity of prey and relative abundance of larger-bodied prey appear to be decreased at many grow sites (Wengert et al., unpublished data), so if this trend is common across all California trespass grow sites, carnivore populations are likely suffering the same effects. In conjunction with the intensified risks of direct poisoning at these sites, species of conservation concern such as the fisher, northern spotted owl, northern goshawk (*Accipiter gentilis*), and Humboldt marten would face cumulative perils from the many factors described above, ultimately risking population-level declines. Indeed, the United States Fish and Wildlife Service (USFWS) has proposed the fisher for listing as threatened under the federal Endangered Species Act, with rodenticides from trespass marijuana cultivation listed as one of the two main causative threats to be considered in the decision to list (USFWS 2014).

LEGACY EFFECTS, UNCERTAINTIES, AND THE REALITIES OF THE ENVIRONMENTAL DAMAGE

It should be clear that the diversity, spatial extent, and cumulative effects of marijuana cultivation on public lands have the potential to be monumental and formidable. The estimate that California's national forests have seen several hundred newly established cultivation sites each year at least for the past decade is disconcerting, but the fact that a generous estimate of roughly 10 percent of sites are remediated each year underscores the reality that to this day, there are probably thousands of sites with all their associated poisons, infrastructure, and garbage still in place. Consequently, the legacy effects of these sites grow cumulatively over time, as well as across the landscape. Every year, the number of contaminated, compromised patches of forest only grows larger and the cumulative impacts just expand. The hazards of these sites dissipate slowly at best, especially due to many poisons remaining unopened in their original packaging for wildlife to tear into them.

Given the uncertainties surrounding the real number of sites on California's national forests, the changes in the characteristics of sites over time (for example, in all the sites we visited in 2015, a vast majority had carbofuran present, whereas until that year, only a handful of sites did), and the complex ways in which the environmental effects cumulatively mount up, it is difficult to quantify the enormity of this issue. Though we know each cultivation site across the forests has its own array of poisons and overuse of fertilizers, how much is actually making it into the watershed? We know that carnivores are being poisoned directly and through consumption of poisoned prey, but are the fish, amphibians, and benthic invertebrates suffering the same impacts downstream of these sites? There is evidence that prey populations are depressed at and immediately surrounding grow sites, but do they recover quickly if the sites are remediated? We suspect the answers to these questions will become evident over time as the public becomes more aware, as more investigators begin addressing these issues, and as partnerships between researchers and law enforcement continue to grow. New sites continue to stack up each year, creating a backlog of legacy impacts that will be difficult to reconcile with even the greatest public awareness and joint remediation efforts.

All that we know and do not know regarding the cumulative landscape impacts of this illicit activity on our public lands and the daunting quantity and distribution of cultivation sites can be overwhelming. Despite this reality, agencies, tribes, nongovernmental organizations (NGOs), and individual citizens are approaching this problem head-on, tackling site cleanups wherever they can and with the little funding available. In fall of 2014, in an immense six-day effort by NGOs, California state and federal agency scientists and law enforcement officers, citizens and local tribal members, and National Guard soldiers, the chemicals, infrastructure, and garbage from ten separate sites on Six Rivers and Shasta-Trinity National Forests were removed; the total haul-out amounted to five tons of cultivation infrastructure and garbage, including several hundred pounds of fertilizer and pesticides. In another effort in 2015 with the same collaboration of participants, five sites on tribal land and ten sites on Northern California's national forest were reclaimed. But cleanups are not limited to northern California. In 2014 a joint effort between the US Forest Service, California Department of Fish and Wildlife, and nonprofit partners remediated thirteen trespass grow sites on the Sierra and Sequoia National Forests, removing 3.5 tons of garbage, 15 miles of irrigation tubing, and over thirty containers of pesticides and rodenticides. In addition to these comprehensive, focused efforts, the multi-agency law enforcement teams tasked with locating, surveilling, and eradicating trespass cultivation sites often haul a few net loads of trash and pesticides out of many of the sites they raid, even though they are under no mandate and have no funding to do so. Though this problem may cause many a feeling of helplessness, small steps to initiate the recovery of our public lands by these partnerships are a start and can inspire the public to be more involved and aware. Likewise, more complete investigation and documentation of the scope of this problem can encourage policy makers to draft support for continued monitoring, remediation efforts, and enforcement to prevent this clandestine activity from taking root in the first place. While the forests wait for a more permanent solution to safeguard them from this ruthless invasion, these new partnerships will continue chipping away at this enduring insult to California's vast and exquisite public lands.

WORKS CITED

Ferreras, P., A. Travaini, S. C. Zapata, and M. Delibes. 2011. "Short-Term Responses of Mammalian Carnivores to a Sudden Collapse of Rabbits in Mediterranean Spain." *Basic and Applied Ecology* 12: 116–124.

Gabriel, M. W., G. M. Wengert, J. M. Higley, S. Krogen, W. Sargent, and D. L. Clifford. 2013. "Silent Forests? Rodenticides on Illegal Marijuana Crops Harm Wildlife." *Wildlife Professional* 7: 46–50.

Gabriel, M. W., G. M. Wengert, L. W. Woods, N. Stephenson, J. M. Higley, C. Thompson, S. M. Matthews, R. A. Sweitzer, K. Purcell, R. H. Barrett, S. M. Keller, P. Gaffney, M. Jones, R. Poppenga, J. E. Foley, R. N. Brown, D. Clifford, and B. N. Sacks. 2015. "Patterns of Natural and Human-caused Mortality Factors of a Rare Forest Carnivore, the Fisher (*Pekania pennanti*) in California." *PLOS ONE* 10, 11: e0140640. doi:10.1371/journal.pone.0140640.

Gabriel, M. W., L. W. Woods, R. Poppenga, R. A. Sweitzer, C. Thompson, S. M. Matthews, J. Mark Higley, S. M. Keller, K. Purcell, R. H. Barrett, G. M. Wengert, B. N. Sacks, and D. L. Clifford. 2012. "Anticoagulant Rodenticides on our Public and Community Lands: Spatial Distribution of Exposure and Poisoning of a Rare Forest Carnivore." *PLOS ONE* 7, 7:e40163.

Medel, M., and Y. Lu. 2015. "Illegal Drug Cultivation in Mexico: An Examination of the Environmental and Human Factors." *Cartography and Geographic Information Science* 42, 2: 190–204. doi: 10.1080/15230406.2014.985716.

Nores, J., Jr., and J. A. Swan. 2010. *War in the Woods: Combating the Marijuana Cartels on America's Public Lands.* Guilford, CT: Globe Pequot.

Partelow, C. D. 2008. "Using GIS to Depict Resource Risk from Probable Cannabis Cultivation Sites." MA thesis, San Jose State University.

Pereira, J. A., N. G. Fracassi, M. M. Uhart. 2006. "Numerical and Spatial Responses of Geoffroy's Cat (*Oncifelis geoffroyi*) to Prey Decline in Argentina." *Journal of Mammalogy* 87: 1132–1139.

Richards, N., ed. 2011. *Carbofuran and Wildlife Poisoning: Global Perspectives and Forensic Approaches*. Hoboken, NJ: Wiley.

Schmidt, K. 2008. "Behavioural and Spatial Adaptation of the Eurasian Lynx to a Decline in Prey Availability." *Acta Theriologica* 53: 1–16.

Thompson, C. M., R. A. Sweitzer, M. W. Gabriel, K. Purcell, R. H. Barrett, and R. Poppenga. 2013. "Impacts of Rodenticide and Insecticide Toxicants from Marijuana Cultivation Sites on Fisher Survival Rates in the Sierra National Forest, California." *Conservation Letters* 7. DOI: 10.1111/conl.12038.

Wengert, G. M., M. W. Gabriel, S. M. Matthews, J. M. Higley, R. A. Sweitzer, C. Thompson, K. Purcell, R. H. Barrett, and L. W. Woods. 2014. "Using DNA to Describe and Quantify Interspecific Killing of Fishers in California." *Journal of Wildlife Management* 78: 603–611.

USFWS. 2014. Draft Species Report, Fisher (*Pekania pennanti*), West Coast Population. Washington, DC: US Fish and Wildlife Service.

CHAPTER 3

Effects of Illegal Marijuana Cultivation on Wildlife

Pesticide Exposure in a Native Carnivore and Consequences for the Species' Survival

Craig Thompson, Mourad W. Gabriel,
Greta M. Wengert, and J. Mark Higley

In April 2009 technicians with the University of California Sierra Nevada Adaptive Management Project recovered the carcass of an adult male fisher in the Sierra National Forest just south of Yosemite National Park. As part of the project, researchers were monitoring fisher response to forest and fuel management projects in the area by tracking their movements and survival. Fishers, a large, secretive member of the weasel family, were being considered for listing under both the California and federal Endangered Species Acts, and researchers were attempting to understand how forest management, designed to reduce the prevalence of large wildfires in the western United States, would impact the species.

This particular fisher presented a bit of a mystery, however. The animal appeared young and healthy, with no telltale signs of disease of injury. Its body was completely intact, lying adjacent to a large log, ruling out predation by a larger carnivore (a common cause of death for fishers). Based on the lack of evidence in the field, the carcass was submitted to the University of California, Davis veterinary pathology lab for a full necropsy, and results indicated the animal had died of acute toxicosis associated with ingesting anticoagulant rodenticides (ARs) (Gabriel et al. 2012). Here the mystery deepened further; while there is a long history of wildlife being accidently poisoned with ARs it is typically associated with agricultural or residential areas where landowners use the poisons to protect

Figure 3.1. Packets of rodenticide found at an illegal grow site.
Courtesy of Hoopa Tribal Forestry

crops or homes from damage. This animal, tracked for most of its adult life, had not gone near these areas, instead spending its time in a relatively remote section of the Sierra National Forest.

Perplexed by the source of the poison and the quantity the animal must have encountered to cause such a rapid death, researchers first began testing samples from fishers that had died of other causes and had been previously collected as part of ongoing research projects in the Sierras and northwestern California. They were astounded to realize that almost 80 percent of all fishers collected within the Sierra National Forest over the past three years tested positive for AR exposure (Gabriel et al. 2012). And they tested positive for not just one toxic compound but many compounds. A total of six different AR compounds were identified, with individual animals showing exposure to as many as four toxicants (Gabriel et al. 2012). Ultimately, the diversity of compounds identified provided a clue to the source; discussions with local law enforcement agents revealed that many of the same toxicants were being found at illegal marijuana cultivation sites located on public lands throughout California and southern Oregon.

Covert marijuana gardens on public lands are unique within the realm of wildlife ecotoxicology. Most wildlife poisoning is associated either with the use or misuse of pesticides associated with agricultural or residential areas, or with a single, large contamination event (Berny 2007). In comparison, marijuana gardens are small, generally half to 4 acres, yet the level of contamination within that area is severe, with fertilizers, pesticides, and other toxicants being distributed in orders of magnitude greater volume than manufacturer recommendations (Gabriel et al. 2013). Often compounds banned within the United States, such as carbofuran and DDT, are found (EPA 2009; Thompson et al. 2014). The use of toxicants is also not limited to protecting the plants from damage by rodents or insects. Often cans of tuna, cat food, or sardines are found, mixed with concentrated insecticides and distributed around the garden and associated camp in an effort to kill any animal approaching the area (Levy 2014). Furthermore, hundreds to thousands of these sites are located on public land in the western United States, often as many as five or six within the home range of a single fisher (USFWS 2014; Thompson et al. 2014). In a three-year period, almost 50 metric tons of marijuana were con-fiscated on public lands, and this may represent as little as 15 percent of the total production (Miller 2012; Bricker et al. 2014). Together, the intensity and scale of the problem create a unique threat to wildlife that has the potential to negatively impact individuals as well as populations (USFWS 2014).

In 2015 another study was published providing updated and expanded data on the exposure rates of fishers not only to AR compounds but also to other pesticides such as carbamate and organophosphate (OP) insecticides (Gabriel et al. 2015). The study reported that exposure rates statewide had increased to 85 percent, and the percentage of fisher mortalities that could be directly attributed to acute pesticide poisoning rose from 5.6 percent to 18.7 percent (Gabriel et al. 2015). Evidence has also begun to emerge that other species are being poisoned as well. The California Department of Fish and Wildlife (CDFW) reported detecting ARs in bears legally harvested from the Sierra National Forest (D. Fidler, CDFW personal communication), and barred owls from the Hoopa Valley Reservation in Northern California tested positive as well (Higley, unpublished data).

That same year, CDFW proposed to list fishers as threatened under the CA En-dangered Species Act. The US Fish and Wildlife Service also proposed to list the species as threatened under the federal Endangered Species Act, and the potential impacts of illegal marijuana gardens played a significant role in both decisions (USFWS 2014). Here, we outline the variety of ways in which the type, scale, and pattern of poisoning may contribute to the species' threatened status while recognizing that fishers are not alone in this struggle. Evidence of impacts to other species are continuing to emerge.

INDIVIDUAL (DIRECT) IMPACTS

Historically, wildlife ecotoxicology studies have focused on understanding the impacts to individual animals; the LD_{50} value (value at which 50 percent of study animals die) or the exposure rate among individuals (Hayashi et al. 2009; Kohler and Triebskorn 2013) has often been considered as indicative of impacts on individuals and populations. As a result, extensive information exists on the potential direct effects of rodenticides or insecticides on wildlife. While responses are species-specific (Berny 2007) and little is known about fishers' sensitivity per se, much can be extrapolated from studies involving other species. Even experimental studies involving insects or fish can be used to better understand how toxicants may interact with each other or act in concert with other environmental stressors.

Fishers in the western United States are primarily carnivorous; however, they exploit a wide variety of prey resources including small mammals, insects, vegetation, and carrion (Zielinski and Duncan 2004). As a result, they may ingest a lethal dose of toxicants secondarily, through the consumption of poisoned rodents and/or insects (Fournier-Chambrillon et al. 2004) or directly, through the consumption of flavored baits. Many over-the-counter rodenticides include flavorizers, such as bacon or cheese, to increase the attraction to small mammals (Gabriel et al. 2012).

Anticoagulant rodenticides are designed to kill mammals by inhibiting an animal's ability to recycle vitamin K, thereby limiting the animal's production of critical blood-clotting factors. This results in symptoms such as bleeding nose, fatigue, and trouble breathing. In acute cases, it causes damage to small blood vessels throughout the body, resulting in widespread internal hemorrhaging (Berny 2007; Rattner et al. 2014). Many anticoagulant rodenticides currently used are referred to as *second generation* due to the increased toxicity and the ability of a target animal to consume a lethal dose in a single feeding bout. However, just because a rodent consumes a lethal dose in one sitting does not mean it dies immediately; it can take up to nine days for the animal to succumb to the poison, during which time it may act lethargic and erratic, increasing the likelihood of predation by a fisher or other carnivore (Cox and Smith 1990; Bradbury 2008; Gabriel et al. 2012). In one controlled study, Norway rats (*Rattus norvegicus*) given a choice of rodenticide bait and untreated food consumed 40 to 80 times the lethal dose over 6.5 days (Erickson and Urban 2004). If toxicants are present in large quantities—and they typically are—a single rodent may contain sufficient rodenticide to impact a larger predator such as a fisher or bobcat. Furthermore, small mammals are not the only source of anticoagulant rodenticide at illegal grow sites. Invertebrates do not utilize vitamin K in the same manner as mammals, and as a result they can accumulate large doses of rodenticide compounds without negative effects. Bioaccumulation of ARs has been documented in both earthworms (*Aporrectodea caliginosa*) and snails (*Cantareus aspersus*) (Booth et al. 2003), and secondary AR poisoning of insectivores has been documented in European hedgehogs (Dowding et al. 2010).

OP and carbamates are referred to as *anticholinesterase inhibitors*, and they act by interfering with neurotransmitter activity within the brain and central nervous system. In acute cases, seizures and respiratory failure are the primary cause of death (Galloway and Handy 2003). While it is possible to accumulate a lethal or sublethal dose of these toxicants through secondary poisoning and the consumption of scavenged rodents or insects (Berny 2007; Elliot et al. 1996; Wobeser et al. 2004), the most likely source of carnivore poisoning with these toxicants is intentional poisoning by growers. In Northern California, researchers observed hot dogs laced with concentrated methomyl, a potent carbamate insecticide, hung in a perimeter around a grow site. Nearby, a dead fisher was found with pieces of a hot dog still lodged in its throat, suggesting it had died before it even fully ingested the bait. In Southern California, a tuna can collected from a grow site tested positive for carbofuran, a highly lethal carbamate insecticide banned in the United States. Nearby, a dead juvenile coyote tested positive for carbamate poisoning. Given the lethality of these toxicants in concentrated form (Arnot et al. 2011), death is presumably very rapid.

Chronic exposure to low doses of organophosphate pesticides has been shown to significantly reduce the immune response through reduced activity of the Th1 and NK cells (Li and Kawada 2006; Janeway et al. 2007; Zabrodskii et al. 2012), as well as through damage done to immune organs (Galloway and Handy 2003). Pheasants exposed to a single sublethal dose showed impacts to lymphoid organs and lesions on both the thymus and spleen (Day et al. 1995). Vidal et al. (2009) found that voles exposed to the anticoagulant chlorophacine had a higher incidence of infection by the zoonotic pathogen *F. tularensis*. A high level of correlation between AR exposure and notoedric mange in bobcats and mountain lions in Southern California has led several authors to speculate about a link between AR exposure and immune system compromise in these species (Riley et al. 2007; Serieys et al. 2015). Host-parasite relationships may also be influenced by sublethal pesticide or rodenticide exposure. While this is difficult to document in free-ranging wildlife, laboratory experiments have shown a strong, synergistic relationship between pesticide exposure and parasite infestation, resulting in reduced survival (Coors et al. 2008; Coors and Meester 2008). Anecdotally, Gabriel et al. (2012) noted high levels of tick infestation in two fishers that died of rodenticide poisoning, compared to sympatric mesocarnivores (Gabriel et al. 2009).

Animals exposed to sublethal doses of ARs or insecticides are sluggish and weak, and they often behave in odd or erratic manners (Cox and Smith 1992; Fournier-Chambrillion et al. 2004; Berney 2007). This leads to greater predation risk due to preferential targeting of weak or disabled individuals by predators (Lafferty and Morris 1996; Elliot et al. 1977; Milinski and Lowenstein 1980) as well as a failure to respond appropriately when threatened. For example, Rudeback (1950) observed that raptors were twice as successful when attacking injured or abnormally behaving prey. Rats exposed to sublethal doses of ARs showed dramatic changes in anti-predator behavior: abandoning nocturnal behavior, failing to use cover when available, and standing still when threatened as opposed to seeking security (Cox and Smith 1990). Tadpoles exposed to sublethal doses of DDT were more likely to be predated by newts (Cooke 1971), and Farr (1977) found that grass shrimp (*Palaemonetes pugio*) exposed to an organophosphate insecticide were more easily captured by predatory fish. And in an extremely telling experiment, Hunt et al. (1992) reported that house sparrows exposed to a single sublethal dose of the organophosphate pesticide fenthion were sixteen times more likely to be captured by a predator than unexposed sparrows within the same flock. While it is difficult to quantify any additional risk of predation upon fishers exposed to sublethal doses of toxicants at illegal marijuana gardens, we can safely assume that (1) exposed animals will behave erratically, and (2) erratic behavior in a wild animal leads to increased predation risk.

The ability of an animal to recover from physical injury has also been shown to be negatively impacted by exposure to OP pesticides and ARs. OP exposure at sublethal doses, combined with physical injury, increased the likelihood of mortality in injured rats due to reduced immune system activity (Zabrodskii et al. 2002). Similarly, secondary sublethal exposure to ARs has been shown to reduce the blood-clotting activity in numerous animals, including screech owls (*Otus asio*: Rattner et al. 2012), weasels (*Mustela nivalis*: Townsend et al. 1984), barn owls (*Tyto alba*: Webster 2009), and rats (*Rattus norvegicus*: Bailey et al. 2005). Erickson and Urban (2004) reported multiple instances where predators with liver concentrations of ARs as low as 0.03 µg/g died as a result of excessive bleeding from minor wounds inflicted by prey. For example, the authors reported a necropsy of a red-tailed hawk that "seemed to have exsanguinated through a minor toe wound" and was found to have a 0.46 µg/g liver concentration of the rodenticide BRD, and another necropsy of a great horned owl (*Bubo virginianus*) with 0.27 µg/g BRM (another AR) and 0.08 µg/g BRD that "died from hemorrhaging of minor wounds inflicted by prey." It has also been demonstrated that while internal hemorrhaging associated with AR exposure can be spontaneous, it is often initiated and/or exacerbated by trauma, which "is not that unusual in free-ranging wildlife" (Rattner et al. 2014).

Underlying all concerns about direct effects is the lack of information available regarding the potential for additive or synergistic effects of exposure to multiple compounds. *Additive effects* refers to an animal suffering symptoms associated with two or more toxicants. Synergism may occur when one toxin influences the activation, transportation, absorption, or detoxification of another (Thompson 1995).

In a synergistic interaction, the total effect is "greater than the sum of the parts." Gabriel et al. (2015) reported that the average number of toxicants detected in an exposed fisher was 1.7, ranging from 1 to 5, and interactions between toxicants has been documented in other species. Macek (1969) conducted a controlled experiment looking at the effect of thirty-seven different pesticide combinations in bluegill (*Lepomis macrochirus*) and reported that effects were additive in 59 percent of combinations and synergistic in 35 percent. In another experiment, the organophosphate pesticides malathion and EPN, dosed at one-fortieth and one-fiftieth of the LD_{50} doses, respectively, resulted in 100 percent mortality in domestic dogs (Cope 1971), indicating the potential for strong synergistic interactions between these compounds. Similar synergistic interactions have been reported in mice, rats, pigeons, fish, quail, and partridge (reviewed in Thompson 1995). Given the variety of insecticides, rodenticides, herbicides, molluscicides, fungicides, and so on found at these sites (see Table 3.1; Gabriel et al. 2012; Thompson et al. 2014) and the fact that fishers showed exposure to as many as five AR compounds alone, the risk of chemical interactions inflating the behavioral and physiological effects must be considered.

LOCAL (INDIRECT) EFFECTS

Researchers have paid far less attention to the potential indirect effects of pesticide contamination on a sensitive wildlife population. Indirect effects can be considered as "local scale," impacting multiple animals living in the vicinity of a grow site. Indirect effects include changes to prey availability and habitat quality, as well as potential interactions with local stressors such as weather (Morris et al. 2005; Gibbons et al. 2015).

Research on the impacts of pesticide or rodenticide contamination to food web interactions is rare, and conclusions are mixed. Often studies are small and confounded by the ability of larger animals to move into and away from treated areas (Gibbons et al. 2015). For example, Norelius and Lockwood (1999) studied the impact of pesticide treatments on grassland bird densities. While insect densities were markedly reduced following treatment, bird densities were unaffected. Comparatively, Peveling et al. (2003) found that locust control efforts in Madagascar led to an unintended reduction in harvester termite (*Coarctotermes clepsydra*) populations, followed by decreases in termite predators including iguana (*Chalarodon madagascariensis*), skink (*Mabuy elegans*), and the hedgehog tenrec (*Echinops telfairi*). It is difficult to predict how local reductions in small mammal or insect densities would impact fishers; however, the documented relationship between female fisher mortality and the number of marijuana plots within her home range (Thompson et al. 2014) indicates that the potential for negative effects should not be ignored.

Table 3.1. Summary of Toxicants Collected at Covert Marijuana Grow Sites on Sequoia-Kings Canyon National Park and Whiskeytown National Recreation Area, California

Active Ingredient	Category	Class	Brand Names (found at sites)	Bioaccumulation Potential[a]	Mammal Toxicity[b]	Bird Toxicity[c]	Fish Toxicity[d]
Acephate	Insecticide	Organophosphate	Orthonex	Low	Moderate	Moderate	Low
Aldicarb	Insecticide	Carbamate	Temik	Low	High	High	Moderate
Bifenthrin	Insecticide	Pyrethroid	Ortho Bug-B-Gone, Ortho-Klor	High	High	Moderate	High
Brodifacoum	Rodenticide	Anticoagulant	D-Con	High	High	High	High
Bromethalin	Rodenticide	Unclassified	Real Kill Rat and Mouse Killer	High	High	High	High
Carbaryl	Insecticide	Carbamate	Sevin	Low	Moderate	Moderate	Moderate
Carbofuran	Insecticide	Carbamate	Furadan	Low	High	High	Moderate
Chlorpyrifos	Insecticide	Organophosphate	Ortho Dursban	High	High	High	High
Cyfluthrin	Insecticide	Pyrethroid	Bayer Advanced Garden Insect Killer	Moderate	High	Moderate	High
Diazinon	Insecticide	Organophosphate	Ortho Diazinon	Moderate	Moderate	High	High
Diphacinone	Rodenticide	Anticoagulant	JT Eaton Gopher Poison, Tomcat Bait Chunx, Wilco Ground Squirrel Bait	High	High	Low	Moderate
d-trans Allethrin	Insecticide	Pyrethroid	Real-Kill Ant Killer	High	Moderate	Low	Moderate
Fenbutatin-oxide	Insecticide	Organotin	Orthonex	Moderate	Low	Moderate	High
Gamma-Cyhalothrin	Insecticide	Pyrethroid	Specracide Triazicide	High	High	Low	High
Hydramethylnon	Insecticide	Trifluoromethyl aminohydrazone	Grants Ant Bait	Low	Moderate	Moderate	Moderate
Malathion	Insecticide	Organophosphate	Ortho Malathion	Low	Moderate	Moderate	High

(continued on next page)

Table 3.1. (*continued*)

Active Ingredient	Category	Class	Brand Names (found at sites)	Bioaccumulation Potential[a]	Mammal Toxicity[b]	Bird Toxicity[c]	Fish Toxicity[d]
Permethrin	Insecticide	Pyrethroid	Orthomax Garden and Landscape Insect Killer; KGRO Ready to Use Multi-Purpose Insect Killer Granules, Ortho Ant-B-Gone	Moderate	Moderate	Low	High
Phenothrin	Insecticide	Pyrethroid	Ortho Flying Insect Killer	Moderate	Low	Low	High
Pyrethrum	Insecticide	Pyrethroid	Ortho Ant-B-Gone	Low	Moderate	Low	High
Tetramethrin	Insecticide	Pyrethroid	Ortho Flying Insect Killer	Low	Low	Low	High
Tralomethrin	Insecticide	Pyrethroid	Real-Kill Ant Killer	High	High	Low	High
Triforine	Fungicide	Piperazine derivative	Orthonex	Low	Low	Low	Low
Zinc Phosphide	Rodenticide	Unclassified	Sure Stop Gopher Killer, Sweeney's Poison Peanuts, Grant's Gopher Killer	Low	High	High	Moderate

Source: Jeffcoach 2012.
Note: All thresholds are derived from EPA regulatory guidelines.
a. Octanol-water partition coefficient (Log P) where < 2.7 = low bioaccumulation, 2.7–3.0 = moderate, and > 3.0 = high.
b. Acute oral LD50 (mg kg-1) where > 2,000 = low, 100–2,000 = moderate, and < 100 = high.
c. Acute LD50 (mg kg-1) where > 2,000 = low, 100–2,000 = moderate, and < 100 = high.
d. Acute 96-hour LC50 (mg l-1) where > 100 = low, 0.1–100 = moderate, and < 0.1 = high.

The impact of illegal marijuana cultivation on water resources has been well-established. Throughout the region, streams may be completely dewatered as they are diverted into catchment ponds or irrigation systems. In an analysis of four watersheds in Northern California, Bauer et al. (2015) found that demand for water, based on the number of marijuana gardens observed in the watershed, could exceed the maximum flow rates for three of the four streams. And flow in the fourth steam, the largest, would be reduced by 23 percent. In the southern Sierra Nevada, a more xeric environment, the lead author has observed numerous small streams and seeps drained for the irrigation of clandestine marijuana plots (C. Thompson, USFS personal observation). Additionally, water that is diverted is often mixed with chemicals and fertilizers before being used for irrigation. The risk of these contaminants returning to the hydrologic system appears to vary, being greater in mesic areas where the hydrologic system is more active (Thompson and Gabriel, unpublished data). More information is needed to better understand how reductions in water availability and quality will impact fishers, a species already pushing the southern extent of its range in the Sierra Nevada mountains.

Sublethal exposure to pesticides can influence local reproductive rates in a variety of ways. Exposure of rats to low doses of insecticides has been implicated in reduced sperm production, reduced pregnancy rates, and higher rates of spontaneous abortion, stillbirth, and premature birth (Bal et al. 2012; Cox 2001; Gawade et al. 2013; Tingle et al. 2003). Yet, in addition to these physiological effects, several additional factors may exacerbate the impact of grow site contamination on fishers; timing, movement, and weather.

The majority of documented fisher mortality due to acute rodenticide poisoning occurs in the spring (Gabriel et al. 2015), when growers are aggressively protecting young marijuana plants and fishers are actively breeding, giving birth, and provisioning dependent kits. Fishers mate during a brief period only, immediately after females give birth in the spring. Females may remain in estrus for only 3–5 weeks (Frost et al. 1997), and to maximize their reproductive potential, male fishers move widely during this period, visiting as many females as they can. GPS telemetry collar data indicate that males do not search randomly but move long distances rapidly and directly between female dens, indicating a familiarity with the landscape and memory of female den sites (Thompson, unpublished data).

Experiments with migratory birds indicate that adults given low doses of insecticides over several days lost their ability to properly orient themselves for migration for almost a week post-exposure. However, juveniles given the same treatment were unaffected, and researchers hypothesized that the mechanism for disorientation somehow involved memory of the migration routes (Vyas et al. 1995, 1996). While the evidence is scarce, any disruption in male fishers' ability to navigate

Figure 3.2. Pacific fisher near Hoopa. *Courtesy of Hoopa Tribal Forestry*

during the brief reproductive window could have significant consequences to local reproductive rates.

Female fishers give birth in early spring, using tree cavities as den sites. Fisher kits are unable to adequately thermoregulate until they are approximately thirty days old, so females may select den sites to maximize solar exposure and are only absent from the den for limited periods to hunt. Sublethal exposure to pesticides has been shown to cause short-term hypothermia in a number of birds and mammals (Jaques 1959; Ahdaya et al. 1976; Martin and Solomon 1991; Gordon 1994). Given that the risk of exposure appears to peak in the spring, when weather is highly variable and females are already stressed with provisioning kits, reduced thermoregulatory capacity could result in reduced hunting efficiency, kit abandonment, and female mortality. Furthermore, evidence exists that AR compounds can be transferred from a female fisher to dependent kits through lactation (Gabriel et al. 2012), and female fishers frequently provision weaned kits with small mammals. This raises the concern that kits may die of exposure or secondary poisoning during this sensitive period.

POPULATION-LEVEL EFFECTS

Understanding the population-level impacts of pesticide poisoning is a difficult and complex task, one that is rarely attempted. Historically, most ecological risk assessments have relied on what are commonly referred to as *benchmark assessments* (Sample et al. 1993; Salice et al. 2011), where contaminant levels in either the environment or sampled species is compared to some threshold presumed to represent no adverse effect. However, this fails to account for myriad potential population-level factors, such as variable effects according to age (Caswell 1996), the interaction of multiple toxicants and other environmental stressors (Thompson 1995; Coors and Meester 2008), and the impact of sublethal dosages on demographic parameters (Forbes et al. 2001; Knillmann et al. 2012). Furthermore, it has been established that a species' ecology may have as great an influence on population-level impacts as the toxicity of a particular substance (Dalkvist et al. 2009). Yet despite these challenges, moving beyond individual impacts is critical in assessing the potential impact of widespread contamination on a threatened species such as the fisher (Kohler and Triebskorn 2013).

One critical question is the relationship between toxicant impacts and density dependence, meaning that the negative impacts of poisoning could be mitigated by a density-dependent response in a territorial species such as the fisher. Schipper et al. (2013) modeled the population-level impacts of pesticide contamination on peregrine falcons (*Falco peregrinus*). They found that initially, toxicant-induced reductions in population density were buffered by the filling of open territories by young falcons. However, once density was no longer a limiting factor, the population dropped rapidly. Salice et al. (2011) incorporated toxic effects into a density-dependent, individual-based population for mink in order to evaluate potential remediation strategies. They found that stable populations were driven toward extinction with the addition of pesticide-related mortality, and the speed at which remediation was implemented was the strongest factor in population recovery.

Spencer et al. (2011) modeled fisher population density for the southern Sierras and suggested that the population was failing to expand, despite over fifty years of protection, due to high mortality rates. The authors demonstrated that a 10–20 percent increase in mortality would be sufficient to limit population growth. Zielinski et al. (2013) analyzed long-term monitoring data and concluded that fisher occupancy rates had remained stable over the past eight years despite the fact that Gabriel et al. (2015) documented an increase in toxicant-related direct mortality from 5.6 percent to 18.7 percent between 2007 and 2014. Given that fishers are a territorial species subject to density-dependent population control, it is possible that they would exhibit a similar population response to that observed by Schipper et al. (2013): population stability while density dependent buffers the effect of increased mortality until a threshold is reached, after which the population drops rapidly. Independent of this speculation, it is clear that pesticide-related mortality levels have reached those identified by Spencer et al. (2011) as sufficient to limit population expansion even without accounting for sublethal effects.

Fishers are currently the "canary in the coal mine" regarding wildlife poisoning associated with illegal marijuana gardens on public lands. The problem is clearly extensive, with 85 percent of fishers tested in the state of California testing positive for exposure, and exposure rates increasing (Gabriel et al. 2015). The problem was only discovered by accident; had researchers not been looking at fisher population dynamics for other reasons it is unlikely the scope of the problem would have been realized. There is no reason to assume that other species inhabiting the same landscape are not similarly impacted, though their susceptibility is likely to vary according to ecology, physiology, or population status. Fishers are clearly susceptible to many of the direct effects described above, ranging from direct mortality to increased disease and predation rates. And while the relationship is complex and not yet well-understood, the sheer number of marijuana cultivation sites throughout the region and the diversity of threats they pose argues for a strong population-level impact.

WORKS CITED

Ahdaya, S. M., P. V. Shah, and F. E. Guthrie. 1976. "Thermoregulation in Mice Treated with Parathion, Carbaryl, or DDT." *Toxicology and Applied Pharmacology* 35, 575–580.

Arnot, L. F., D. J. H. Veale, J. C. A. Steyl, and J. G. Myburgh. 2011. "Treatment Rationale for Dogs Poisoned with Aldicarb (Carbamate Pesticide)." *Journal of the South African Veterinary Association* 82: 232–238.

Bailey, C., P. Fisher, and C. T. Eason. 2005. "Assessing Anticoagulation Resistance in Rats and Coagulation Effects in Birds Using Small Volume Blood Samples." *Science for Conservation* 249: 5–22.

Bal R., G. Türk, O. Yılma, E. Etem, T. Kuloğlu, G. Baydaş, and M. Nazıroğlu. 2012. "Effects of Clothianidin Exposure on Sperm Quality, Testicular Apoptosis and Fatty Acid Composition in Developing Male Rats." *Cell Biology and Toxicology* 28: 187–200.

Bauer, S., J. Olson, A. Cockrill, M. van Hatten, L. Miller, M. Tauzer, and G. Leppig. 2015. "Impacts of Surface Water Diversion for Marijuana Cultivation on Aquatic Habitat in Four Northwestern California Watersheds." *PLOS ONE.*

Berny, P. 2007. "Pesticides and the Intoxication of Wild Animals." *Journal of Veterinary Pharmacology Therapy* 30: 93–100.

Booth, I. H., P. Fisher, V. Heppelthwaite, and C. T. Eason. 2003. "Toxicity and Residues of Brodifacoum in Snails and Earthworms." *DOC Science Internal Series* 143. Wellington: New Zealand Department of Conservation.

Bradbury, S. 2008. "Risk Mitigation Decision for Ten Rodenticides." Washington, DC: US Environmental Protection Agency, Office of Prevention, Pesticides and Toxic Substance.

Bricker, K. S., M. T. J. Brownlee, and J. R. Rose. 2014. "Illegal Marijuana Cultivation on Public Lands: Management Perspectives." Unpublished report. Salt Lake City: University of Utah College of Health, Department of Parks, Recreation, and Tourism.

Caswell, H. 1996. "Demography Meets Ecotoxicology: Untangling the Population Level Effects of Toxic Substances." In *Ecotoxicology: A Hierarchical Treatment*, eds. Michael C. Newman and Charles H. Jagoe, 255–292. Boca Raton, FL: CRC Publishers.

Cooke, A. S. 1971. "Selective Predation by Newts on Frog Tadpoles Treated with DDT." *Nature* 229: 275–276.

Coors, A., E. Decaestecker, M. Jensen, and L. De Meester. 2008. "Pesticide Exposure Strongly Enhances Parasite Virulence in an Invertebrate Host." *Oikos* 117: 1840–1846.

Coors, A., and L. De Meester. 2008. "Synergistic, Antagonistic, and Additive Effects of Multiple Stressors: Predation Threat, Parasitism, and Pesticide Exposure in *Daphnia magna*." *Journal of Applied Ecology* 45: 1820–1828.

Cope, O. B. 1971. "Interactions between Pesticides and Wildlife." *Annual Review of Entomology* 16: 325–364.

Cox, C. 2001. "Insecticide Factsheet: Imidacloprid." *Journal of Pesticide Reform* 21: 15–21.

Cox, P. R., and R. H. Smith. 1990. "Rodenticide Ecotoxicology: Assessing Non-target Population Effects." *Functional Ecology* 4: 15–320.

Dalkvist, T., C. J. Topping, and V. E. Forbes. 2009. "Population-Level Impacts of Pesticide-Induced Chronic Effects on Individuals Depend More on Ecology than Toxicology." *Ecotoxicology and Environmental Safety* 72: 1663–1672.

Day, B. L., M. M. Walser, J. M. Sharma, and D. E. Andersen. 1995. "Immunopathology of 8-Week-Old Ring-Necked Pheasants (*Phasianus colchicus*) Exposed to Malathion." *Environmental Toxicology and Chemistry* 14: 1719–1726.

Dowding, C. V., R. F. Shore, A. Worgan, P. J. Baker, and S. Harris. 2010. "Accumulation of Anticoagulant Rodenticides in a Non-target Insectivore, the European Hedgehog (*Erinaceus europaeus*)." *Environmental Pollution* 158: 161–166.

Elliot, J. E., K. M. Langelier, P. Mineau, and L. K. Wilson. 1996. "Poisoning of Bald Eagles and Red-Tailed Hawks by Carbofuran and Fensulfothion in the Fraser Delta of British Columbia, Canada." *Journal of Wildlife Diseases* 32: 486–491.

Elliot, J. P., I. McTaggart Cowan, and C. S. Holling. 1977. "Prey Capture by the Africa Lion." *Canadian Journal of Zoology* 55: 1811–1828.

EPA (Environmental Protection Agency). 2009. Carbofuran; Final Tolerance Revocations; Final Rule. Federal Register 74: 23045–23095.

Erickson, W., and D. Urban. 2004. "Potential Risks of Nine Rodenticides to Birds and Nontarget Mammals: A Comparative Approach." Washington, DC: US Environmental Protection Agency, Office of Pesticides Programs, Environmental Fate and Effects Division.

Farr, J. A. 1977. "Impairment of Antipredator Behavior in *Palaemonetes pugio* by Exposure to Sublethal Doses of Parathion." *Transactions of the American Fisheries Society* 106: 287–290.

Forbes, V. E., R. M. Sibly, and P. Calow. 2001. "Toxicant Impacts on Density-Limited Populations: A Critical Review of Theory, Practice, and Results." *Ecological Applications* 11: 1249–1257.

Fournier-Chambrillon, C., P. J. Berny, O. Coiffier, P. Barbedienne, B. Dasse, G. Delas, H. Galineau, A. Mazet, P. Pouzenc, R. Rosoux, and P. Fournier. 2004. "Evidence of Secondary Poisoning of Free-Ranging Riparian Mustelids by Anticoagulant Rodenticides in France: Implications for Conservation of European Mink (*Mustella letreola*)." *Journal of Wildlife Diseases* 40: 688–695.

Frost, H. C., W. B. Krohn, and C. R. Wallace. 1997. "Age-Specific Reproductive Characteristics in Fishers." *Journal of Mammalogy* 78: 598–612.

Gabriel, M. W., R. N. Brown, J. E. Foley, J. M. Higley, and R. G. Botzler. 2009. "Ecology of Anaplasma phagocytophilum Infection in Gray Foxes (*Urocyon cinereoargenteus*) in Northwestern California." *Journal of Wildlife Diseases* 45: 344–354.

Gabriel, M. W., G. M. Wengert, J. M. Higley, S. Krogan, W. Sargent, and D. L. Clifford. 2013. "Silent Forests?" *Wildlife Professional* 7: 46–50.

Gabriel, M. W., L. W. Woods, R. Poppenga, R. A. Sweitzer, C. M. Thompson, S. M. Matthews, J. M. Higley, S. M. Keller, K. L. Purcell, R. H. Barrett, G. M. Wengert, B. N. Sacks, and D. L. Clifford. 2012. "Anticoagulant Rodenticides on our Public and Community Lands: Spatial Distribution of Exposure and Poisoning of a Rare Forest Carnivore." *PLOS ONE* 7: e40163.

Gabriel, M. W., L. W. Woods, G. M. Wengert, N. Stephenson, J. M. Higley, C. Thompson, S. M. Matthews, R. A. Sweitzer, K. Purcell, R. H. Barrett, S. M. Keller, P. Gaffney, M. Jones, R. Poppenga, J. E. Foley, R. N. Brown, D. L. Clifford, and B. N. Sacks. 2015. "Patterns of Natural and Human-Caused Mortality Factors of a Rare Forest Carnivore, the Fisher (*Pekania pennanti*) in California." *PLOS ONE*.

Galloway, T., and R. Handy. 2003. "Immunotoxicity of Organophosphorous Pesticides." *Ecotoxicology* 12: 345–363.

Gawade, L., S. S. Dadarkar, R. Husain, and M. Gatne. 2013. "A Detailed Study of Developmental Immunotoxicity of Imidacloprid in Wistar Rats." *Food Chemical Toxicology* 51: 61–70.

Gibbons, D., C. Morrissey, and P. Mineau. 2015. "A Review of the Direct and Indirect Effects of Neonicotinoids and Fipronil on Vertebrate Wildlife." *Environmental Science Pollution Research* 22: 103–118.

Gordon, C. J., 1994. "Thermoregulation in Laboratory Mammals and Humans Exposed to Anticholinesterase Agents." *Neurotoxicology and Teratology* 16: 427–453.

Hayashi, T. I., M. Kamo, and Y. Tanaka. 2009. "Population-Level Ecological Effect Assessment: Estimating the Effect of Toxic Chemicals on Density-Dependent Populations." *Ecological Research* 24: 945–954.

Hunt, K. A., D. M. Bird, P. Mineau, and L. Shutt. 1992. "Selective Predation of Organophosphate-Exposed Prey by American Kestrels." *Animal Behavior* 43: 971–976.

Janeway, C. A., P. Travers, and M. Walport. 2007. *Immunobiology*, 7th ed. New York: Garland Science.

Jaques, L. B. 1959. "Dicoumarol Drugs and the Problem of Haemorrhage." *Canadian Medical Association Journal* 81: 848–854.

Jeffcoach, D. 2012. "Assessment of Chemical Contaminants Used in Illegal Marijuana Cultivation in California National Parks." Unpublished report to the National Park Service. Fresno: California State University.

Knillmann, S., N. C. Stampfli, Y. A. Noskov, M. A. Beketov, and M. Liess. 2012. "Interspecific Competition Delays Recovery of *Daphnia* spp Populations from Pesticide Stress." *Ecotoxicology* 21: 1039–1049.

Kohler, H. R., and R. Triebskorn. 2013. "Wildlife Ecotoxicology of Pesticides: Can We Track Effects to the Population Level and Beyond?" *Science* 341: 759–765.

Lafferty, K. D., and A. K. Morris. 1996. "Altered Behavior of Parasitized Killifish Increases Susceptibility to Predation by Bird Final Hosts." *Ecology* 77: 1390–1397.

Levy, S. 2014. "Pot Poisons Public Lands." *BioScience* 64: 265–271.

Li, Q., and Kawada, T. 2006. "The Mechanism of OP Pesticide-Induced Inhibition of Cytolytic Activity of Killer Cells." *Cellular and Molecular Immunology* 3: 171–178.

Macek, K. J. 1969. "Screening of Pesticides against Fish." *Progress in Sport Fishery Research*, 92.

Milinski, M., and C. Lowenstein. 1980. "On Predator Selection against Abnormalities of Movement: A Test of an Hypothesis." *Zeitschrift fur Tierpsychologie* 53: 325–340.

Miller, C. 2012. *Public Lands, Public Debates.* Corvallis: Oregon State University Press.

Morris, A. J., J. D. Wilson, M. J. Whittingham, and R. B. Bradbury. 2005. "Indirect Effects of Pesticides on Breeding Yellowhammer (*Emberiza citrinella*)." *Agriculture, Ecosystems, and Environment* 106: 1–16.

Norelius, E. E., and J. A. Lockwood. 1999. "Effects of Reduced Agent-Area Insecticide Treatments for Rangeland Grasshopper (*Orthoptera: Acrididae*) Control on Bird Densities." *Archives of Environmental Contamination and Toxicology* 37: 519–528.

Peveling, R., A. N. McWilliam, P. Nagel, H. Rasolomanana, L. Rakotomianina, A. Ravoninjatovo, C. F. Dewhurst, G. Gibson, S. Rafanomezana, and C. C. D. Tingle. 2003. "Impact of Locust Control on Harvester Termites and Endemic Vertebrate Predators in Madagascar." *Journal of Applied Ecology* 40: 729–741.

Rattner, B. A., K. E. Horak, R. S. Lazarus, D. A. Goldade, and J. J. Johnston. 2014. "Toxicokinetics and Coagulopathy Threshold of the Rodenticide Diphacinone in Eastern Screech-Owls (*Megascops asio*)." *Environmental Toxicology and Chemistry* 33: 74–81.

Riley, S. P., C. Bromley, R. H. Poppenga, F. A. Uzal, L. Whited, and R. M. Sauvajot. 2007. "Anticoagulant Exposure and Notoedric Mange in Bobcats and Mountain Lions in Urban Southern California." *Journal of Wildlife Management* 71: 1874–1884.

Salice, C. J., B. E. Sample, R. M. Neilan, K. A. Rose, and S. Sable. 2011. "Evaluation of Alternative PCB Clean-up Strategies Using an Individual-Based Population Model of Mink." *Environmental Pollution* 159: 3334–3343.

Sample, B. E., R. J. Cooper, and R. C. Whitmore. 1993. "Dietary Shifts among Songbirds from a Diflubenzuron-Treated Forest." *Condor* 95: 616–624.

Schipper, A. M., H. W. M. Hendriks, M. J. Kauffman, A. J. Hendriks, and M. A. J. Huijbregts. 2013. "Modelling Interactions of Toxicants and Density Dependence in Wildlife Populations." *Journal of Applied Ecology* 50: 1469–1478.

Serieys, L. E. K., J. Foley, S. Owens, L. Woods, E. E. Boydston, L. M. Lyren, R. H. Poppenga, D. L. Clifford, N. Stephenson, J. Rudd, and S. P. D. Riley. 2015. "Serum Chemistry, Hematologic, and Post-mortem Findings in Free-Ranging Bobcats (*Lynx rufus*) with Notoedric Mange." *Journal of Parasitology* 99: 989–996.

Spencer, W. D., H. Rustigian-Romsos, J. Strittholt, R. Scheller, W. Zielinski, and R. Truex. 2011. "Using Occupancy and Population Models to Assess Habitat Conservation Opportunities for an Isolated Carnivore Population." *Biological Conservation* 144: 788–803.

Thompson, C., R. Sweitzer, M. Gabriel, K. Purcell, R. Barrett, and R. Poppenga. 2014. "Impacts of Rodenticide and Insecticide Toxicants from Marijuana Cultivation Sites on Fisher Survival Rates in the Sierra National Forest, California." *Conservation Letters* 7: 91–102.

Thompson, H. 1995. "Interactions between Pesticides: A Review of Reported Effects and Their Implications for Wildlife Risk Assessment." *Ecotoxicology* 5: 59–81.

Tingle, C. C. D., J. A. Rother, C. F. Dewhurst, S. Lauer, and W. J. King. 2003. "Fipronil: Environmental Fate, Ecotoxicology and Human Health Concerns." *Reviews of Environmental Contamination and Toxicology* 176: 1–66.

Townsend, M. G., P. J. Bunyan, E. M. Odum, P. I. Stanley, and H. P. Wardall. 1984. "Assessment of Secondary Poisoning Hazard of Warfarin to Least Weasels." *Journal of Wildlife Management* 48: 628–632.

USFWS (United States Fish and Wildlife Service). 2014. 50-CFR Part 17, Endangered and Threatened Wildlife and Plants; Threatened Species Status for West Coast Distinct Population Segment of Fisher: Proposed Ruling. Federal Register Docket No FWS–R8–ES–2014–0041. 2014:1–94.

Vidal, D., V. Alzaga, J. J. Luque-Larena, R. Mateo, L. Arroyo, and J. Vinuela. 2009. "Possible Interaction between a Rodenticide Treatment and a Pathogen in Common Vole (*Microtus arvalis*) during a Population Peak." *Science of the Total Environment* 408: 267–271.

Vyas, N. B., E. Hill, J. R. Sauer, and W. J. Kuenzel. 1995. "Acephate Affects Migratory Orientation of the White-Throated Sparrow (*Zonotrichia albicollis*)." *Environmental Toxicology and Chemistry* 14: 1961–1965.

Vyas, N. B., W. J. Kuenzel, E. F. Hill, G. A. Romo, M. V. S. Komaragiri. 1996. "Regional Cholinesterase Activity in White-Throated Sparrow Brain Is Differentially Affected by Acephate (Orthene®)." *Comparative Biochemistry and Physiology* 113: 381–386.

Webster, K. H. 2009. "Validation of a Prothrombin Time (PT) 613 Assay for Assessment of Brodifacoum Exposure in Japanese Quail and Barn Owls." MA thesis, Simon Fraser University.

Wobeser, G., T. Bollinger, F. A. Leighton, B. Blakley, and P. Mineau. 2004. "Secondary Poisoning of Eagles Following Intentional Poisoning of Coyotes with Anticholinesterase Pesticides in Western Canada." *Journal of Wildlife Diseases* 40: 163–172.

Zabrodskii, P. F., V. G. Germanchuk, V. F. Kirichuk, V. S. Birdin, and A. N. Chuev. 2002. "Combined Effects of Toxicants with Various Mechanisms of Action and Mechanical Trauma on the Immune System." *Bulletin of Experimental Biology and Medicine* 6: 594–596.

Zabrodskii, P. F., V. G. Lim, and E. V. Strel'tsova. 2012. "Disturbances of Immune Status and Cytokine Profile Caused by Chronic Intoxication with OP Compounds and Their Correction by Administration of Imunofan." *Eksperimental'naya i Klinicheskaya Farmakologiya* 75: 35–37.

Zielinski, W. J., J. A. Baldwin, R. L. Truex, J. M. Tucker, and P. A. Flebbe. 2013. "Estimat-

ing Trend in Occupancy for the Southern Sierra Fisher (*Martes pennanti*) Population."
Journal of Fish and Wildlife Management 4: 3–19.

Zielinski, W. J., and N. P. Duncan. 2004. "Diets of Sympatric Populations of American Martens (*Martes americana*) and Fishers (*Martes pennanti*) in California." *Journal of Mammalogy* 85: 470–477.

CHAPTER 4

The Marijuana Green Rush Is Anything but Green

A Report from the Hoopa Tribal Lands

J. Mark Higley, Greta M. Wengert, Dawn M. Blake, and Mourad W. Gabriel

The Hoopa Valley Indian Reservation contains 144 square miles of land, includes the Trinity River and Hoopa Valley, and the Hupa people consider it the center of the world. It encompasses many of the Hupa people's ancestral village sites. The valley is home to many acres of prime agricultural land and once was considered the breadbasket of Humboldt County. The vast majority of the Hoopa Reservation, however, is mountainous, forested land rich in timber resources, water, fish, and wildlife habitat. Tribal administrators have taken great pride in developing a forest management plan and practices that balance economic needs with traditional and cultural values over the past two decades. The plan has been certified as Ecologically Sustainable by the Forest Stewardship Council since 1996. There is no pesticide or herbicide use within these forestlands. Some of those management practices may have left the door open for outsiders to exploit the reservation's natural resources for personal gain. Large-scale clandestine marijuana growing operations, often supported by drug-trafficking organizations, have sprung up on and around the reservation, leaving a path of destruction, poisons, and animal carcasses. In this chapter, we will describe how we discovered the shocking impacts of such growing operations on the Pacific fisher, a federally proposed threatened species, and the potential for threats to other wildlife that we are uncovering through our collaborative research projects.

We will discuss the Hoopa Reservation's forest management plan and how the implementation of certain management practices may contribute to the exploitation of the reservation by criminal organizations. Finally, we will discuss how tribal members use the reservation and how this illegal activity may be impacting their cultural, spiritual, and recreational activities.

While attending an interdisciplinary team meeting in June 2013, Mark Higley received a somewhat disturbing text message from one of his northern spotted owl field crew leaders: "AWC hasn't come out of the woods yet and we have been waiting for over an hour and we're getting kinda worried." Knowing the area where they were working and the possibility for illegal marijuana growing, Higley and the crew leader became worried about the young Hupa field technician (whose initials are AWC). He emerged from the brush a short time later, and was really shaken up as he told his story. He had entered the stand from a road located above the owl activity center along with three other people, each charged with taking a route through one portion of the stand in search of spotted owls. The site is extremely brushy with evergreen huckleberry, making travel through the stand very difficult. A third of the way down the steep slope, he encountered a makeshift water impoundment with black plastic pipe diverting water downhill. Given his assignment and the difficult terrain he had already covered he opted to continue downhill, albeit away from the apparent direction the water line was heading. A short distance below he came across some fresh garbage, including food wrappers. He pushed on. Eventually, as he was approaching the bottom of the stand and the lower road where he was supposed to meet the rest of the crew, he heard something "human like" and saw an opening that included a pond, and he became unnerved. He froze for about an hour in hiding before feeling that the coast was clear enough for him to make a run for the road below.

These types of experiences and some much worse have become commonplace in the forests of California among wildlife and forestry workers, hunters, and recreationists. Other tribal forestry personnel have come face-to-face with armed growers while laying out timber sales. The tribe's owl night crew also has seen numerous vehicles in the woods that they know do not belong there, given that the forested portion of the reservation is closed to all nontribal members.

The Hoopa Valley Tribal Forestry Department is charged with managing the tribe's forest resources within the reservation, located in northeastern Humboldt County, California. The Bureau of Indian Affairs (BIA) had been in charge of this task from the 1930s until 1989, when its staff uprooted and left the reservation literally overnight in May of that year. The tribe then became one of only ten self-governing tribes at that time and assumed responsibility for all natural-resource management on the reservation. The tribal forestry department began the task of developing the first Forest Management Plan (FMP) in May 1991 and completed that effort in 1994. Following completion of the plan the tribe was invited to present at a United Nations conference using the recently completed FMP as a model for community-based management planning. Shortly thereafter the Forest Stewardship Council (FSC), which sets forestry standards approved by the Sierra Club, World Wildlife Fund, Natural Resources Defense Council, and Greenpeace, approached the tribe and requested that it submit its FMP for consideration of FSC certification as an Environmentally Sustainable management plan. Hoopa forest management has remained FSC-certified since 1996.

Among many self-imposed restrictions, tribal administrators have banned the use of all herbicides and pesticides in the forested lands of the reservation. This has resulted in the need for a great deal of manual stand improvement projects to ensure that young regenerating stands are free to grow. Without the use of herbicides, people with chainsaws are needed to cut competing brush and trees from around the retained future crop trees. If this work is not completed, the developing stands will grow far more slowly at best, and, at worst, may not contain any commercial-sized conifers at all. Therefore, the tribe has hired contractor crews to conduct the majority of the stand improvement work since the early 1990s. Contractors have included tribal members with tribal member laborers as well as outside contractors with outside laborers, or a combination of the two. The outside laborers often are Hispanic, most frequently from Mexico, as indicated by the required worker eligibility paperwork submitted by the contractors to the Tribal Employment Rights Office. These crews have been very productive and have saved the tribe the hassle of logistics and financial costs associated with manual labor. The US Forest Service and Bureau of Land Management also often employ contractors for stand improvement and fuel reduction projects, and such crews work on tribal and federal land across Northern California. Unfortunately, on the Hoopa Valley Reservation, many of the known large-scale marijuana grow sites are within or very close to stands that have been thinned by contract crews at some time in the recent past. Therefore, it is conceivable that either members of these contract crews or the contractors themselves could be involved in the reconnaissance scouting, site development, and/or operation of tribal trespass grow sites since their layout reflects an intricate familiarity with the landscape.

In addition to the labor-intensive stand improvement projects, the tribe leaves all drivable roads open year-round for tribal members to have access to the forest lands for wood cutting; hunting; gathering of acorns, mushrooms, and other forest products; and general recreation. There are over 600 miles of such roads within the reservation and five independent entrances, in addition to California Highway 96, providing access to the north and south ends of the reservation. There is at least one entrance in each quarter of the square reservation boundary. Although the forested portion of the reservation is technically closed to all nontribal members, there are no barriers (i.e., gates) or security points that would dissuade any individual from entering the reservation from any public roads or highways. A tribal-trespass ordinance explicitly states that nontribal members cannot leave their vehicles while driving through the forested portion of the reservation. Yet, because there is little or no enforcement of rules or culpability for those caught breaking these regulations, those who wish to violate them are likely not impeded. Although the tribe has its own police force, it has fluctuated greatly in its effectiveness due to staffing levels and emphasis on policing the urban zone rather than the backcountry of the reservation. It is fairly easy for outsiders to trespass, steal, or abuse tribal resources such as firewood, fungi, and game animals—as well as the growing of marijuana in hidden locations around the reservation. The situation on adjacent and nearby public lands throughout Northern California is quite similar to that on the Hoopa Valley Reservation. Relatively good road access and very limited-to-no law enforcement presence provide a haven for illegal activity.

DEATH BY RODENTICIDE

In 2009 an adult male fisher was discovered dead, lying on the forest floor in the Sierra National Forest, and was later confirmed to have died from anticoagulant rodenticide poisoning (Chapter 3; Gabriel et al. 2012). By 2010 four radio-collared fisher mortalities were confirmed to be poisonings from rat poisons. Two of those animals were from Hoopa. Since 2005 the tribe has collaborated with researchers from several universities and two nonprofit conservation organizations while beginning and maintaining the longest-running fisher demographic study in western North America. The resulting work includes the development of field studies to document the impacts of trespass marijuana cultivation on fishers and the broader environment.

So, why did the tribe initiate a fisher study in the first place? First, the tribe manages the forest of Hoopa for its economic and ecological functions. The overall forest management goal is as follows: "Provide for the conservation and development of natural resources for the present and future benefit of the Hoopa Tribe, while *protecting* Tribal cultural integrity *including fish, wildlife, plants and their habitats.*" On the ecological function side, several species of wildlife that are of high cultural importance are also closely associated with mature and older forest conditions. This includes the fisher, which had been proposed for listing but subsequently denied protection under the federal Endangered Species Act (USFWS 2014, 2016).

Although the tribe's forest management is regarded as ecologically sustainable, the tribe continues to cut mature forest stands while developing the second-growth stands for future management in the near future. Documenting the effects of implementing the FMP on a select few species helps to gauge the tribe's management in terms of maintaining favorable conditions for those species associated with a mature forest. With that in mind, the tribe began studying fishers in 1992 using sooted track plates and remote camera stations to document presence of fishers across the reservation landscape. That was followed by a brief radio telemetry study aimed at determining fisher rest site selection (1996–1999). Then, in 2004, after five years of no fisher study activity, the tribe received its first grant from the USFWS through its Tribal Wildlife Grant program. This also corresponded with the elevation of the fisher's status to that of a "Candidate for Federal Protection."

A NEW TWIST TO AN OLD STORY

Humboldt County has long been known for growing marijuana, production that is often hidden in the forests of public and private lands. That part of this story is nothing new, but the detection of rat-poisoned fishers and a subsequent link to trespass marijuana cultivation was significant news within the scientific community and media. This discovery gave rise to an impassioned journey to investigate the potential environmental impacts stemming from this clandestine activity. We were initially in disbelief that growing cannabis illegally could possibly be "that bad." However, finding that 79 percent (46 of 58) of fishers tested positive for anticoagulant rodenticide across all of California's fisher study areas and from both remaining natural West Coast populations of fishers raised a significant red flag (Gabriel et al. 2012). This was especially apparent in the spatial data gathered for several of the southern Sierra animals that had spent nearly their entire lives within national parks or federally designated wilderness areas. The Hoopa tribe and the Integral Ecology Research Center (IERC) have been working on this issue since it came to light in 2009–2010 with the first confirmed fisher mortalities, a collaboration that intensified in 2012 with the securing of the first grant funding aimed at studying the link between rodenticides and fisher mortality.

We created a team of scientists to visit sites while federal, state, and local law enforcement (LE) was conducting eradication efforts. This has been a critical aspect of our research effort as we have been present to see firsthand the abuse and destruction of our natural resources that criminal organizations have perpetrated. This has afforded us the opportunity to begin to quantify and document the impacts. Still, this research is far more difficult to conduct than most ecological studies in North America. The sites are hidden, and when they are in use they are typically defended by armed workers. The value of the crops they are protecting is generally in the tens to hundreds of thousands of dollars, and therefore their guards are likely to protect their crops with violence. To conduct our research, then, requires us doing so under the protection of large groups of LE at the time of eradication; even if we visit in the nongrowing months of winter, we still need

LE presence for safety concerns, albeit fewer of them. In addition, we are generally limited to visiting and documenting sites that have been recently eradicated by LE. LE does not share information about active sites due to their status as ongoing crime scenes and concurrent investigations.

This effort began in 2012 on the Hoopa Valley Reservation at the request of the Hoopa tribal chairman. The first grow site we visited was located in the Mill Creek watershed: it was large, spread out over a mile along Mill Creek, and situated within an area that had been set aside from future timber management under the tribe's FMP for the purpose of protecting water quality, fish, and wildlife resources as well as a tribal archaeological site. Although the area was not old-growth forest habitat—much of it had been logged by the BIA in 1968, 1975, and 1977—the area had over thirty-five years of regeneration following those harvests.

Within this Mill Creek area, marijuana plants had been planted in at least six sites, distinct patches that ranged from one-quarter acre to a full acre in size. Four of those had been cleared of most of the native trees that had regenerated, and several residual mature hardwood trees had been fallen with the use of hand saws. We documented well over a ton of empty chemical fertilizer bags and 11 pounds of poisoned rat bait on that first visit, among other pesticides, and several gallons of liquid fertilizers. Human waste was common within feet of the main channel of Mill Creek; this creek is a key domestic water source for the tribe as well as one of the most important anadromous fish-bearing streams on the reservation. Our in-depth investigation into this first site was an eye opener: it was hard to believe what we were seeing. Intricate trail systems connecting the patches, camps, dumps, drying areas, and water sources were extensive throughout this grow-site complex. At least three major water sources were used, and we noted several miles of ¾- and 1-inch black plastic source lines in addition to miles of ½-inch irrigation lines within patches, fitted with drip lines and emitters. The cultivators also had small numbers of corn stalks, cucumber, squash, and other garden vegetable plants still standing during the eradication.

We removed all of the pesticides that we found on that and subsequent visits and then made additional plans for full reclamation of the site. All that we observed at Mill Creek and two other cultivation sites visited in Hoopa in 2012 contributed to our contemplation of systematically documenting various aspects of the impacts we were seeing. For example, we asked: "What would be most important, and what might be feasible to accomplish, given the difficulty in gaining access to sites and the limited window of opportunity available to do so?"

The initial documentation included mapping the sites as best we could, using resource-grade GPS instruments to mark patches, trails, camps, dumps, water sources, and drying areas. We also deployed remote trail cameras to document the various wildlife species we suspected were visiting the main dumpsite at Mill

Creek. These cameras ran for a period of five months. We were able to capture numerous visits by black bears, fishers, ringtails, gray foxes, and bobcats as well as rodents that many of these carnivores are dependent on.

In the course of our research, we learned that fishers are vulnerable to predation by carnivores such as coyotes, bobcats, and mountain lions, which had not been previously documented (Wengert et al. 2014). Preyed-upon fishers on the Hoopa Valley Reservation are often found near man-made linear features such as roads and skid trails. Of course, some are found along natural game trails and, occasionally, in places that have no obvious sign of where and how the predator killed the fisher. Still, the intricate trail system found in large complex grow sites, coupled with the attractants found in camps and dumps, may contribute to an increase in fisher vulnerability to predation there. This would be an extremely difficult hypothesis to test, but it might be one of several plausible explanations for why female fishers in the southern Sierra had significantly lower survival rates when higher numbers of grow sites were present within their home ranges (Thompson et al. 2014).

In 2013, we visited six more sites on the reservation and three on US Forest Service land. All but two of the sites had been active in 2013; two of the Hoopa sites were eradicated in 2010. On a July morning in 2013, LE had completed their eradication effort of a small site (376 plants) and discovered a dead animal along the trail, which officers recognized as likely being a fisher. We were taken back to the site to collect the carcass and document the site and situation. We had very little time, as the escorting officer who led us back into the site was nervous about being there alone, with no nearby backup. We quickly put our gloves on, confirmed the carcass to be a male fisher, photographed the animal, and tagged and bagged it. We noticed that it had been frothing at the mouth and had not entered rigor yet. There were still bubbles coming from the mouth; the animal had been dead for only a short time, less than an hour. We suspected poisoning, given the location of the animal and the frothing at the mouth. A full necropsy was completed early the following week, and it confirmed that the animal had died of acute methomyl poisoning (a restricted-use carbamate insecticide) and had remnants of hotdog in its esophagus and stomach (Gabriel, unpublished data). This was yet another new twist on the use of toxicants at grow sites that we had never previously encountered. Clearly there had been poisoned baits placed around the grow, as LE had taken photos of a hotdog hanging from a large fish hook. The poison, a strong neurological toxicant, was most likely placed at the site to kill carnivores that might damage the crop or water system.

Though we had heard of such use of poisons, this was our first experience seeing its deadly consequences. Unfortunately, it was not the last. In fact, after receiving the necropsy results, we returned to the grow with two Humboldt County sheriff's deputies to collect the fish hooks. As we arrived at the trail leading to the grow, two dozen turkey vultures flushed out of the brush. We all jumped a bit, thinking that the growers had returned, before we recognized the avian source of the commotion. As we climbed up the hill we could smell decomposition. We found a mostly skeletonized gray fox lying on the ground very near to where we had collected the fisher, but it was not the source of the smell of decomposition. That was coming from somewhere 30–50 meters up the hill in the brush. In my experience, large numbers of turkey vultures congregate around large dead animals, such as bears or deer; our time was limited and although we searched in the brush for a while we did not find the source of the smell. Subsequent testing revealed that the fish hooks were positive for methomyl.

WHAT CAN BE DONE?

We have joined in with a handful of other researchers who are working to inform the public about the damage being done to our public and tribal lands by criminal organizations exploiting our natural resources. We have been interviewed by local, national, and international journalists from print, radio, and television mediums; contributed to short documentary films; and written one general research article (Gabriel et al. 2013). We have collectively conducted close to 100 presentations in California and in several other states on the subject in professional wildlife meetings and LE symposiums, and we have met with congressional representatives, museum staff, and educational institutions. We were also invited to present at a TEDx Talk and have received awards from both the Executive Office of the White House and the US Forest Service for assisting law enforcement in the scientific documentation of grow sites. However, that we lack steady financial support to continue this research highlights a major barrier to a fuller understanding of the impact of illegal grows on Hoopa and public lands.

Additionally, we have taken journalists into the field on occasion so they could experience for themselves some of what we have been experiencing and evaluating. One experience that comes to mind is the visit one warm day in September 2013 at the request of the Trinity County sheriff, Bruce Haney. Mark Higley climbed into a helicopter with a Trinity County sheriff sergeant, a news reporter, and her cameraman, and we headed out to a 40,000-plant trespass grow that had been eradicated that August. As the pilot was firing up the engine, the sergeant mentioned that one of the people from "that group cleaning up sites in the Sierras" (High Sierra Volunteer Trail Crew) had fallen from a helicopter while doing grow site cleanup the morning before. Higley immediately felt a chill and became uneasy as he had been in close contact with the leader of that organization while planning cleanup efforts for Hoopa. We lifted off and headed out to the site without knowing anything more until later that afternoon.

Shane Krogen died in that incident. Higley had spoken to him the evening before he passed. He was tired but in great spirits, having spent the day rolling up drip line and nursing bruises from the day before. We were falling behind on paperwork and finalizing a cleanup effort at the tribe's end a few weeks prior when Operation Pristine, led by Shane, was scheduled to come to the Hoopa Valley Reservation. Shane just shook it off when Higley told him he would not blame them if they gave up on us. He laughed and said in his most optimistic voice, "Don't worry, buddy, we have to do it for the animals." Although Higley never met Shane personally, he had communicated with him regularly by phone and email for over a year. From those exchanges, he formed a vision of a man passionate about the environment and dedicated to reclaiming sites following the egregious damage that greedy criminals perpetrated on our public and tribal lands. His passion, enthusiasm, and dedication were contagious and impressive.

As we have worked to document potential impacts, we have also been striving to clean up as many of the sites as we can. The first cooperative cleanup effort on the reservation involved the Hoopa tribe, IERC, the High Sierra Volunteer Trail Crew (Environmental Reclamation Team), The California Department of Fish and Wildlife Law Enforcement division, the California National Guard counter drug task force, and Dr. Craig Thompson, a US Forest Service collaborator who was seeing an actual grow site for the first time. We cleaned up six sites in two days in November 2013; most still had several pounds of rodenticide (including one site that had been eradicated in 2010) and other pesticides present, which were all removed.

The cleanup efforts currently on tribal lands involve several key and essential steps, first among them mapping out the entirety of the site so that when it comes time to clean it we know the level of effort that will be needed and where to send workers. Second, we organize and coordinate a cleanup crew including LE personnel and qualified and trained volunteers, and create a detailed plan of operations. On the day of cleanup we roll up the irrigation pipe within each grow patch, pull and roll the source lines, and bag up all of the trash and other items at camps and dumps. Then everything is moved to staging areas that are appropriate and safe for a helicopter long-line to operate in order to pick up net loads and move them out of the forest to a refuse disposal site. The helicopter work does not necessarily have to be done on the same day as the staging of materials, but it should be completed within a few weeks to ensure that the bags are not torn open by wildlife or break down naturally by the elements.

A TRIBAL PERSPECTIVE

The Hupa people have lived in the Hoopa Valley since time immemorial. Radiocarbon dating of material from fire pits at ceremonial sites on the reservation indicates that they have been used for 7,000 to 10,000 years. As participants in ancient customs, the Hupa continue to be consumers of their forest. Materials used to construct baskets and ceremonial regalia in addition to food and medicine items are gathered from the forest seasonally. As Dawn Blake spoke with a tribal elder about the changes that result from the trespass marijuana grows, she was informed that the elder used to enjoy gathering materials alone but now is encouraged to only go out with others as a matter of security. Because the Hupa's gathering practices involve prayers and a one-on-one connection with Ninis'a:n (interpreted as both Creator and Mountain), these new security concerns compromise the ceremony and its sacred purposes.

The by-products of these unregulated plantations also can have implications upon forest consumers. In addition to general interruption of the gathering process, posed risks that have been previously advocated against by traditional forest consumers quickly become an issue. Cultural, spiritual, and recreational activities of the Hupa are compromised twofold. First, the presence of potentially violent defenders of marijuana patches creates a risk to going into the forest in the first place, which has become a deterrent. Second, the chemicals used are a concern for protected resources, such as fish-bearing streams, as well as trophic level effects that can reach human consumers. Fishers, ringtails, and bears are all important species to the tribe, and, seemingly, they are specifically targeted at grow sites; anadromous fish, which are a food staple, can be impacted by runoff. Pesticides find their way into weaving materials, thus potentially affecting basket weavers as they place the materials in their mouths.

SAVED BY PROPOSITION 64?

California's Proposition 64, which passed in November 2016, legalizes the growing and recreational use of marijuana by adults twenty-one years of age and older. Many proponents of the new legislation have stated that this will make the trespass-growing problem simply go away. We are skeptical at best about that result, primarily because a large black market still exists throughout the United States and around the world. Most of the marijuana grown on California's public and tribal lands has been destined for places outside of California, and this continues to be the case. It is likely that drug-trafficking organizations may attempt to grow more on private lands in the open with the hope of going undetected by regulators, but our concerns are that increasing land prices in culturally prime yet ecologically sensitive locations within the state and the scrutiny and fees associated with the new regulations may force drug-trafficking organizations to venture back to the woods to maximize their monetary gain. Finally, the much-needed expansion of scientific knowledge on impacts associated with this activity may not be met with the current proposition wording. As it stands, funding received through fees and taxes will be distributed to two state natural-resource agencies and then "may be" distributed as grants to address environmental impacts and remediation of damages on public lands. However, over 90 percent of the current scientific knowledge and published material was funded via grants to nonstate governmental agencies. In addition, the majority of complete remediation of trespass sites within the state for the past three years has been via grant funding to joint partnerships between public and nonprofit organizations. We recommend that funding via competitive grants that clearly demonstrate partnerships between state and federal agencies, NGOs, tribes, and academia should be encouraged to avoid pitfalls of the needless redundancy of developing new pathways toward the same goals.

WORKS CITED

Gabriel, M. W., G. M. Wengert, J. M. Higley, S. Krogan, W. Sargent, and D. L. Clifford. 2013. "Silent Forests?" *Wildlife Professional* 7: 46–50.

Gabriel, M. W., L. W. Woods, R. Poppenga, R. A. Sweitzer, C. M. Thompson, S. M. Matthews, J. M. Higley, S. M. Keller, K. L. Purcell, R. H. Barrett, G. M. Wengert, B. N. Sacks, and D. L. Clifford. 2012. "Anticoagulant Rodenticides on Our Public and Community Lands: Spatial Distribution of Exposure and Poisoning of a Rare Forest Carnivore." *PLOS ONE* 7: e40163.

Thompson, C., R. Sweitzer, M. Gabriel, K. Purcell, R. Barrett, and R. Poppenga. 2014. "Impacts of Rodenticide and Insecticide Toxicants from Marijuana Cultivation Sites on Fisher Survival Rates in the Sierra National Forest, California." *Conservation Letters* 7: 91–102.

USFWS (United States Fish and Wildlife Service). 2014. 50-CFR Part 17 Endangered and Threatened Wildlife and Plants; Threatened Species Status for West Coast Distinct Population Segment of Fisher: Proposed Ruling. Federal Register Docket No. FWS–R8–ES–2014–0041. 2014:1–94.

———. 2016. 50-CFR Part 17, Endangered and Threatened Wildlife and Plants: Withdrawal of the Proposed Rule to List the West Coast Distinct Population Segment of Fisher; Proposed Rule. Federal Register Docket No. FWS–R8–ES–2014–0041; 4500 030113.

Wengert, G. M., M. W. Gabriel, S. M. Matthews, J. M. Higley, R. A. Sweitzer, C. M. Thompson, et al. 2014. "Using DNA to Describe and Quantify Interspecific Killing of Fishers in California." *Journal of Wildlife Management* 78, 4: 603–611.

CHAPTER 5

Managers' Perceptions of Illegal Marijuana Cultivation on US Federal Lands

Jeff Rose, Matthew T. J. Brownlee, and Kelly S. Bricker

Illegal drug production in protected areas is an international issue that disrupts natural resources (Wiant 1985; McSweeney et al. 2014). For example, cocaine production in South America often requires systematic removal of forests, is preceded by the construction of illicit airstrips, and destroys water resources (Farah 1990). The United Nations Office on Drugs and Crime (UNODC) reports that "although most coca is grown in forests protected by law, the Governments of Bolivia, Colombia, and Peru have had considerable difficulty in slowing the rate of deforestation; as a result, some of the most important ecosystems in the upper Amazon basin have been destroyed" (UNODC 2014). Other geographic contexts show similarly devastating ecological effects. In Southeast Asia, millions of acres of mountain rain forests have been removed by damaging slash-and-burn techniques for cultivation for illicit opium, the base component for heroin (UNODC 2014). After opium production, heroin processors in and near protected areas dump thousands of gallons of poisonous by-product into critical watersheds. As a result, Doi Inthanon National Park and Doi Chiang Dao Wildlife Sanctuary in Thailand have been severely damaged, compelling the International Union for Conservation of Nature Commission on Parks and Protected Areas to list Doi Inthanon as a "threatened park" due to illegal drug production (UNODC 2014).

In the United States, a pressing threat to the management of natural resources is illegal and rampant marijuana (*Cannabis sativa*) cultivation on public lands, including national forests, national parks, and special management areas. In 2012 the

US Attorney's Office stated that illegal drug production on public lands "pose[s] a safety threat to the public and an environmental threat to the land and to wildlife [and] the problem is severe" (US Attorney's Office 2012). This statement can be partially attributed to the substantial increases in marijuana cultivation on public lands during the past two decades. For example, marijuana plants seized annually on public lands increased from fewer than 1 million in 2004 to 2.6 million in 2009 (ibid.). In California alone, land management agencies witnessed a 300 percent increase in grow sites from 2006 to 2010 (US Office of National Drug Control Policy 2012).

As a result of these increases, law enforcement eradication efforts have resulted in more than $1.45 billion (user price, or street value) in marijuana seizures on public lands across seven western states (US Attorney's Office 2012). During the summer of 2012, approximately 67 percent of marijuana plants captured in the West occurred on public lands (ibid.), and within a three-year period, 49,105 metric tons of marijuana were confiscated on California's public lands (Miller 2012). However, such seizures represent only 15 percent of estimated cultivation on public lands (US Office of National Drug Control Policy 2012). These data reveal the enormity of the issue confronting US federal agencies.

Within the United States, media have highlighted this issue, but empirical investigation of the ecological consequences of illegal marijuana cultivation on public lands remains scarce (National Research Council 2001; cf. Martin 2012; Miller 2012). Research on illegal activity on public lands has used "less than systematic data sources" (Cohen et al. 2007, 262) and focused on enforcement and substance prevalence. What currently is lacking is research that seeks to effectively understand the extent of harm to environments and communities (Reuter 2002; US Government Accountability Office 2010). Further, while the frequency and amount of seizures, estimated street value, and indictments have been documented, research to understand the perspectives of professionals who engage with these concerns on a daily basis is lacking. In short, research addressing this issue from federal land managers' perspectives is "necessary and overdue" (Tynon and Chavez 2006, 154).

This chapter seeks to fill this gap in our knowledge in three ways: to understand managers' challenges, successes, ideas, and experiences regarding marijuana cultivation; highlight specific drivers that prohibit, assist, and influence the prevention, mitigation, and response to marijuana cultivation on public lands; and use the design principles of common pool resources (CPRs) as an analytical lens to further understand the results. The chapter provides background on CPRs, explaining the complexities associated with public resource management. It next reports the results from the interviews with managers confronting illegal marijuana cultivation on public lands and analyzes results through the use of CPR design principles

(Ostrom 1990). It concludes with recommendations to further understand illegal marijuana cultivation on public lands and a discussion of evolving legality of the use, consumption, and growth of marijuana in the United States.

COMMON POOL RESOURCES

Garrett Hardin's "Tragedy of the Commons" (1968) highlighted the philosophical, moral, environmental, and managerial conundrums associated with distributing the benefits and costs of shared resources. While Hardin's metaphor has been widely embraced as a way of understanding various natural resource management strategies (cf. Brown and Harris 1992; Honey-Roses 2009; Leong 2009; Pandit and Thapa 2004), it has also been the subject of debate and critique. Hess and Ostrom (2007) argued that Hardin's (1968) conceptualization of the commons was mistaken for four reasons: (1) The commons were open rather than managed, (2) there was no communication among stakeholders, (3) there was no account for priorities beyond self-interest, and (4) there existed alternatives to privatization or regulation.

Subsequently, Ostrom (1990) offered the notion of common pool resources (CPRs; e.g., fisheries, forests, water supplies, grazing lands). This work examined the management of CPRs, building upon Hardin's (1968) thesis and identifying mechanisms to avoid potential "tragedies." This chapter considers various US federal lands as CPRs, which are a "resource system that is sufficiently large as to make it costly (but not impossible) to exclude potential beneficiaries from obtaining benefits from its use" (Ostrom 1990, 30). In the case of US federal lands—typically though not exclusively managed by the Bureau of Land Management (BLM), US Forest Service (USFS), National Park Service (NPS), or the Fish and Wildlife Service—traditional perspectives of these spaces (Wilson 2014) indicate alignment with CPR characteristics.

How then have public-land managers confronted and been challenged by illegal marijuana cultivation on public lands? To answer this question, we adopted the following eight design principles that researchers believe are conducive to the long-term survival of a CPR (Ostrom 1990):

1. Clearly defined boundaries: Individuals or households who have rights to withdraw resource units from the CPR must be clearly defined, as must be the boundaries of the CPR itself.
2. Congruence between rules and local conditions: Rules restricting time, place, technology, and/or quantity of resource units are related to local conditions. There should be simple rules that are related to the access and resource use patterns agreed upon by the appropriators.

3. Collective-choice arrangements: Most individuals affected by the rules can participate in modifying the rules. There is a need to remain adaptable, to be able to modify the rules with regard to membership, to have access to and use of the CPR, and to remain responsive to rapid exogenous change.

4. Monitoring: Monitor who actively audits CPR conditions and appropriator behaviors, and who is accountable to the appropriators. The enforcement of rules is shared by all appropriators and sometimes assisted by official observers and enforcers.

5. Graduated sanctions: Appropriators who violate rules are assessed graduated sanctions (depending on the severity and context of the offense) by other appropriators, officials, or both.

6. Conflict-resolution mechanisms: Appropriators and officials have rapid access to resources to resolve conflicts, including adapting the rules to changing conditions, problems, and scales.

7. Recognition of rights to organize: The rights of appropriators to devise organizations are not challenged by external entities. Appropriators have freedom to legally sustain their ownership of the CPR.

8. Nested enterprises: For CPRs that are part of a larger system, the appropriation, provision, monitoring, enforcement, conflict resolution, and governance activities must take into account the larger organization(s) in which they are nested (Ostrom 1990, 90).

US federal lands and their management, as they are commonly conceptualized, align with Stern's (2011) CPR characteristics and Ostrom's (1990) CPR design principles (Wilson 2014). We therefore use these principles to (a) understand the experiences of US federal managers as they successfully and unsuccessfully engage with illegal marijuana cultivation, and (b) highlight a variety of forces that prohibit, assist, and influence the prevention, mitigation, and response to illegal marijuana cultivation on public lands.

To address these goals, we audio-recorded twenty-nine in-depth, semistructured, confidential interviews with a variety of key informants involved in addressing illegal marijuana cultivation on public lands. Paradigmatically aligned with qualitative research and to gain greater context for the management implications, we also engaged in multiple on-site visits to already interdicted marijuana grow sites on federal lands, accompanied by agency personnel. Those visits enabled us to better understand information gleaned from the in-depth interviews. The combination of on-site visits and interviews provided greater insight into experiences than quantitative approaches because little knowledge existed concerning the potential views expressed by respondents (Seidman 2013). Since no social science research has systematically evaluated marijuana cultivation on public lands, an initial qualitative investigation of the perspectives of those associated with this issue was appropriate.

Study participants were selected using a purposive snowball approach where key informants and previous study participants recommended other potential interviewees (Creswell and Plano Clark 2011). Ultimately, study participants were selected based on their potential diversity of opinions and ability to provide robust insight into the issue (Creswell and Plano Clark 2011). We selected key informants from a variety of US federal agencies, from different types and levels of divisions, including law enforcement, resource management, and varying levels of administration. Some of the respondents engaged with illegal marijuana cultivation only incidentally; however, most indicated they confronted the issue as either a major part or exclusive focus of their position. Although reports and media suggest that illegal marijuana cultivation on public lands is of particular concern in the western United States, researchers sought to spatially diversify the respondent sample to increase geographic representation, interviewing individuals from federal agencies located in California, Washington, Nevada, Idaho, Montana, Utah, Arizona, Wisconsin, Oklahoma, Kentucky, Virginia, and Washington, DC. This purposive sampling ensured that a diversity of opinions, influenced by different ecosystems, cultures, institutions, and social dynamics, was incorporated. Out of this array of responses emerged six themes—collaboration, grows and growers, challenges of interdiction, ecological impacts, complexity, and future concerns. Each of these themes is briefly defined and discussed, with representative and supporting participant quotes in Table 5.1.

Respondents consistently referenced collaboration within and between agencies and cited it as contributing to interdiction success, while simultaneously acknowledging that more collaboration would increase perceived accomplishments. Multiple interviewees recognized that interdiction methods on their lands were successful but also likely led to increased illegal grows on adjacent lands, both public and private; respondents felt they were effectively "pushing" the problem elsewhere. Consequently, respondents identified that collaboration is needed at multiple spatial and bureaucratic scales, identifying the necessity of collaboration within their agency, between agencies, and between agencies and other collaborators. Further, they suggested that outside agencies included a variety of obvious and less-than-obvious support. For instance, collaborating with local law enforcement agencies (e.g., police, sheriffs) or federal law enforcement agencies (DEA) supported interdiction efforts, but they also acknowledged that visitor informants provided useful tips on grow sites. Nonprofit environmental agencies were also often vital sources of information related to grow site restoration efforts, and civic organizations were effective avenues for informing the public.

The illegal marijuana grows themselves and the individuals associated with these grows were another important theme. Respondents reported an increasing size, complexity, flexibility, and sophistication of grow sites, growers, and techniques. Grow sites and farming techniques were far from monolithic, and respondents suggested that growers were very responsive to past interdictions, such that growers change conditions, locations, sizes, methods, and other techniques regularly, making detection and intervention difficult. Further, respondents suggested a futility with engaging the plots and growers on the local scale: more effective law enforcement intervention would address higher organizational levels that are thought to be involved in networks of multiregional cultivation and distribution.

One of the major challenges of interdicting these growers and grow sites was the impact this had on existing financial, human, and material resources. Respondents emphasized that human safety in and around these sites is increasingly problematic, as federal employees are often exposed to automatic and semiautomatic weapons (cf. Pendleton 1996; Tynon and Chavez 2006; Wing and Tynon 2006; Beckley 2010), human traps (Batiste 2013), and harmful fertilizers, pesticides, herbicides, and rodenticides. Respondents lamented that serious direct physical conflicts between growers and visitors are inevitable. Finally, managers repeatedly emphasized the importance of dismantling existing infrastructure at grow sites, including sleeping platforms, kitchens, hoses, water receptacles, chemicals, human-waste systems, and litter that remained after interdiction.

ECOLOGICAL IMPACTS

Administrators, land managers, and ecologists alike voiced significant concerns about the ecological impacts associated with illegal marijuana grows. While impacts to water quality and surrounding ecosystems are beginning to be understood, there has been substantial research examining the bioaccumulation of associated toxins in mesocarnivores, particularly in fishers (cf. Gabriel et al. 2012; Gabriel et al. 2013; Thompson et al. 2013). Respondents reported a number of ecological impacts have yet to be addressed, including human health. For example, respondents acknowledged that the rodenticides and fertilizers used in illegal marijuana production may eventually enter municipal water sources or agricultural areas with unknown impacts to humans. Intensification of drought conditions for downstream communities was another recurrent concern for managers. In addition to the needed ecological research, interviewees discussed the importance of clearly and effectively communicating these results to interested parties, including local and regional political entities and media outlets, as well as the visiting public.

Participants from the USFS, NPS, and BLM indicated that their agency response was not uniform, with these inconsistencies leading to a variety of oversights and frustrations. They also suggested that there were complexities associated

Table 5.1. Themes, Subthemes, and Direct Quotes of Illegal Marijuana Growth on US Federal Lands

Themes and Subthemes	Direct Quotes
Collaboration	
Interagency	"Different federal agencies don't talk. Within this region there are XX DEA offices, YY forest districts, ZZ divisions, and not each division will take the same stance on marijuana. Here we make it the feather in our cap, but —— says they don't care and then someone else can run the show [responding to marijuana cultivation on public lands]. . . . Just not aggressively pursuing it with the same tenacity, even within one agency, much less with a lot of agencies working together."
	"You're dealing with multiple jurisdictions, multiple experience levels, some people are talking to each other, working together."
	"Whenever you get into this you're dealing with egos and people try to do it themselves, alone, take the glory for the bust, make the front page, it makes a good article, a good story, but they're probably missing a lot of grows too. It is too much for one agency."
Intra-agency	"We've got to have the resource people talking to the law enforcement folks. And then we try to communicate our operations to other folks in the Forest Service, because they're dealing with these same issues. . . . It really requires all of us being on the same page."
Beyond Agency	"We need to join the federal land management people with the university people. People are truly engaged but are 3,000 miles away in many cases, and out of the field, and don't even know who is working on this. Having research to support taking it to the Hill, real research documents to say this is really what's going on out there and why. . ."
	"We collaborate locally and regionally. . . . We have worked with state partners, local partners, utilized state assets, aviation assets, very strong in deterring activity . . . can be an effective tool in reducing demand."
	"Taskforce is the model that should be pushed; you are not really going to combat the entire organization without this approach."
Grows and Growers	
Dynamic Production Tactics	"These grows are no longer Mom and Pop operations. . . . Twenty years ago, it was small cultivation operations. Parks that historically had no connections to local (drug) areas have

(continued on next page)

Table 5.1. (*continued*)

Themes and Subthemes	Direct Quotes
Grows and Growers	
Dynamic Production Tactics	experienced marijuana growth on a scale of not five or ten plants, but hundreds of thousands of plants. . . . The nature of it has changed to a sizeable operation, greater sophistication than one can do on their own."
	"Now they get two, sometimes three harvests, when they used to get one. We used to look in drainages, water sources, you know, but they will pipe water now over into dry drainages and even grow in shade. They know where we look and try to get in where we don't."
	"When the growers change tactics and locations, we can't just jump on the plane and helicopter and go, because in my agency we have to follow the aviation protocol and we can't keep up."
Law Enforcement Investigations	"There has been a bigger emphasis placed on the investigation side. We're trying to tie it all together . . . getting people camping at the grows, means nothing."
	"If you arrest the people, the growers, it does not matter. We learned that you need to prosecute the management of the growers."
Challenges of Interdiction	
Safety	"Visitor safety is our number-one priority, but I worry about our rangers also . . . 99 percent of the grows I go into I find weapons."
Challenge to Resources	"We need a new model; we are public land managers, not international drug cartel enforcement officers. . . . These are complex and different from what we are trained to do."
	"You have to pick and choose—you can only do so much with so much out there."
	"Complex cases can be expensive."
	"At the end of the day, it's the people at the top who will decide if they want to fund these efforts or not."
Removal of Infrastructure	"One of the market disruptions we look at is we have to remove the infrastructure. If we don't, many of the growers will come back within the same grows the following year and use the facilities that have been left behind. That is why for reclamation we now remove everything in the grow site, trash, piping. If we leave that stuff, it takes minimal effort to get the grow site up and running again."

Ecological Impacts

Known	"One of the challenges is the support from the public and support from the Hill as to what the environmental impacts actually are, and the biggest challenge is being able to educate everybody . . . that it's a huge impact related to public lands. What we need to do better and what a lot of people don't know is the environmental impacts."
Unknown	"We really don't know, I mean, we don't know about water quality . . . some of the wildlife issues, clear-cutting issues. It's a big deal."

Complexity

Resource Degradation	"There was a complete disconnect of management with law enforcement—they were flabbergasted that this was occurring [toxins in the environment]—completely unaware of [ecological impacts], of magnitude of what is going on out there."
Interagency Involvement	"You're dealing with multiple jurisdictions, multiple experience levels, some people are talking to each other, working together."
Encroachment and Access	"We've had people build houses on FS [Forest Service] system lands to house their illegal grow workers; . . . squatters use mining law in order to evade another law; . . . access issues where people are crossing FS lands to access illegal grows, including building a road adjacent to a creek."

Future Concerns

Ambivalence and Ambiguity of Legality	"Whatever happens [with legalization], we've got a job to do. So legalization isn't a question for us. You're not allowed to grow corn or potatoes in national parks, so we would go after those grows too."
	"There will still be a market for it, because there's always a black market for something. It's not real clear how it [legalization] will impact public lands."
	"If they decriminalized it to one or two plants, you may not see it like you see it now."
Uncertainty of Success	"Not sure we've made any headway . . ."
	"We've certainly made gains . . ."

with laws governing ways in which illegal grows were accessed across federal lands, in grow sites adjacent to federal lands, and in using other legal rights as a cover (i.e., mining law) to "squat" on federal lands for illegal cultivation purposes. Organizationally, there were frustrations in combining agency personnel and programs effectively and efficiently. For instance, respondents acknowledged that illegal marijuana grows are not singular issues for law enforcement and ecologists but rather an integrated, systematic problem. While many respondents identified circumstances where agencies are increasingly responding to illegal marijuana grows in cohesive ways, they also revealed that it has taken time and the agencies have suffered setbacks. Administrators found difficulties in directing these multiple structures to work together in an integrated fashion while maintaining efficiency and agility. Further, while respondents identified a few examples of interagency cooperation to address best practices and share challenges (i.e., National Park Service, n.d.), they also identified a lack of national interagency dialogue concerning this issue due to complexity. Confusion was echoed not only as an interagency concern but as an issue to be addressed in an intra-agency manner.

A final theme was lack of clarity around the future of illegal marijuana cultivation on public lands. Not only did interviewees state that they do not have a clear and consistent assessment of the efficacy of intervention strategies, but there was also uncertainty about the current and future legality of marijuana in general. Many respondents indicated an objective sense that the unpermitted growing of anything on public lands is illegal, and many also indicated that the seemingly dynamic legal status of marijuana in many states gives them pause as to how vehemently illegal marijuana cultivation is and should be addressed. Current and future conflicts between state and federal laws were cited as confounding issues for managers. Others even addressed potential collaborative solutions between agencies and marijuana growers, where marijuana cultivation would be permitted and regulated similarly to grazing or timber harvesting on particular federal lands.

TRAGEDY, COMMON POOL RESOURCES, AND MARIJUANA CULTIVATION

These results are further illuminated when analyzed using Hardin's (1968) "Tragedy of the Commons" and the design principles of CPRs (Ostrom 1990; 1992). The "tragedies" (cf. Hsu 2006) of marijuana cultivation on public lands are numerous but can be generalized into four categories. First, there is the tragedy associated with damaging effects to ecosystems: watershed pollution, impacts to wildlife and vegetation, biodiversity disruption, and landscape change (e.g., widespread erosion, tree clearing, water diversion). Second, there is the tragedy of various human communities adjacent to these areas that are negatively disrupted. Agency personnel are often endangered through violence or through exposure to harmful chemicals, as are individuals immediately responsible for the grow operations. Third, there is a social component within the illegal grows themselves, where the results indicated that many growers are potentially exploited by often unmet promises of permanent transnational relocation, improved livelihoods, familial protection, and high wages. Finally, there is the tragedy of the allocation of tax-related resources—financial, material, and human—that are distributed toward addressing illegal marijuana grows to the detriment of other services typically provided by land managers, such as recreation and biodiversity protection.

With Stern's (2011) characteristics of CPRs in mind, we suggest that a particular resource's "appropriators" share "a common cultural and institutional context." However, the CPR framework becomes complicated in the case of illegal marijuana cultivation because growers are not always aligned with local and national legal structures, even as these structures are in the midst of uneven changes. For instance, it is difficult to believe that individuals or groups growing marijuana on federal lands have common cultural understandings of US federal lands and their management institutions (e.g., national parks as "America's Best Idea" and the NPS as "protectors" of valuable lands). Therefore, growers may not conceptualize, perceive, or identify with these lands in the same ways as land management agencies or the public at large envision them, resulting in a potential fundamental disagreement about the nature of and appropriate use of common pool resources.

Illegal marijuana cultivation on federal lands actively contests many traditionally understood assessments of these spaces; revisiting these design principles in light of marijuana production provides new insight into managing these contested spaces.

Clearly defined boundaries: While federal lands are clearly defined through managerial and political boundaries, it is unclear whether these boundaries are universally understood and recognized.

Congruence between rules and local conditions: Interviewees regularly expressed frustration at the variegated ways in which growers violated rules within management parcels, emphasizing the dynamism associated with many of the grow operations. Land management and law enforcement practices and protocols in one area often could not be replicated elsewhere, for various place-based and bureaucratic reasons.

Collective-choice arrangements: The results indicated that most managers agree that marijuana growth on federal lands should not be allowed. However, since marijuana growth on public lands is currently an illegal activity, it is clear that the growers did not participate in decision-making processes for how US federal land, the common resource, would be governed. Marijuana growth on federal lands also challenges traditional notions of growers as appropriators. If growers are not considered appropriators then this conceptualization violates Ostrom's (1990) recommendation that successful CPRs need to remain adaptable to modify rules regarding membership, and for access to and use of the CPR (e.g., growers). While the researchers are not advocating for considering growers as appropriators, this tension may obfuscate alignment between CPRs and managers' response to illegal marijuana cultivation. Also related to collective-choice agreements, many federal agencies are relatively slow to adapt due to lengthy waits for policy change (although results indicate some exceptions). There remains uncertainty as to how federal agencies may respond to recent legislation regarding marijuana's more locally recognized legality (e.g., Colorado, Oregon, Washington, and California).

Monitoring: As grow sites are often discretely hidden in deep, inaccessible areas, current efforts at monitoring are often unsuccessful. Agencies with advanced remote sensing mapping and access to helicopters and planes are often more successful in monitoring potential grow sites, a fact that will likely evolve with the increasing acceptance and use of unmanned aerial vehicles (drones). Monitoring was cited by respondents as critical to interdiction success, and without consistent and detailed approaches to monitoring, interdiction was largely ineffective.

Graduated sanctions: Nearly all respondents indicated a "no-tolerance" policy for marijuana growth on federal lands, primarily because marijuana is currently illegal at the federal level. These positions suggest that graduated sanctions as a tenet of CPRs does not apply well to the no-tolerance policy for illegal marijuana cultivation. Alternatively, sanctions for illegal marijuana cultivation range from dismissal of charges to multiple years in federal prison, indicating that sanctions often reflect the severity of the action. However, graduated sanctions may be partially attributed to inconsistent legal processes and outcomes, as described next.

Conflict-resolution mechanisms: Interview results reveal that many managers perceive that current conflict-resolution mechanisms concerning illegal marijuana production are largely ineffective or nonexistent. Viewing legal strategies as conflict-resolution mechanisms, almost all respondents suggested that the antiquated avenues for indictments poorly address the complex and current state of marijuana cultivation on public lands. For example, respondents discussed that profound ecological impacts from cultivation are often not pursued by prosecutors because the necessary laws do not exist or are differentially supported by courts. As a result, prosecutors are left with pursuing less aggressive violations concerning general cultivation, evading the law, and extended human inhabitancy on federal lands, which although important may be dismissed by courts or result in reduced sentences. Regarding interagency collaboration, numerous respondents described their beliefs that management policies would change and adapt with presumed changes in upcoming legislation, which may increase the availability and use of some conflict-resolution mechanisms (e.g., potentially more administrative and financial support).

Recognition of rights to organize: The majority of US federal land appropriators (i.e., visitors, tax payers, concessionaires, agency personnel) can legitimately challenge the management of these spaces. However, illegal marijuana growers are not considered or perceived as legitimate by civil society and therefore have limited avenues to formally organize or challenge governmental authority. This may result in more violence as growers attempt to assert their "rights" through potentially armed confrontations. Alternatively, the rights of the majority of appropriators to formally organize may provide distinct advantages over growers and their associated organizations.

Nested enterprises: Federal lands and management agencies are regularly organized in a nested manner, with each enterprise (land management unit) operating with some limited degree of independence. Also recognized is that individual growers and grow sites are often nested within larger enterprises of multinational cartels and regional distribution networks. The nested nature of the agencies' or illicit organizations' positions, divisions, and regions may contribute to the overall effectiveness of interdiction or growth success through sharing and linking resources. Alternatively, this nestedness may increase inefficiencies born from bureaucratic or organizational layering, intra- or interagency organizational disagreements, and lack of budgets or budgetary autonomy.

FUTURE RESEARCH

Because illegal marijuana cultivation on public lands is relatively uninvestigated, there are numerous avenues for future research. Ecological research in and around marijuana grow sites is in its initial stages, and themes from this current study point to a growing demand from managers to have more empirically focused studies that detail the impacts to water, wildlife, soil, and ecological systems. The international community appears aligned and states:

> Government, academic, and private scientific research institutions and foundations should be encouraged systematically to monitor environmentally affected areas through remote sensing, aerial surveys and other resource evaluation technologies. Research on and assessments of forest resource loss and ecosystem contamination by dangerous products and wastes that have environmental and health implications should be advanced on an urgent basis. (UNODC 2014)

This research also implies that there are impacts felt in local human communities due to illegal marijuana grows. For instance, illegal grows and their associated activities and infrastructure (e.g., rudimentary housing, armed weaponry, and pesticides) may potentially decrease site-specific visitation and regional tourism, which may further stress agencies' budgets and lead to decreased political support. Further, it is likely that some local economies may become at least partially dependent on revenue related to illegal cultivation, such as purchases of large quantities of irrigation pipes, food, and other resources. Over time, this reliance could become pervasive and offset other traditional revenue sources for a particular community, such as legal agriculture.

Although this chapter provides but a small entry into the complex management concerns associated with illegal marijuana grows, its in-depth case studies provide context-specific results. Conversely, a more expansive quantitative assessment of managers and local human communities might provide greater insight into the generalizability of the views discovered in this research. Such an investigation could provide quantitative comparisons within and across positions, agencies, and regions.

Other important actors in this complex system are the actual growers and the often transnational networks (Martin 2012; Batiste 2013) that support and facilitate their involvement in the grow sites. Tracing this lineage may connect grows to specific organizations, inform law enforcement policies, and help to understand the effects on domestic and international political economy. Furthermore, investigating the growers themselves may highlight, explain, and increase collective understandings of social justice issues and what is effectively a contemporary version of indentured servitude, with growers being forced into managing illegal grows by larger, multinational criminal organizations.

The legality of marijuana for recreational use in the United States also complicates future scenarios. For example, as the demand for recreational marijuana and the amount of energy required to produce marijuana at indoor facilities increase (Mills 2012), a market-based incentive to grow marijuana on public lands may intensify. While recreational use of marijuana is as of 2017 legal in eight states (Alaska, California, Colorado, Maine, Massachusetts, Nevada, Oregon, and Washington) and the District of Columbia, there are differential levels of institutional infrastructure available to facilitate this process. California, the most populous state, passed Proposition 64 in 2016, allowing adults age twenty-one and older to possess up to one ounce of marijuana and grow up to six plants in their homes, though many aspects of the law have an effective date of January 2018. Our research suggests that much of the law enforcement activity on federal public lands also takes place in California, so these legal status changes may have short- and long-term impacts on land management agencies. In addition to recreational marijuana, medicinal marijuana is currently legal in a total of twenty-eight states and the District of Columbia, with varying levels of access and distribution. Applied to the context of this research, these uneven state legalization and criminalization policies, as well as contradictions between federal and state policies, may have implications for the cultivation of marijuana on public lands. If marijuana cultivation on private lands is widely legalized but heavily monitored and regulated similarly to sustainable agricultural practices, appropriate yields, levels of potency, and labor and wages, then unregulated grows on public lands may increase so growers can escape these complex layers of institutional oversight. Legalization of recreational and medicinal use may also increase demand for marijuana, and matched supply may not be accomplished by regulated growers on private parcels alone, potentially incentivizing grows on public lands.

Alternatively, if recreational and medicinal use of marijuana is widely legalized, production farms close to distribution centers may reduce the need to hide production in remote and difficult locations with less-than-adequate resources, hence reducing the need to produce on public lands. Such a scenario may also result in a cost–benefit deficiency where the cost of growing on public lands does not match crop and economic yield, shifting illicit organizations' focus to more profitable substances (e.g., methamphetamines). Legalization, along with the public's increasing general detachment from nature (Louv 2006), including outdoor recreation on public lands (Pergams and Zaradic 2008), may aggregate, resulting in general public apathy about the social and ecological impacts of marijuana cultivation on public lands. Such a decrease in public awareness, concern, and support may drastically influence the tax-based resources allocated to address illegal marijuana cultivation and further increase the challenges currently expressed by managers, particularly those challenges related to inadequate financial and human resources.

In addition to lessons from previous efforts at interagency and intra-agency collaboration concerning illegal activities (Foster et al. 2009), this research complements a growing body of popular media by providing a more systematized understanding of the multiple ecological, managerial, and administrative concerns that managers face with illegal marijuana cultivation on federal lands. As managers, domestically and internationally, confront complex illicit activity on public lands, more public discussion and scholarly research will be necessary to inform management decisions concerning nature–society relations in an uncertain future.

WORKS CITED

Batiste, J. 2013. "Continued Decrease in Large Marijuana Grows on Public Land." Washington State Patrol media release. http://www.wsp.wa.gov/information/releases/2013_archive/mr112613.htm (accessed March 1, 2013).

Beckley, B. 2010. "Keeping Safe if You Come across a Marijuana Grow Site." USFS Technology & Development Program Safety and Health Law Enforcement and Investigations. http://www.fs.fed.us/t-d/pubs/pdfpubs/pdf10672317/pdf10672317dpi72.pdf.

Brown, G., and C. C. Harris. 1992. "National Forest Management and the 'Tragedy of the Commons': A Multidisciplinary Perspective." *Society and Natural Resources* 5, 1: 67–83.

Cohen, K., N. Sanyal, and G. E. Reed. 2007. "Methamphetamine Production on Public Lands: Threats and Responses." *Society and Natural Resources* 20, 3: 261–270.

Creswell, J. W., and V. L. Plano Clark. 2011. *Mixed Methods Research*. London: Sage.

Farah, D. 1990. "Cocaine Chemicals Foul the Amazon Basin." *Washington Post*. http://www.washingtonpost.com/archive/politics/1990/11/20/cocaine-chemicals-foul-amazon-basin/7121bd32-37e5 4ff2-93c7-a6066fecf316/ (accessed September 8, 2015).

Foster, A., C. Partelow, A. Demetry, S. Shackelton, and B. Alberti. 2009. "Science and Strategies: Collaboration to Combat Marijuana Cultivation on Public Lands." In *Proceedings of the 2009 George Wright Society Conference*, ed. S. Weber, 175–178. Hancock, MI: George Wright Society.

Gabriel, M. W., J. M. Higley, G. Wengert, L. Woods, and R. Poppenga. 2013. "Intentional Poisoning of a Fisher (*Martes pennanti*) with a Carbamate Insecticide Laced Bait at an Illegal Marijuana Trespass Cultivation Site." Unpublished data retrieved from http://www.iercecology.org/wp-content/uploads/2013/08/Fisher_Poisoning_July_2013.pdf.

Gabriel, M. W., L. W. Woods, R. Poppenga, R. A. Sweitzer, C. Thompson, S. M. Matthews, J. M. Higley, S. M. Keller, K. Purcell, R. H. Barrett, G. M. Wengert, B. N. Sacks, and D. L. Clifford. 2012. "Anticoagulant Rodenticides on Our Public and Community Lands: Spatial Distribution of Exposure and Poisoning of a Rare Forest Carnivore." *PLoS ONE* 7, 7: 1–15.

Hardin, G. 1968. "The Tragedy of the Commons." *Science* 162: 1243–1248.

Hess, C., and E. Ostrom. 2007. *Understanding Knowledge as Commons: From Theory to Practice*. Cambridge, MA: MIT Press.

Honey-Roses, J. 2009. "Illegal Logging in Common Property Forests." *Society and Natural Resources* 22, 10: 916–930.

Hsu, S. 2006. "What Is a Tragedy of the Commons? Overfishing and the Campaign Spending Problem." *Albany Law Review* 69: 75–138.

Leong, K. M. 2009. "The Tragedy of Becoming Common: Landscape Change and Perceptions of Wildlife." *Society and Natural Resources* 23, 2: 111–127.

Louv, R. 2006. *Last Child in the Woods*. Chapel Hill, NC: Algonquin.

Martin, R. 2012. "The National Park Service and Transnational Criminal Organizations: Is a Crisis Looming?" MA thesis, West Virginia University.

McSweeney, K., E. A. Nielsen, M. J. Taylor, D. J. Wrathall, Z. Pearson, O. Wang, and S. T. Plumb. 2014. "Drug Policy as Conservation Policy: Narco-deforestation." *Science* 343: 489–490.

Miller, C. 2012. *Public Lands, Public Debates*. Corvallis: Oregon State University Press.

Mills, E. 2012. "The Carbon Footprint of Indoor Cannabis Production." *Energy Policy* 46: 58–67.

National Park Service. n.d. "Pacific West Region Marijuana Eradication Framework and Goals." Washington, DC: Department of the Interior. 16 pages.

National Research Council. 2001. "Data Needs for Monitoring Drug Programs." In *Informing America's Policy of Illegal Drugs: What We Don't Know Keeps Hurting Us*, ed. C. F. Manski and J. V. Pepper, 77–123. Washington, DC: National Academy Press.

Ostrom, E. 1990. *Governing the Commons: The Evolution of the Institutions for Collective Action*. New York: Cambridge University Press.

———. 1992. "The Rudiments of a Theory of the Origins, Survival, and Performance of

Common-Property Institutions." In *Making the Commons Work: Theory, Practice, and Policy*, ed. D. W. Bromley, 293–318. San Francisco: ICS Press.

Pandit, B. H., and G. B. Thapa. 2004. "Poverty and Resource Degradation under Different Common Forest Resource Management Systems in the Mountains of Nepal." *Society and Natural Resources* 17, 1: 1–16.

Pendleton, M. R. 1996. "Crime, Criminals, and Guns in Natural Settings: Exploring the Basis for Disarming Federal Rangers." *American Journal of Police* 15, 4: 3–25.

Pergams, O. R. W., and P. A. Zaradic. 2008. "Evidence for a Fundamental and Pervasive Shift away from Nature-Based Recreation." *Proceedings of the National Academy of Sciences of the United States of America* 105, 7: 2295–2300.

Reuter, P. 2002. "The First Agenda for Drug Enforcement Research." *Addiction* 97: 653–654.

Seidman, I. 2013. *Interviewing as Qualitative Research*, 2nd ed. New York: Teachers College Press.

Stern, P. 2011. "Design Principles for Global Commons: Natural Resources and Emerging Technologies." *International Journal of the Commons* 5, 2: 213–232.

Thompson, C., R. Sweitzer, M. Gabriel, K. Purcell, R. Barrett, and R. Poppenga. 2013. "Impacts of Rodenticide and Insecticide Toxicants from Marijuana Cultivation Sites on Fisher Survival Rates in the Sierra National Forest, California." *Conservation Letters* 7: 91–102.

Tynon, J., and D. Chavez. 2006. "Crime in National Forests: A Call for Research." *Journal of Forestry* April–May: 154–157.

UNODC (United Nations Office on Drugs and Crime). 2014. "Illicit Narcotics Cultivation and Processing: The Ignored Environmental Drama." US Department of State technical report. http://www.unodc.org/unodc/en/data-and-analysis/bulletin/bulletin .html.

US Attorney's Office. 2012. "US Attorneys Announce Final Statistics on Operation Mountain Sweep." United States Attorney Benjamin B. Wagner, Eastern District of California. http://www.justice.gov/usao/cae/news/docs/2012/09-2012/09-05-12 MountainSweep%20Update.html (accessed September 1, 2013).

US Government Accountability Office. 2010. "Federal Lands: Adopting a Formal, Risk-Based Approach Could Help Land Management Agencies Better Manage Their Law Enforcement Resources." http://www.gao.gov/new.items/d11144.pdf (accessed September 20, 2012).

US Office of National Drug Control Policy. 2012. Office of National Drug Control Policy Data Sets. http://www.whitehouse.gov/ondcp/ondcp-data-sets (accessed December 4, 2012).

Wiant, J. A. 1985. "Narcotics in the Golden Triangle." *Washington Quarterly* 8, 4: 125–140.

Wilson, R. 2014. *America's Public Lands: From Yellowstone to Smokey Bear and Beyond*. New York: Rowman and Littlefield.

Wing, M., and J. Tynon. 2006. "Crime Mapping and Spatial Analysis in National Forests." *Journal of Forestry*, September: 293–298.

PART TWO

Downwind Consequences

CHAPTER **6**

Mission Croy Road

Gunmen, a K9, and a Pack Mule Named Stanley

John Nores Jr.

I am prepared to go anywhere—provided it be forward.
—David Livingston, 1875

The grower struggled and kicked under the duress of Phebe's bite as our relentless K9 kept pressure on the man's right calf. Running full speed to catch up to Phebe and her suspect just 10 yards ahead, Brian and I could see this man was tough. Unlike other dangerous growers under the duress of a seasoned K9's control, he did not scream or yell out.

Running just a few yards ahead of me, Brian could not focus on Phebe or her suspect; he was locked on to a second grower a few feet away, armed with a bright stainless-steel handgun. Now, just a few feet away from Phebe and her struggling felon, I saw the man leaning up on his side and kicking his legs, still fighting to shake our K9 loose. He pulled out an automatic pistol from the waistline of his cargo pants. My breath hitched; I could not get to the man fast enough, as everything around me moved in slow motion. Unknown to our team at that moment, the next few seconds would validate a change in the progression of apprehension strategies for these dangerous men. Mission planning and tactics for our Marijuana Enforcement Team (MET), and later other teams throughout the state, would change forever.

Four months earlier . . .

Before her retirement in late 2012, Nancy Foley, who served as chief of the California Department of Fish and Wildlife's Law Enforcement Division, often told those of us in her ranks that change is inevitable, but growth is optional. That provocative statement had never been more relevant than in the spring of that year. It was late March 2012, and so many changes had taken place within our allied-agency Marijuana Enforcement Team (MET) since 2010, the ending time period covered in my first book, *War in the Woods*. When writing *War in the Woods*, I focused on the development of our Silicon Valley MET, including the environmental crime enforcement and restoration efforts we practice and promote on marijuana cultivation operations throughout the Silicon Valley foothills. The book covered our team's evolution from its inception in 2004 through the spring of 2010, and naturally, our team's tactics and policies evolved significantly during that time period. The lessons learned from what worked safely and effectively, and what didn't and needed to be changed, engendered significant tactics and awareness changes during those years, and this progression naturally continued following the end of that era.

Since then, marijuana cultivation–related environmental crime operations have become more prevalent within our traditional game warden ranks. Besides our allied-agency brotherhood in Santa Clara County, Captain Nate Arnold and his progressive assistant chief, John Baker, in the Fresno-based Central Enforcement District (CED), were making our involvement in large-scale, allied-agency task force marijuana operations a priority. Also supported by progressive-minded assistant chief Mike Carion in the Redding-centered Northern Enforcement District (NED), a handful of tactically minded wardens were building allied-agency bridges and working with agencies like the US Forest Service, Shasta County Sheriff's Office, and Bureau of Land Management on marijuana enforcement operations.

In all of these cases, reclamation—defined as the restoration of water quality and the rectification of environmental damages done throughout these cultivation sites—was becoming as important as suspect apprehension and plant eradication. The Law Enforcement Division's three-pronged approach to clandestine outdoor cultivation operations (apprehension, eradication, and environmental reclamation) started to spread throughout California, and we were pleased when several of our allied-agency partners began to incorporate this approach.

The Santa Clara County Sheriff's Office MET experienced many changes during this timeframe. Snake and Rails, my first two allied-agency partners on the Sheriff's Office MET, had rotated off their MET assignments in late 2010 and were replaced by Spag and Hunter in late 2011. Spag is a Spec Ops sergeant, past sniper team leader, and decade-long friend. Hunter is young, motivated, and quick-witted with a dry sense of humor, a direct yet soft-spoken deputy with a love for hunting, fishing, and all things outdoors.

I met Hunter, a fellow south Santa Clara County native, in the 1990s when he was in high school and doing ride-alongs with local law enforcement agencies. Hunter was more of a partner than a ride-along that day, and I liked him immediately. Knowing he would make a great game warden, I was disappointed a few years later to hear he had joined the Sheriff's Office. Our loss was the Sheriff's Office gain, and I didn't expect to work with him directly in the future. But we did, as on this cold and clear March day, a day perfect for a recon scout. Also with us was the newest addition to our MET family, my six-month-old K9 companion dog, Apollo. An English lab, Apollo had passed her companion obedience testing on her first attempt, just a few days previous. Today would be her first time on a scout, and a test of her focus, noise discipline, and K9 field craft in the woods.

Although March is an unusually early month for marijuana cultivators to begin planting in California, this site was an exception. With the start of the biggest drought in California's recent history, the extremely light rains throughout Silicon Valley during the 2011–2012 winter season were catalyzing an early start of grow operations throughout the county. Area residents had witnessed unusual vehicle traffic up and down Croy Road (a remote roadway surrounded by densely wooded and lush, steep hills a few miles west of rural Morgan Hill in southern Silicon Valley). Witnesses had seen small lights moving through the underbrush and tree canopy in the middle of the night on the vast wooded ridgeline on the south side of Croy Road, activity that had continued nightly over the past week.

Our plan was simple and had been tested on past scouting missions many times previous. Our scout team would access the suspected grow site from the west, far from the location of the suspected cultivation activity. We would hike to the top of the ridge and work quietly and carefully along the edge of the eastern border of the grow site, approaching it from the west and above if possible. Tactical advantage was the goal, and it would dictate our route once we reached the target area. Fortunately, we knew the terrain and possessed the ability to move through it quietly and discreetly. With Hunter on point and Spag following a few yards behind him, Apollo and I fell into the tail position, gaining elevation slowly as we ascended the ridge above. The ground was soft and the brush and tree limbs were wet from recent rains, making the climb virtually silent. This was unusual for a scout, as the terrain throughout our county is usually much noisier and tactically less forgiving later in the season. The lush green terrain smelled fresh, and our sweat dried quickly in the cool winter air as we climbed carefully and quietly through the brush. Apollo, showing a little puppy energy at times, maintained her noise discipline and focus as she followed carefully behind Spag at the end of her leash. She was excited and doing a good job on her first recon scout.

Approximately an hour after beginning our climb, we had ascended 700 feet and were less than a quarter mile from the top of the ridge. Up on point, Hunter was the first to see signs of a grow operation and froze in place. Holding his AR-15 rifle at the high ready position with it pointed ahead of him, he carefully whispered into his radio microphone, "We've got a brush wall 20 yards ahead at 10 o'clock." Spag pivoted toward that position and froze ahead of us, his AR-15 now pointed in that direction. Hearing this in my ear mic, I gave Apollo the hand signal to "hold." She sat down ahead of me, looking up to see what I would do next. I raised my POF AR-10 carbine and scanned the brush line ahead through my Aim point micro red dot site. Having a feeling of being watched and concerned with a threat moving up behind us, I turned slowly to check our 6 o'clock. For the next few minutes, the four of us remained frozen as I verified we had no threats or movement beyond the brush wall with my pocket binoculars. When we resumed movement toward the wall, we could see that multiple coyote brush, chemise, and manzanita branches had been freshly cut, interwoven, and piled into a short boundary line. These brush-built boundary walls are common to grow operations all over California, with growers using them not only to enclose and disguise their cultivation site but also to make it difficult for law enforcement teams like ours to penetrate quietly without detection. We all knew we were now on the edge of an active grow site.

As we slowly paralleled the brush wall looking for an unobstructed and quiet entry point into the grow, Hunter found the first good spot to cross the boundary, just 20 yards south of our position. Carefully tiptoeing through the few openings of the stacked trimmings, we crossed the boundary one at a time. Hunter moved through the boundary as Spag covered him with his rifle. I did the same for Spag. Spag then turned to cover me as I untethered Apollo's leash before she silently slid through the brush pile. Once Apollo was at Spag's side, I moved across the boundary and fell into the tail gun position on our team once again. A few seconds later, Hunter whispered into his mic: "Fresh digging and a shovel 10 yards ahead at 12 o'clock." Again, Spag, Apollo, and I froze as we all scanned ahead. Sure enough, we could see a shovel on the ground with moist dirt on its blade. This shovel had been used that morning, possibly even minutes earlier, and we now knew we had growers in the perimeter ahead of us. While the digging was fresh, we did not see any signs of marijuana plants in the ground. Clearly this crew was just getting started, preparing the ground and their irrigation system for an imminent planting phase of their operation. Apollo turned her head, her ears now cocked forward, and alerted on something in the brush ahead of us. Sitting at my feet, she remained frozen and looking intently ahead. I scanned behind us once again as I heard Hunter in my ear mic say, "two voices ahead, Spanish speaking, unknown distance, at our 10 o'clock." A dose of adrenaline shot through us as we knew we were dangerously close to the men running this grow. When the voices ahead of us faded to silence, and Hunter was confident the growers had moved further away, he signaled us to move. Covering each other with our rifles once again, we carefully crossed the brush barrier one at a time. Now on point, I guided our team to some brush cover, well outside of the grow site perimeter. Well concealed in the brush, we took a long break and listened for movement behind us. We would patiently monitor this site for the next several months and confirm plants in the ground before organizing one of our first allied-agency takedowns of 2012.

Following our scout in late March, we all agreed that an aerial flyover of the site to verify plants in the ground was necessary. We needed to solidly link cultivation, and the multitude of other associated felony and misdemeanor environmental crimes, to any suspects we encountered the day of the takedown. But with the Sheriff's Office helicopter down for multiple repairs and my agency's air assets tied up on other details, we had no choice but to wait. After following up on other early season cultivation reports, and conducting many hours of late-night Croy Road surveillance after dark, the Sheriff's Office helicopter was finally up and running the last week of May. Spag called me on a Friday afternoon, excited to share the good news about their bird. Since we only had the chopper for that Sunday afternoon, we jumped on the opportunity to fly. We met at Moffett Field to meet Rob, the seasoned Sheriff's Office helicopter pilot. While I'd flown with a lot of skilled and confident law enforcement and military helicopter pilots in the past, I was impressed with Rob's attention to detail and his low-key, confident demeanor. With Spag up front, and Rob and me in the back seat with both side doors removed, we were ready to roll. Being careful not to compromise the Croy Road grow, Spag asked Rob to make a single pass of the target site and to fly it from west to east, the same direction our scout team had hiked it over a month before. Given our high altitude and constant speed over the site, Spag and I knew we had to find plants quickly and get an immediate and accurate GPS coordinate once we did. If our GPS waypoints were marked even a few seconds too late during the flyover our coordinates could be as far as a quarter mile or more off target. Not good for our ground team trying to vector in on the grow site with an inaccurate location later.

We flew south along the top of Loma Prieta, just a few hundred feet above the radio repeater towers, before banking east and making corrections toward the Croy Road ridgeline. Spag picked up key landmarks quickly, giving Rob navigation adjustments as we rapidly approached the target site below. Flying several hundred feet above and in line with the southern ridgeline, Spag and I simultaneously smiled as we saw large marijuana plants below us. We both marked waypoints on our individual handheld GPS units, and Rob could hear our excitement over the intercom as we articulated what we saw below. The grow site was big. It stretched much farther to the east than we had suspected, and with all the tree

Figure 6.1. Metaphos poison, common in trespass grow sites throughout California. The toxic pink liquid is applied and dried on marijuana plants, in waterways, and in and around grow site camps. A single tablespoon of this substance can destroy several miles of waterway wildlife species, and the poison must be handled as a deadly hazardous material when encountered.

canopy and thick brush cover below we were likely seeing only a fraction of the plants on the ground. With the late afternoon sun setting slowly behind us, we continued east for some time before slowly banking northwest and heading back to Moffett.

After verifying the Croy Road site was actively under cultivation, Spag, Hunter, and I quickly developed a plan to end this operation immediately. Of particular concern was the location of this site in relation to the Uvas Creek watershed, less than a mile down canyon from the grow site. With all of this site's drainages flowing into tributaries of Uvas Creek and Uvas Reservoir, we were concerned with the environmental impacts not only to water quality but also to sensitive wildlife species. With migrating steelhead trout and red-legged frog (both threatened and/ or endangered species) residing in those watersheds, we could only imagine the level of damage this grow site's fertilizers, pesticides, and other grow poisons were causing downstream.

Figure 6.2. Poisoned gray fox found in the Silicon Valley foothills on a public land trespass grow site.

After pulling together our best operators from the Sheriff's Office and the California Department of Fish and Wildlife, we were ready to go on June 7, 2012. That day's mission consisted of eight sheriff's deputies and six game wardens. Up front and on point were our apprehension-and-arrest team's long gunners, Hunter and Mia, the latter a Sheriff's Office sergeant, sniper, and seasoned MET operator. In the constant effort to progress tactically, and increase officer and suspect safety, we were changing up tactics on today's operation once again. Until now, we had utilized light runners behind our two riflemen on point to pursue and capture any unarmed suspects encountered on these operations. Today, however, we were adding a specialized apprehension K9 to do the job of our light runners.

Positioned right behind Mia in our entry team were Brian and his legendary dual-purpose K9, Phebe. Phebe is one of the most highly skilled and versatile dogs in the Department of Fish and Wildlife's K9 program. Because of the excessively violent and deadly nature of the growers we encounter on these operations, any tactical advantage we can gain to keep us safe is critical.

Since finding my first trespass marijuana cultivation site in 2004, I along with my teammates have raided approximately 300 trespass drug trafficking operations (DTOs) grow sites throughout California. In the majority of these complexes

Figure 6.3. Camp waste at a national forest trespass grow site polluting an adjacent pristine steelhead trout stream.

we find firearms either on the growers themselves or somewhere in the growers' sleeping camp or kitchen area. Since 2006 our team members have been involved in five officer-involved shootings where armed growers did not give up when confronted by law enforcement officers. In 2010, for example, there were ten officer-involved shootings during trespass DTO grow operations with armed and aggressive growers throughout California. During our first gunfight in 2005, our team was ambushed by growers positioned tactically and waiting to shoot anyone who entered their grow site from a hidden position in the northwestern foothills above the city of Los Gatos in Santa Clara County (See *War in the Woods*, chapter 2: "Gunfight on Sierra Azul"). During that horrible day, our partner warden was shot through both legs by a trespass grower shooting an AK-47–type rifle, an assault rifle developed for the Soviet military and intended for combat. My young partner was just a year into his career on that August day and thankfully survived that deadly encounter. That event, and the ambush mindset of the growers in that site, catalyzed a change in the way operators and administrators throughout numerous US law enforcement agencies deal with these grow site operations. For our agency in particular, the support in trauma medicine and tactical training, in addition to the advanced equipment, personnel resources, and helicopter air support dedicated to this dangerous work, would increase substantially to good effect following the events of August 5, 2005.

Also alarming is the danger posed to outdoor recreationalists when they inadvertently encounter armed and violent trespass growers. In one case, a father and his young son were shot at by growers on public land in Calaveras County when the pair stumbled into a 3,000-plant clandestine marijuana grow complex while deer hunting.

In another encounter with a trespass marijuana grow complex, Fort Bragg city council member Jere Melo was murdered in August 2011. Jere was an exceptional leader in the region and an environmental steward of California's wildlife and natural resources, and this tragic incident exemplifies the violent nature of many trespass growers willing to kill for their cash crop.

An apprehension K9 that is skilled in working effectively in these remote wooded grow site areas is rare and invaluable. Over the 2011 season, Brian and Phebe worked with us half a dozen times, becoming a much-desired duo of our Santa Clara County team. Our friendship grew, and while we did not apprehend any growers during those missions, we did develop team-wide stalking and apprehension tactics designed around Phebe's detection and tracking skills during those operations. As Brian's K9 lethal cover support on all of these missions, I transitioned from the light runner role to following closely behind Brian and Phebe, providing arrest and lethal cover support as needed.

With the Croy Road mission being a large operation with a high likelihood of encountering suspects, I asked for Brian's and Phebe's help once again. Before dawn the next morning, our team was staged below and west of the grow site. Brian and Phebe were positioned directly behind Hunter and Mia on point today, for maximum effectiveness. As Brian's K9 support and cover, I was positioned behind him, with Phebe eagerly looking around ready to hike. Behind me was Quell, new to the team from the Sheriff's Office and a multitour Iraq veteran from the Marine Corps. In the tail gunner position of our apprehension team was Harp, a Coast Guard Spec Ops veteran and seasoned deputy who was also on the Sheriff's Office special emergency response team. Approximately 25 yards behind Harp was Markos, who would serve as the point man on our secondary team, the quick reaction force (QRF), following not far behind us on the apprehension team. Backing them up, and strategically positioned below the grow site and not far above Croy Road, was our perimeter team. Carefully placed to catch any fleeing suspects that might get lucky and make it out of the grow site when contacted by our apprehension team, these wardens were invaluable.

Hundreds of feet above and a half mile west of our perimeter team, our entry team was now hiking up the ridge, below and west of the grow site. The dry and crunchy leaf litter under the trees, coupled with the dry grasses, made it almost impossible to remain silent as we ascended. As a result, we moved extremely slow, focusing concentration on our field craft and stalking tactics to remain undetected. Slow and deliberate foot placement, combined with smooth upper body and facial movement, kept us nearly invisible as our team closed the distance to the complex. An hour into the hike, Hunter stopped and radioed back for the rest of us to hold. We were getting close. Holding in place and scanning for movement around us, we were only 100 yards west of the target now. Following this brief stop, our point team continued moving east toward the grow site, as Spag paused the QRF a little longer before falling in behind us. After slowly covering the final 100 yards Hunter stopped the team again. The trail we had used to enter the complex had been completely altered. Dry manzanita branches and tree limbs covered the entrance and were scattered all over the footpath into the complex. This noisy trail trap would at best spook the growers into fleeing when they heard our team entering the grow site, and at worst allow them to set up an ambush and shoot us to pieces as we entered. Reminiscent of August 2005, when Mojo was shot and almost killed after our team moved through a similar noisy brush tunnel, we were much more prepared now.

As usual, I was carrying only my handgun, a Taser, arrest tools, and a light pack to support Brian and Phebe as a light runner and K9 support. Also on my belt was a pair of small brush clippers to deal with the obstacle ahead of us. Knowing this, Hunter called me up to cut a trail through the labyrinth of brush ahead. With Brian and Phebe moving to the side of the trail, I slowly slipped past them, reaching Mia and Hunter up on point covering the trail with their AR-15s. I looked at them both as they nodded slowly, signaling that they were in position with their rifles and ready for me to move ahead.

Dropping down on my knees, I crawled slowly ahead, looking carefully for hidden booby traps while clipping brush and branches out of the way for our team behind. Found in several trespass grow sites throughout California and other western states, these traps are designed specifically to maim or kill humans and animals that enter the grow site. From Vietnam War–era guerrilla warfare punji pits (disguised holes in the ground with a series of sharpened stakes carefully placed and pointed upward to severely puncture the feet, legs, and body of any person or animal that steps into them) to camouflaged wire-snare traps designed to strangle anyone or anything that steps through them, these booby traps would at best slow our team down and at worst critically wound or kill one of us. While not found in every trespass grow site, these antipersonnel traps are prolific enough in these complexes that our team exercises extreme caution when moving through grow sites.

In slow motion, I moved each freshly cut branch to the right or left of the trail, placing it quietly on the ground out of our way. Now on point, with Mia and Hunter covering me with their long guns, I crawled through the brush, unable to look ahead through the tangle at any threats ahead. My heart raced with adren-

Figure 6.4. Trespass grower in the Silicon Valley back country posing with a poisoned golden eagle killed from banned toxic pesticides used on and around his marijuana crop.

aline as I cut away at the obstruction, smoothly moving cut brush to the side of the trail and out of the way of my teammates behind. With my handgun trained ahead and down the trail, I pushed forward another 10 feet and froze. Seeing no movement ahead, I transitioned to a kneeling position, raising my body and pistol higher off the ground to see more peripherally. Directly ahead and as far down the hillside as I could see were thousands of large budded marijuana plants. I radioed back to the team advising them the trail was clear and that I was holding on the edge of endless marijuana plants.

We observed that the plants around us had not been watered and knew the growers could be walking down our trail at any moment to do so. We waited five minutes, letting the woods settle, looking and listening for movement around us. Seeing and hearing nothing threatening, Hunter signaled the team to move further down the trail into the grow site. Contact with the growers felt imminent. The temperature had risen steadily. Ahead of us now, the hillside dropped in elevation as the plantation curved slightly downhill. With the main trail in the middle of a downhill slope, we were positioned at an ideal choke point to watch the trail below, safely detect, and ambush the growers when they worked up the ridge to water their cash crop.

Phebe's keen sense of smell would surely detect suspects approaching us, well before they saw any of our team members. Like other K9s, Phebe's sense of smell is at least 10,000 times greater than ours. Affectionately known as the "fur missile," Phebe is unstoppable once she has identified and locked onto a dangerous suspect. Just as important, and as witnessed with Jordan and Apollo many times before, Phebe's ability to alert our team to the presence of dangerous suspects around us before we see them or they see us is a significant officer safety advantage.

Our timing and movement were perfect. Within five minutes of setting up on an uphill advantage Brian and I spotted two growers emerge from the bottom of the grow site ahead of us. Both were dressed in green military pants and moved carefully through the grow site toward us, quietly speaking in Spanish, seemingly oblivious to our presence. We were alarmed to see a large, bright, and holstered pistol on the right hip of one of the men. Brian immediately notified the team on the radio, whispering: "Two suspects at 12 o'clock, 25 yards out, headed toward us. Be advised, one has a handgun on his right hip so this will be a silent release." Brian was preparing all of us for a K9 deployment with this transmission.

Given the presence of at least one handgun, the gun violence we've experienced from growers in the past, and several brutal grower assaults on Phebe during similar apprehension missions, we weren't taking any chances. To ensure our safety and the safety of the growers we were about to engage, the apprehension would be as silent and surprising as possible. When approximately 20 yards out, the two men turned north and began moving diagonally away from us. Brian was reading my mind when he gave Phebe the apprehension command, released her from the leash, and whispered over the radio, "Dog's away!" Phebe shot toward the two men at 30 miles per hour, with Brian and me sprinting behind her as fast as we could run. Pushing forward with our Glock pistols trained on the men, we identified ourselves, yelling, "Police! Put your hands up and don't move!" We needed to get to the men quickly, capitalize on the element of surprise, and prevent them from drawing and engaging us with a pistol. Realizing something was wrong and sensing movement ahead of them, the growers stopped in mid-track and focused ahead just in time to see our speedy K9 closing in. With their eyes as wide as silver dollars and their mouths opened in shock, the men did not see us closing in behind Phebe until it was too late. Before the men could turn to run, Phebe tackled the felon on the right, bit down on his right calf, and forced him to the ground. Unfortunately, the armed grower with the pistol was behind his partner and not yet under control. He looked at his partner on the ground being subdued by Phebe before noticing Brian and me closing in. Seeing us, the gunman squared off and faced us. His right hand reached for his holstered pistol. As this man represented the most-immediate threat, Brian realized he could not deal with Phebe and her suspect on the ground now. He yelled to me, "John, take my dog!" and ran past Phebe's struggle to deal with the armed grower further out.

In a split-second decision during the chaos of the chase, Brian and I had switched roles. I now had to handle Phebe and her suspect as Brian worked to keep the armed gunman ahead from harming our team. Phebe's grower struggled and kicked under the duress of her bite, as our relentless K9 kept pressure on the man's right calf. Unlike other dangerous growers under the duress of a seasoned K9's control, he did not scream or yell out. Instead, he just grunted on the ground, clearly furious and focused on fighting his way through the K9's bite.

As I was just a few yards away from Phebe and her struggling face-down felon, I saw the man leaning up on his side, kicking his legs, and fighting to shake our K9 loose. Worse yet, he was now holding an automatic pistol in his left hand and pushing through the pain of the bite to point it toward us. Brian, now face-to-face with his gunman a few yards ahead of me, had his Glock trained solidly on his suspect's chest. The man hesitated for a moment before releasing the grip on his holstered pistol and putting his hands up to surrender. With Mia and Hunter covering, Brian placed the man in handcuffs and removed a loaded Taurus Judge .44 magnum/.410-gauge shotgun combination pistol from his holster.

I could not get to my suspect fast enough. Thankfully, Phebe's bite pressure was slowing the grower down. She was making it difficult for him to train the pistol on any of us, affording me the opportunity to close the gap and take control. From a sprint, I jumped on the suspect's back as Phebe continued to keep bite pressure on his calf. I struck the gunman between the shoulder blades, yelling at him to drop the pistol. I grabbed both of his hands and placed them in handcuffs. Now that my gunman was no longer a threat, I had to call Phebe off her bite and handle her. Fortunately, Brian had trained all of us on the team to handle Phebe during a deployment in the event he was ever injured or tied up on another threat, and today that training was invaluable. With our point team's attention focused solely on our two suspects, I heard Spag behind me moving the QRF up to support us. Telling Markos, Raptor, Fleck, and Beric to secure a perimeter around our two suspects and keep a tight 360, I knew Spag's concern. Since we had only cleared a small part of the grow complex and had not found a kitchen or a camp yet, we were not safe. More armed growers could be in the area, along with any number of environmental threats including booby traps and toxic grow poisons and pesticides.

Harp was now at my back, covering me with his AR-15. After a quick patdown search of the suspect's pockets and waistband, I picked up the handgun (a WWII-era semiautomatic .32-caliber Russian Tokarev combat pistol) off the ground. I unloaded it and removed a full magazine of ammunition from the pistol and a live, unexpended .32 caliber cartridge from the firing chamber. I turned to Harp and showed him the pistol and live cartridge before he said, "That was close, Lieutenant, and that round was intended for us." I let out a breath of relief

Figure 6.5. Semiautomatic pistol used by Phebe's suspect and pulled on our team during the apprehension.

before responding, "Way too close, brother! And God bless Phebe. She saved us from another gunfight today."

Once the scene was secured, our team divided up to tackle the numerous tasks of processing the grow site. Brian, Phebe, Mia, Hunter, and Quell hiked out and cleared the rest of the complex for any more threats. Spag cleaned and dressed the gunman's wound before sitting him down in the shade under a small tree in the center of the grow site. The gunman still had to be walked out of the grow site and medically treated and cleared at the hospital later that day. Within thirty minutes, Hunter's team found the gunmen's camp, their kitchen, their marijuana processing area, and multiple check dams and water diversions throughout the complex. Like all of these complexes, the grow site was a mess. With several tons of camp trash, human and cooking waste, fertilizers and pesticides, and thousands of feet of black plastic irrigation hose littering the ground as far as the eye could see, we knew we had our work cut out for us.

The two growers we had just caught were the only men present and running the operation at that time. With the grow site a few weeks away from being harvested, the two men did not yet need additional workers on site. While most of the marijuana within the grow site had budded, none of it was quite ready to be

Figure 6.6. MET operators with K9 Phebe shortly after their apprehension of the two armed Croy Road suspects.

harvested or taken out of the woods. With both growers handcuffed and seated apart from each other in the center of the complex we could move forward with processing, eradicating, and reclaiming (environmentally restoring) the grow site. Hunter told us all that they had found several containers of Furadan, the highly toxic pesticide banned from use in the United States, within the site. Alarming to everyone, we realized our gunmen had used this poison throughout the complex and likely throughout the site's watering system. With a tablespoon of this substance being enough to decimate all the fish and other aquatic wildlife for miles in Croy Creek below us, everyone was extra careful to avoid exposure. Before eradicating and reclamating the site later that morning, we all donned Nitrile protective gloves to protect us from the numerous poisons throughout the grow site.

Although we were pleased we caught the growers before they could harvest the crop or move any of the budded marijuana out of the woods and into distribution nationwide, we had a problem. Without helicopter support to long-line the budded plants out of the woods, we were going to have to move it all by hand. Given the heat of the day, with the temperature steadily climbing, and the long hike through dense woods to get to our vehicles to transport and dispose of the cash crop, none of us looked forward to that part of the operation. We needed a way to get this dope out of the grow site without having to hike it all down on our backs.

Unforeseen obstacles like this are common to MET operations, and the ability to adapt to these challenges and come up with improvised solutions is a necessity. With our MET motto being "fill and flow," we all know that bouncing from one plan or solution to a problem to another within seconds is often needed. Fortunately, John, a friend of mine who runs pack mules in the Sierra Nevada during the summer, lived close by. We were relieved to learn that John had one mule left on his ranch. Stanley was an older, seasoned, and trail-savvy black mule that was only a day from joining the rest of his pack train in the Sierras when we called for help. Quin and Bones escorted John and Stanley up the ridgeline and into the grow site, and I will never forget the smiles on all three of the men's faces when they reached us with Stanley in tow. This was not a common method for MET to use when eradicating and removing a budded crop from a mountaintop; we were all laughing at the novelty of it.

For the next two hours, Quin, Brian, Beric, Quell, Harp, Mia, Fleck, and Hunter cut and stacked massive bundles of budded marijuana plants on Stanley's pack board before walking him down the hill to the transport trucks. Even with Stanley's help, many of us were carrying and dragging bundles down the hill as well to expedite the haul-out process. By midafternoon we had transported both armed suspects to jail and removed and eradicated all 7,000 budded marijuana plants from the complex. Even without a helicopter to assist on environmental cleanup and reclamation that day we were able to restore the water diversions, collect and pile the thousands of feet of black plastic water line, and contain all of the camp and grow site trash for helicopter removal at a later date.

Tired, thirsty, and content with another mission completed safely, our MET walked single file out of the grow site and down the ridgeline to much-needed cold drinks in our trucks below. What we experienced that day was a game changer and an indication of how much officer safety and effectiveness is improved with the use of well-trained K9s like Phebe. Growth may be optional, but that is not the case with our MET. Growth is mandatory for success and survival; we had proven that on this operation.

Like many of the hundreds of trespass DTO growers we have apprehended over the past decade, the two gunmen we captured during this operation were not US citizens and told us they were responsible for starting and maintaining this grow site. They were doing so voluntarily, with their financial rewards of this site being directly contingent on the successful harvest of their lucrative crop. Both men admitted to working for others above them in a larger organization, but would not elaborate any further. Typical of trespass DTO operations, these growers were selected and put in place to cultivate marijuana given their skill sets in di-

Figure 6.7. MET operators and Stanley the mule removing budded marijuana from the Croy Road grow site.

verting water from remote water sources and growing marijuana covertly to avoid detection from law enforcement teams like ours. Before being embedded in the United States under fictitious identification, vetted and skilled growers are smuggled across the border along with their banned poisons and pesticides to cultivate highly lucrative marijuana. Even more alarming is the fact that this marijuana is often tainted with those banned toxic poisons before being sold and distributed all over the United States. While we have heard rumors of growers being transported into the country under duress to cultivate marijuana for the DTOs, we have never seen evidence of this during the hundreds of suspect apprehensions and missions completed in the past twelve years.

The two gunmen growers spent the next few months in the Santa Clara County jail, working through the courtroom process before sentencing. Shortly after testifying in a preliminary hearing with Hunter, both men pleaded guilty to numerous charges, including possession of firearms while committing felonies, water diversion, water pollution, littering, and using banned and toxic poisons while illegally cultivating marijuana. In addition, the gunman Phebe and I apprehended was charged with assault on a law enforcement officer since he was drawing his pistol on our team when apprehended. That gunman pleaded to the long list of misdemeanor and felony charges, including the assault charge, and received a prison sentence of five years as a first-time offender. The second gunman (charged with everything listed above, except assault on a law enforcement officer) pleaded to a two-year prison sentence, also as a first-time offender.

While we unfortunately did not have the resources to reclaim the grow site during the day of the raid, we did rectify the water diversions on site and stabilized the rest of the complex to insure against water pollution runoff and the poisoning of Croy Creek below us. In the fall of 2013 we returned to the Croy Road cultivation site with a helicopter team to remove all the camp, kitchen, and other grow site trash, fertilizers, and miles of poly pipe irrigation line. Since we removed the infrastructure of the grow site and naturalized the complex, the DTOs have not returned to this location to cultivate. For this area in particular, the dangers, logistics involved, and costs of doing the arrest, eradication, and reclamation phase of this operation were well worth it. Given the environmental concerns and sensitive waterway within and below the grow site, we needed to put the time and effort into completing all three phases of our marijuana enforcement program on this site. As experienced on the Croy Road mission and numerous others we've been involved in, the unavoidable delays in completing some missions engendered by officer safety and resource needs are frustrating. In the case of trespass DTO grow sites operating on county, state, and national park lands especially, these delays not only hinder client access and enjoyment of pristine parts of our nation's wildlands but also maintain an unavoidable public safety threat until removed.

Three years later . . .

Over years of countless hours of training together, Brian and Phebe have developed into an exemplary K9-handler team. As of January 31, 2017, Brian and Phebe have had 114 bite apprehensions of violent grow site suspects since 2007 on marijuana operations throughout California. The number of suspects who surrendered before being subjected to Phebe's physical control is eight times that, at approximately 800. To put the significance of these numbers in perspective, we must remember that every one of these men caught not only were cultivating marijuana for sale illegally throughout California's wild lands but also were poisoning and destroying a diversity of wildlife species and waterways throughout the state. In light of the record drought facing California in recent years, the massive amounts of water diverted and stolen (approximately 1.3 billion gallons of water in 2013 and 2014 alone) by clandestine outdoor growers was significant—as was the amount of water saved by shutting down illegal grow sites. Because most of these men were armed with firearms to defend their cash crop, the public safety threat that was eliminated when removing these felons from our wild lands was even more critical.

Those successes in 2013 led the CDFW to test-pilot a new initiative, in collaboration with the California Air National Guard's counter drug focused Team Hawk, from the 129th Air Rescue Wing out of Moffett Field. Dubbed Operation PRISTINE (Protecting Resources Involving Specialized Team in Narcotics Enforcement), the combined agency-force conducted a whirlwind of operations in August 2013, and by the end of that month those involved were exhausted but pleased with the results. The operation had yielded good numbers in all areas, and based on the immediate success of the pilot program, CDFW chief Carion and the rest of his command staff green-lighted the development of the agency's first full-time Marijuana Enforcement Team. By the end of 2016 and after four years of operations, our MET has eradicated 2.1 million poisoned plants on trespass DTO grows all over California, along with 36,000 pounds (18 tons) of poisoned processed marijuana seized and destroyed during operations. Our team has also seized 433 firearms being used by DTO growers, arrested 745 DTO suspects, removed 335 tons of grow site waste, removed 1.65 million feet (311 miles) of black irrigation pipe, removed 82,718 pounds (41 tons) of fish and aquatic killing fertilizer, removed 134 containers of prohibited poisonous pesticides, and removed 614 illegal water impoundments statewide. Removing these water diversions and dams has saved approximately 756 million gallons of California's depleted water during the most severe drought our state has experienced in a century.

In November 2016 recreational marijuana use in California was legalized through the passing of Proposition 64. Many believe that because of medicinal and recreational legalization, the market for DTO trespass marijuana will be eliminated, hence thwarting the DTOs' environmental crime and public safety threats throughout the state. Unfortunately, a large majority of DTO trespass marijuana produced in California is sold on the black market to Midwest and East Coast states that do not allow either recreational or medicinal cannabis use. Given the high demand outside of California for DTO trespass cannabis, and the multi-million-dollar black market for this illegal and unregulated product, these new laws are unlikely to slow down DTO operations throughout California. Because Proposition 64 also reduced public and private land trespass cultivation penalties from felonies to misdemeanors, deterrence to DTO activity throughout California was not enhanced. With our agency's mandate to enforce compliance of legal medicinal and recreational cannabis production facilities and continue to fight the public safety and environmental crime threats posed by DTO trespass cultivation operations, the challenge for our agency's wildlife officers working in these programs has never been greater.

Figure 6.8. Military Pave Hawk helicopter removing loads of trespass grow site pollutants, poisoned marijuana, and camp waste for CDFW MET operators during Operation PRISTINE.

Yet given the historical significance and progress of our newly formed unit, we feel lucky to be the foundation of the MET's development since the beginning. The tangible environmental crime-fighting effectiveness thus far, coupled with the resource-protection and restoration results we experience on a daily basis, are deeply rewarding for all MET operators. It is good news for the land, too.

CHAPTER 7

Double Bind

The Intractability of Undocumented Immigrant Trespass Marijuana Grow Operations in US National Forests

Amos Irwin

This chapter informs our understanding of the "balloon effect" using case studies of undocumented immigrants growing marijuana in national forests. These trespass grows have remained intractable for decades due to weaknesses in immigration policy and the criminal justice system. As this chapter demonstrates, the illegal status of workers on these trespass grow sites makes it easy for grow organizers to recruit them and for prosecutors to convict them. Their status also prevents law enforcement from effectively pursuing the grow organizers. While further crackdowns on trespass grows and undocumented immigrants would likely be counterproductive, the most effective intervention against trespass grows may be state-level efforts to regulate the marijuana industry.

Scholars have suggested that law enforcement campaigns against illicit drug production follow the "balloon effect," meaning that they displace production rather than suppress it. Like a hand squeezing a balloon, the theory suggests, when law enforcement applies pressure to one production site, it pushes production to expand elsewhere. The expansion itself is not a controversial idea; the key question is whether law enforcement pressure ends up substantially reducing the total volume of production or simply displaces it to a new location. Many studies argue that law enforcement efforts can successfully suppress drug cultivation (Bar and Pease 1990; Windle and Farrell 2012; Clarke and Weisburd 1994). However, these studies track existing producers in a specific region rather than the global universe of potential producers. Studies of coca and opium poppy production show that while law enforcement campaigns may drive out existing producers, the void is filled by new producers in new locations (Salazar and Fierro 1993; Rouse and Arce 2006; Calvani 2002; McCoy 2003; Kramer et al. 2014).

While most balloon effect literature has focused on patterns of displacement for cocaine and heroin (e.g., Rouse and Arce 2006; Calvani 2002; Chin 2009; Meehan 2011), the effect is equally visible for marijuana. In the 1960s marijuana was a high-end agricultural import, grown more like avocados than an illegal, underground commodity. There was almost no US production; prior to 1969, an estimated 80 percent of all marijuana used in the United States was imported from Mexico (Brecher 1972). Commanding prices roughly forty times higher than other crops, marijuana represented about 9 percent of Mexico's total exports (Doyle 2003).

As Nixon's War on Drugs squeezed the marijuana trade, it moved within US borders. Antidrug operations—including Operation Intercept in 1969, paraquat fumigation in the late 1970s, and Operation Wagonwheel in 1984—pushed marijuana production out of Mexico, encouraging cultivation north of the border (Pollan 1995; Weisheit 1992; Robbins 1986). By 1989 the Drug Enforcement Administration (DEA) estimated that 25 percent of all marijuana consumed in the United States was domestically grown (DEA 1992).

At the same time, asset seizures encouraged US outdoor marijuana growers to move to public lands. Civil asset forfeiture provisions of the 1970 Controlled Substances Act allow law enforcement to seize assets tied to the drug trade without charging the owner with a drug offense. Officers began aggressively seizing growers' land, cars, and homes in the early 1980s when new laws allowed police to keep revenue from the seizures. In response, growers moved off their own land to avoid jeopardizing their own property (NDIC 2001). By 1986 trespass grow operations on public land had become so widespread that Forest Service officials persuaded Congress to grant them antidrug law enforcement powers as part of the Anti-Drug Abuse Act of 1986 (Sterling 2015; Anti-Drug Abuse Act 1986). Since then, most national forest grow sites have been operated in remote areas by undocumented Mexican immigrants, who camp out for months at a time to avoid detection (Ruzzamenti 2015). By the mid-1990s trespass grows had spread from the Emerald Triangle in Northern California across the entire state. Trespass growers also gradually adopted advanced techniques to make their crops more potent, from sinsemilla cultivation to smaller hybrid plants and female cloning (Ruzzamenti 2015; Sedgwick 2015).

Growing marijuana on public land magnifies its environmental hazards. Already facing stiff federal penalties if arrested, growers seek to maximize the harvest at the clear expense of the environment. To avoid detection, they place grow sites in remote sanctuaries for endangered species. They divert water and dam streams that are essential to endangered salmon populations, they allow water-soluble fertilizers to drain straight into the water supply and kill the fish, and they douse the plants with carbofuran, a pesticide so powerful it is banned in the United States (Ruzzamenti 2015; Thorsen 2012; Boehm 2014; Thompson et al. 2013).

Despite the best efforts of law enforcement, public land cultivation continues. Forty-six percent of all US marijuana plants eradicated in 2010 were found upon public and tribal lands (ONDCP, n.d.). In 2014 the US Forest Service documented illegal marijuana cultivation in twenty-two states and seventy-two national forests, and trespass grows have also been found in national parks and in parcels managed by the Bureau of Land Management (Boehm 2014). William Ruzzamenti, director of California's Central Valley High-Intensity Drug Trafficking Area (HIDTA), acknowledges that trespass grows have outpaced law enforcement: "Back in the 1990s, we eradicated 90 percent of the marijuana grows that we found. Today, we're hitting maybe 25 percent because they're so prevalent. I could take you up right now and show you 100 marijuana grows. Law enforcement is overwhelmed and we just can't get to them" (Ruzzamenti 2015). The prevalence of undocumented California growers also continues. US Sentencing Commission data show that of the thirty-eight defendants sentenced in federal court in 2015 for growing over 5,000 marijuana plants, thirty-one were in California, twenty-eight were Hispanic, and twenty-five were noncitizens.

As California law enforcement continues to pressure trespass grows, the grows are evolving. Nguyen et al. (2015) and Gallupe et al. (2011) demonstrate that sites shrink in response to law enforcement sanctions. As suggested by the "group hazard hypothesis," splitting up and scattering the sites minimizes the risk of detection (Erickson 1973; Bouchard 2007). The other evolution is regional. Since the 1980s, most trespass grow sites cultivated by undocumented immigrants have been found on the West Coast, particularly in California (Ruzzamenti 2015). However, Ed Shemelya, the National Marijuana Initiative coordinator for Kentucky HIDTA, reports that starting in about 2007, Mexican nationals began establishing grow sites in Appalachia, particularly in Virginia, West Virginia, Kentucky, and Tennessee (Shemelya 2015). Since most marijuana grown in California's national forests is shipped to consumers across the country, it makes sense that operations would spring up closer to the East Coast market. With fewer Mexican nationals in Appalachia, most grow sites are close to areas with a significant Mexican workforce, particularly poultry farms. Because Kentucky HIDTA is accustomed to locally run grow sites, whose operators only visit the sites occasionally, the agency normally plants video cameras to document the growers' activities. However, since the Mexican growers do not leave their sites, the agency has been unable to surprise them and thus has not yet apprehended any of the growers (Shemelya 2015).

Large-scale trespass grows on public land are notable not for being new but rather for sticking around. They are indisputably illegal, easy to spot from a helicopter, and enormously costly in environmental damage. They have been the primary target for law enforcement eradication efforts (ONDCP, n.d.). Yet trespass grow production has remained steady in California and has grown nationwide (Ruzzamenti 2015; Shemelya 2015). How is it possible that the world's strongest law enforcement power cannot more effectively squeeze the balloon within its own borders? First, being within US borders, law enforcement is bound by US laws and norms. Planes cannot fumigate national forests, and few would support flooding the forests with heavily armed troops. In addition, trespass grows are run by undocumented immigrants. For their own safety, undocumented workers avoid any connection with law enforcement and government services in general.

Two case studies help us understand the unique staying power of undocumented immigrant trespass grows. They also reveal how law enforcement's struggles to squeeze the balloon stem not only from physical remoteness but also from the intersection of the criminal justice system and immigration policy. As well, the case studies demonstrate that law enforcement pressure exacerbates the social, environmental, and economic consequences of marijuana production. Finally, they illustrate why intractable trespass grows are in fact evolving in response to law enforcement pressure. While individual grow operations are not reliable indicators of general trends, only a detailed case study can reveal the inner workings of these operations. I interpret the cases cautiously, using court transcripts as well as interviews with lawyers, law enforcement officers, and the growers themselves.

Criminal case studies are even more difficult to use, since only exceptional cases make it to trial. Most undocumented growers flee the grow site before officers arrive and are never caught. Many arrested growers are never prosecuted. When growers do face charges, prosecutors threaten them with harsh mandatory minimum sentences if they do not plead guilty (Ruzzamenti 2015). US Sentencing Commission data show that of the thirty-eight defendants sentenced in federal court in 2015 for growing over 5,000 marijuana plants, only two went to trial. Plea deals do not release detailed accounts of the grow operation. Only trials, with extensive investigation and cross-examination of witnesses, publicly reveal reliable accounts of these operations.

CASE STUDY 1: FREDY FIGUEROA-MONTES

On June 15, 2011, six Mexican nationals were arrested in Oregon's Wallowa-Whitman National Forest, where they had planted 91,000 marijuana plants, the largest known trespass grow operation in the state's history; the individuals arrested at the grow site were the lowest-level workers tending the plants. The others escaped—two armed guards, "lunchmen" who brought food and grow supplies weekly, and the lead organizers and funders. One case went to trial—that of Fredy Figueroa-Montes, a man from Jalisco who had lived in Merced, California, for eleven years with his wife and two young children.

Figueroa-Montes insisted on going to trial because he felt he was innocent. Though he admitted to participating in the trespass grow operation, he claimed that he had been recruited to thin out a pine forest in Washington, not to grow marijuana in Oregon. He had only learned the truth after traveling for days and arriving at the grow site in the middle of the night, hundreds of miles from home and deep inside a national forest. Since Fredy had participated in the grow operation, the jury found him guilty.

He appealed his conviction, mounting a duress defense—meaning that he had been forced to participate. He explained that when he arrived, he learned that the grow site managers were from the Carrasco family, an infamous cartel family that killed people in his hometown in Mexico. He believed that if he left the site, they would execute his family. Asked why he had not shared this information before, he explained that the Carrasco family would retaliate if they thought that he informed on them in court. Indeed, after their arrest, Audel Carrasco-Soto, a fellow grower and a member of the Carrasco family, told family members that Figueroa-Montes was talking to the police, so they killed his cousin. Then it came out that Carrasco-Soto was testifying against his own family in court, so the family accepted Figueroa-Montes's pleas of innocence. He could now mention them without fear of reprisal (*USA v. Fredy Figueroa-Montes* 2013a, 112). Figueroa-Montes was granted a second trial, in which the jury rejected his duress defense and returned a second "guilty" verdict.

CASE STUDY 2: HERIBERTO SICAIROS-QUINTERO

On July 13, 2009, law enforcement personnel were guiding a volunteer crew to clean up old marijuana grow sites in eastern California's Sierra National Forest when they discovered that one old site was being newly cultivated. They found one man at the 7,000-plant site, Heriberto Sicairos-Quintero. Sicairos-Quintero, a legal US resident in his fifties, had been at the site for a month, cooking and cleaning for two marijuana growers. He did not attempt to escape when the officers approached because he had a bad knee (*USA v. Heriberto Sicairos-Quintero* 2009a, 211). They found a handgun tucked into his waistband.

Sicairos-Quintero also insisted on going to trial to prove his innocence. He claimed that he had been recruited to cook for workers at a ranch, with no mention of marijuana. He had only learned the truth upon arriving at the grow site after a long, difficult hike through the forest. He also mounted a duress defense, claiming that the growers were dangerous young men who would have caught and killed him if he tried to hobble off in search of help. Since he had made no attempt to escape from the growers, who had given him a gun to protect himself against wild animals, the jury rejected the duress defense. Because he had aided and abetted the grow operation by cooking for the growers, he was found guilty of marijuana cultivation and firearm possession (*USA v. Heriberto Sicairos-Quintero* 2009a, 163).

The purpose of these case studies is not to argue for or against the convictions but rather to draw out lessons about trespass grow operations by undocumented immigrants. After all, both cases are exceptional. At 91,000 plants, Figueroa-Montes's trespass grow operation was the largest in Oregon's history and one of the largest in the nation. Figueroa-Montes was also the only grower in the operation who both feared for his family's safety and had been brought to the forest on false pretenses. Sicairos-Quintero was also the only one at his grow site who had been brought there on false pretenses. Even more unusual, he was recruited only to cook for the growers, not to grow marijuana himself.

The first lesson is that the illegal status of undocumented immigrants enables recruiters to organize far more successful grow sites. Trespass grows require constant supervision to produce high-quality marijuana. However, daily traffic to these remote sites would give away their presence to law enforcement. As Ed Shemelya of Kentucky HIDTA has noted, absences from the site also enable law enforcement to set up surveillance, collect information, and more easily apprehend and prosecute growers (Shemelya 2015). Successful trespass grows require conditions that no American worker would accept: fourteen-hour-a-day manual labor for four months without a vacation, spent living in tents with no cell phone reception or showers. Fortunately for the recruiters, over 2 million undocumented immigrants in California are already living in fear of the law, many of whom work in agriculture (Walters 2014). They are often accustomed to poor working conditions and desperate to earn money to send home to their families. For Figueroa-Montes, excessively long hours was a selling point, not a concern:

> Q. Did they tell you anything else about how many days a week you'd be working and what your pay would be?
> A. Yes. He told me it would be seven days a week, he said you can work up to 15 hours all day. He said that the people were really good workers and those people had earned about $180, between $180 to $250 for that 15 hours. That's for the people who were good workers. (*USA v. Fredy Figueroa-Montes* 2013a, 74)

Figueroa-Montes was focused on earning money as fast as possible—the more hours per day, the better—and he asked nothing about working conditions. On the phone with me, he explained that secrecy is routine. The recruiter had told him that someone else had injured their foot and he would be working under their name. He added that when he receives a job offer, he never asks questions about the employer or the conditions because he knows they may rescind the offer. The only thing he asks about is the pay (Figueroa-Montes 2015c).

Undocumented immigrants are easy prey for deception because of their illegal status. Recruiters do not have to sign contracts or even provide contact information. Figueroa-Montes was accustomed to taking a job with no paperwork. As he testified at trial:

> Q: Your family didn't have the number of a company you were working for to call, did they?
> A: No. They never—they never take down my boss's phone numbers or who I'm working for.
> Q: And you didn't arrange for a hotel or any lodging where you could be contacted?
> A: Who? My family?
> Q: Correct.
> A: No, I didn't ever do that. I don't ever do that. When I get to the place, that's when the boss man pays for your hotel. (*USA v. Fredy Figueroa-Montes* 2013a, 139)

In the underground labor market, secrecy is expected by both parties. Since recruiters do not have to provide any documentation, they are harder to track and prosecute.

Undocumented immigrants are also safe recruits because they will not turn growers in to the police. Already living in the country illegally, workers like Figueroa-Montes stay away from law enforcement. His defense attorney tried to convey this to the jury:

> Q: Now, did you have the opportunity to tell the police about the Carrascos and these threats?
> A: When?
> Q: When you were arrested.
> A: No, I did not tell them. I did not tell them because I don't trust the police. (*USA v. Fredy Figueroa-Montes* 2013a, 120)

Figueroa-Montes did not explain his lack of trust for the police, but all undocumented immigrants know that trusting the police could lead to deportation

(Theodore 2013). This fear also prevents police from using undercover agents or confidential informants. It is never easy for undercover officers to infiltrate criminal circles, but it would be exceptionally difficult to infiltrate a circle of undocumented growers.

Undocumented immigrants also know that US law enforcement cannot protect their families. Figueroa-Montes explained to me on the phone that he stayed silent about the Carrasco family less out of fear of US law enforcement and more out of knowledge that the police could not protect his family back in Mexico (Figueroa-Montes 2015a). While Mexico is far away, the threat is surprisingly close. Figueroa-Montes reports that even in federal prison in rural Georgia, he is incarcerated with more than twenty individuals who know the Carrasco family. He is working with them to try to resolve any outstanding problems he might have with the family (Figueroa-Montes 2015c).

The same features of the underground labor market that make undocumented immigrants easy prey for recruiters also make them easy prey for conviction-hungry prosecutors. In closing arguments, Sicairos-Quintero's prosecutor argued that when he took the job without learning anyone's real name, he must have expected illegal activity:

> He talked about Guero and Grenas and another Grena, and how they didn't even know each other's names. And there's a couple guys with the nickname "Grenas." Is that really believable? That's something for you to determine. (*USA v. Heriberto Sicairos-Quintero* 2009b, 99)
>
> I would submit to you that persons involved with illegal activities, people who may be part of organized crime generally don't use their full legal names. That they would use their nicknames. They wouldn't want to give their true identifications to someone outside. (*USA v. Heriberto Sicairos-Quintero* 2009b, 111)

The prosecutor also stressed that Sicairos-Quintero left his relatives without even providing contact information:

> I asked Mr. Quintero when he was on the stand, you met these other guys, Grenas and some other guy, and you just left with them. You left with them. They told you you were going to be gone for a month, and you're living with your sister, right? And he said he didn't let her know. He didn't give her a phone number. He didn't give her an address. (*USA v. Heriberto Sicairos-Quintero* 2009b, 98)

Figueroa-Montes's prosecutor also dwelled at length on how foreign the work situation should seem to the jurors:

Just assuming for a moment that what the defendant said was accurate, that he thought he was going to grow pine trees, imagine yourself at that gate, first of all, in the middle of the night. That's a strange way to begin a job. That's a really strange way to begin a job, unloading a bunch of stuff in the middle of night out in the middle of nowhere. And then you're asked to strap on a headlight and only put on the red light as you make your way down the path. That red light should have been a red flag, if what that defendant said was true. That was his moment to get out. Who on earth would try to hike down three-quarters of a mile [of] a steep ravine carrying a bunch of supplies, lit only by a red light? That alone tells you, this isn't going anywhere. This defendant knew what he was getting into. He knew it was going to be secretive, he knew that he was getting into something illegal, and he was doing it willingly and knowing what he was going to do. (*USA v. Fredy Figueroa-Montes* 2013b, 194)

The prosecutors exploited the fact that a normal situation for undocumented workers would be highly suspicious for most Americans. This gap makes it easier both to recruit and to prosecute undocumented immigrants, whether they are told that they will be growing marijuana or pine trees.

The same is true of undocumented immigrants' relationship with law enforcement. Figueroa-Montes's prosecutor seized on his stated distrust of law enforcement in closing arguments:

Now, the defendant says, oh, I don't trust law enforcement. Frankly, that's not a good enough reason. Your standard is the objective standard. Would an objectively reasonable person . . . when offered a law enforcement presence to do something about it, would that person say, oh, my gosh, I have been threatened, help me?. . . He says he doesn't trust law enforcement. He doesn't give a reason for it. There is no rational basis for him to say that. (*USA v. Fredy Figueroa-Montes* 2013b, 165)

The prosecutor in Sicairos-Quintero's case made a similar point in closing:

If you're a prisoner for 25 days and you come up and see the cops, you'll be jumping for joy. You would be just happy as a clam. You'd be saying, "Oh, thank you. Thank you for coming to my rescue." You know, "No, this gun wasn't mine. I'm sorry. These guys, yeah, they were holding me hostage." And, "No, no, why are you restraining me? I didn't do anything, Officer. I was a prisoner." . . . You've heard testimony from three different people that they asked him questions, and never did he say he was a prisoner, that he was forced to be there. You think it's reasonable? (*USA v. Heriberto Sicairos-Quintero* 2009b, 117)

Both prosecutors tried to raise the jurors' suspicions on the grounds that an innocent person would have trusted the police. But in communities of undocumented immigrants, such distrust is completely normal (Theodore 2013).

Regardless of Figueroa-Montes's immigration status, his case would still have been damaged by the divide between Oregon and Jalisco. He explained on the phone that there was no time or money to gather evidence in Mexico (Figueroa-Montes 2015c). Robert Salisbury, his attorney, pointed out that even if there were resources for the investigation, Figueroa-Montes would not want anyone asking questions about the Carrascos on his behalf (Salisbury 2015). With few resources and no desire to stir up trouble in Mexico, the defense could not provide evidence of the Carrascos' criminal involvement.

In the absence of specific evidence on the Carrasco family, the defense planned to call a cartel expert to testify about cartel violence in general. However, the judge rejected the witness because his testimony would not specifically touch on the Carrascos:

The foundation for an expert to testify solely about not even the Carrascos but more generally Mexican drug-trafficking organizations is either missing or so weak here as to not justify or allow for the testimony, since it's two inferential chains away from the decision the jury has to make anyway, and now the evidence supporting why this jury would need to know about the wilds of the Mexican drug-trafficking organization generally, which is, after all, only incremental knowledge to what they've already heard about the more specific group we care about—i.e., the Carrascos—leads me to tentatively conclude I would not allow the expert testimony. (*USA v. Fredy Figueroa-Montes* 2013a, 164).

It is reasonable to exclude testimony about Mexican cartels in general when no evidence established that the Carrascos were even involved with cartels. However, this does not mean such evidence did not exist, but simply that given the time, resources, and danger involved, such a transnational investigation did not take place. As a result, the defense had no chance to illustrate the dangers of Jalisco to the jury in Oregon. In closing arguments, the prosecutor pointed out: "I submit to you that there is nothing that Mr. Figueroa-Montes said about the Carrasco family that has any corroboration from any witness or any piece of evidence in this case" (*USA v. Fredy Figueroa-Montes* 2013a, 194). The statement was true, not because the evidence did not exist, but because nobody had looked for it.

Figueroa-Montes's case was also hurt by the fact that he did not seek help from his family. The prosecutor argued in closing: "He doesn't contact anyone who is not law enforcement related to say, oh, my gosh, there's this threat. Honey, move the kids. Oh, my gosh, family in Mexico, there is this threat, move. He doesn't do any of that. Why doesn't he do that? Because the threat never existed" (*USA v. Fredy Figueroa-Montes* 2013a, 165).

In fact, it is perfectly rational for him not to ask his family in Mexico to uproot their lives so he could flee from the grow site. They would have to flee their home, since US law enforcement could do nothing to protect them. It would also disgrace him, since he was supposed to be sending money to support them, not endangering them and asking for their help. In fact, Figueroa-Montes admitted to me that four years after the fact, he is still keeping the whole situation a secret from his family in Mexico. He told his mother that he had been picked up by immigration authorities, that he was working on getting his papers in order, and that he has been sick for a long time. He doesn't want to scare her or admit that he was involved in growing marijuana, but he needed to explain why he is no longer sending money home (Figueroa-Montes 2015a).

At the same time, both defendants were hurt by their lack of understanding of the US criminal justice system. It is not a coincidence that these defendants were brought to grow sites under false pretenses. They went to trial because they felt they were innocent. Anyone clearly guilty of growing marijuana would gain no advantage from going to trial, since they would face severe mandatory minimum sentences regardless of their mitigating circumstances. The only reason to go to trial is if they believe they can win a "not guilty" verdict. Figueroa-Montes explained on the phone that his lawyer repeatedly urged him to collaborate with the prosecutor in exchange for a plea bargain. Knowing his own innocence and believing that the trial would reveal the truth, he refused the plea offers (Figueroa-Montes 2015a).

While the defendants presented a duress defense, their testimony suffered because they did not understand how to win over a jury. Sicairos-Quintero's attorney said that in person, the defendant was friendly, emotional, and convincing (Salisbury 2015). But on the stand, either because he was reacting to the formal courtroom, imitating the behavior of other witnesses, or simply following masculine norms, he appeared unemotional even while describing threats to his life. Figueroa-Montes fell into the same trap, which his attorney tried to explain to the jury in his closing statement: "You've been given a rare glimpse into the lives of Mexican people. What a scary and dangerous world that they live in. People are killed, people disappeared. They're able to say these things so calmly and casually because they've experienced this their entire lives" (*USA v. Fredy Figueroa-Montes* 2013b, 192). Had the defendants been more familiar with the courtroom, they would have testified less "calmly and casually"—more effectively conveying their fear to the jury.

The criminal justice system is dizzyingly complex for Americans, and much more so for Mexicans. Figueroa-Montes pointed out that he was charged with growing 90,000 plants, an impossible task for a single person. He did not realize that conspiracy laws allow every member of a group to be charged for all of the group's crimes, regardless of their position in the organization (Figueroa-Montes 2015c). Sicairos-Quintero thought that merely cooking meals for the growers was different than growing the plants, but because he "aided and abetted" the growers he was still convicted of cultivation. In the ultimate display of naiveté, both insisted on going to trial to prove their innocence.

With no prior experience of the criminal justice system, Figueroa-Montes did not know to collect valuable information to trade in exchange for a shorter sentence. For the judge to depart downward from a mandatory minimum sentence, a defendant needs to provide investigators with "substantial assistance," usually testimony against codefendants. For this reason, those involved in criminal activity often collect information on their bosses and rivals to trade for leniency in case they are arrested (Strack 2015). Those without any exposure to the criminal justice system do not. Figueroa-Montes explained at trial, "I didn't know anything. I didn't have the name of the boss. The five codefendants, you guys had telephone numbers, and I didn't have anything" (*USA v. Fredy Figueroa-Montes* 2013a, 148). Similarly, Sicairos-Quintero, after a month eating meals with the two growers, had learned nothing more than their nicknames. His attorney, Charles Lee, has worked with many similar clients. "It's always the low guy on the totem pole and they don't have information. If they had information they could actually get a good plea deal. They usually cooperate and get three to five years, assuming they don't have a gun" (Lee 2015). Ed Shemelya of Kentucky HIDTA agreed that the growers have little information to give: "They have no idea who the real players are in the organization" (Shemelya 2015).

By contrast, those who have made a career in crime learn how to use the system to their advantage. Audel Carrasco-Soto, a member of the Carrasco family, had escaped from prison, where he had been incarcerated for cocaine possession. He agreed to testify for the government and had his sentenced shortened from 5 years to 2.5 years for providing "substantial assistance" (*USA v. Fredy Figueroa-Montes* 2013a, 30). The government also reportedly dismissed the remaining prison time from his prison escape and allowed him to stay in the country by removing his Immigration and Naturalization Service deportation hold (Salisbury 2015).

The defendants who are least guilty and least familiar with the criminal justice system serve the longest sentences. Figueroa-Montes is serving twelve years and Sicairos-Quintero is serving fifteen, which was the mandatory minimum for growing 1,000 plants, carrying a firearm, and destroying the forest. The other men at Figueroa-Montes's site, who willingly grew marijuana and carried firearms, all pled guilty and are serving roughly four years. This sentencing disparity is not an anomaly. US Sentencing Commission data from 2015 show that while the median sentence for the thirty-eight offenders charged with growing over 5,000 plants (median size 7,208 plants) was 1.5 years, the two defendants who went to trial (for 6,251 and 6,874 plants, respectively) received sentences of 10.8 and 24 years. Neither was carrying a weapon.

While the circumstances of undocumented immigrants make it easier to obtain a conviction, they make it harder for law enforcement to squeeze the industry. Investigators cannot rely on tips and find it difficult to use undercover agents or informants. Prosecutors struggle to charge anyone other than the lowest-level workers apprehended at the grow site. Worst of all, neither group has much incentive to change this. Agents are rewarded by both their supervisors and the media for seizing large quantities of plants, making successful arrests, and contributing to prosecutions resulting in long sentences. No supervisor in the Justice Department even considers whether those prosecutions will have any impact on the appearance of new grow sites the next year. As a result, though prosecutors know that their defendants are replaceable, they also know that this "low-hanging fruit" offers easy, long convictions.

The success of these trespass grows thus exploits the weak points of the US criminal justice system and immigration policy. These weak points are by no means exclusive to marijuana cultivation. Career criminals of all types trade information for shorter sentences, often throwing their hapless subordinates under the bus. Subcontractors in many industries employ undocumented immigrants to increase profits, evade taxes, and avoid responsibility for substandard working conditions. These weak points are particularly crucial for an illegal industry that depends on secrecy and structural insulation from low-level arrests.

Finally, the case studies suggest that while law enforcement is not squeezing out trespass grows, it is pushing them to evolve. First, undocumented immigrant trespass grows are appearing in Appalachia, and they have shifted from large plantations to decentralized sites. Figueroa-Montes explained on the phone that there were twelve or thirteen growers involved in the 90,000-plant grow operation. But since the sites were spread out, most of the growers escaped when they saw law enforcement officers arriving at his site (Figueroa-Montes 2015b). Ruzzamenti believes that some grow operators plant additional "throwaway" sites with low-quality marijuana, sacrificing them to eradication in the hope that they will distract law enforcement from the real, high-quality sites (Ruzzamenti 2015).

It seems, too, that the organizers are now enticing more workers under false pretenses. As more growers are arrested and sent to prison, it becomes harder for the organizers to find willing recruits. Figueroa-Montes explained that in the years before being deceived into joining this grow operation, he had been asked directly multiple times to join a marijuana grow operation, but he had always refused. He believes that fewer workers are willing to join marijuana plantations today, since many have heard about growers being forced to flee without pay or getting caught and serving long prison sentences. But he is quick to point out that deceiving workers is not getting harder—even after serving time in prison, he still does not plan to push recruiters for details on future job opportunities, for fear of losing them (Figueroa-Montes 2015c).

Deceiving recruits brings additional benefits. Those tricked into participating generally have even less information to reveal. Intimidating the coerced laborers to prevent them from sharing the little information they do know is also easy (Salisbury 2015; Lee 2015). The more law enforcement operations target undocumented growers, the more difficult it will be for organizers to find willing new growers. It will still be easy for organizers to trick workers into the forest, given their armed guards, isolated locations, and an undocumented labor pool that will not demand documentation or seek out law enforcement.

While observers debate whether cartels are directly involved, what matters on the ground is what the growers believe. If they believe that grow organizers have cartel ties, they will obey orders out of fear for their families in Mexico, and growers clearly believe they are dealing with well-connected killers. Robert Salisbury, Figueroa-Montes's attorney, has defended many others in the same position. Unlike Figueroa-Montes, most refuse even to mention the danger in court. "There is a severe undercurrent amongst all these folks—they did not want to get up in an open courtroom and say a word [about the grow organizers]" (Salisbury 2015). Charles Lee, Sicairos-Quintero's attorney, reported the same phenomenon; many of his clients will talk about cartels in confidence but never in court, even at the price of prison time. "They don't want to do a duress defense because they would have to talk about the cartels" (Lee 2015).

POLICY IMPLICATIONS

What are the policy implications of these intractable, if evolving, trespass grows? First, federal officials have recently strengthened pollution penalties for trespass growers. Among other penalties, growers already faced up to ten years in prison plus massive fines for "depredation of government property over $1,000," which prosecutors charged to punish both Figueroa-Montes and Sicairos-Quintero for environmental damage (18USC §1361; Kemp 2014). But Representative Jared Huffman (D-CA), whose district includes the Emerald Triangle, promoted sentencing enhancements for trespass grows, on the grounds that "Environmental damage is almost never fully accounted for. Under current law, environmental damages such as water diversions and vegetation removal are not considered as separate or aggravating offenses" (Kemp 2014). The US Sentencing Commission responded by creating new guidelines that allow prosecutors to charge water diversion and vegetation removal as separate or aggravating offenses (Huffman 2014).

These heightened penalties will most likely exacerbate the social consequences of the grow sites. While Representative Huffman was correct that the guidelines had not included water diversion or vegetation removal, both serious environment harms, he overlooked the fact that adding these charges does nothing to prevent trespass grows. They will not help police catch grow organizers or help prosecutors build cases against them. The people facing these sentencing enhancements will be low-level growers who already face stiff penalties, have no useful information, and are the least culpable and most replaceable members of the operations. In addition, as communities of undocumented immigrants gradually learn of these harsher penalties, they will be less likely to voluntarily join trespass grow operations—encouraging recruiters to use deception instead.

Tougher immigration law enforcement has recently become a key focus for the federal government. President Donald Trump and the Republican-controlled Congress are likely to create tougher sanctions for illegal immigration and increase funding for immigration law enforcement. Such laws will make trespass grows easier. The more US law criminalizes undocumented immigrants, the less reason they have to avoid criminal activity. If we increase their distrust in law enforcement, we will facilitate the recruitment and conviction of low-level growers while making it harder to track down the grow organizers. Immigrant detention will clog the prison system, reducing the resources available to pursue and detain grow organizers.

A very different policy trend is the spread of state-level marijuana legalization for recreational use by adults. As of February 2017, eight states and the District of Columbia have passed ballot initiatives to legalize the drug. Trespass grows are concentrated in California and Oregon, where legal marijuana markets are displacing the illegal market. Still, even before legalization, California and Oregon trespass grows primarily exported their marijuana to other states. So even as demand for illegal marijuana in California and Oregon falls, trespass grow marijuana will remain.

Still, widespread marijuana legalization has the potential to make trespass grows on public lands economically unviable. Just as legalization replaces illegal dealers on street corners with regulated dispensaries, it replaces marijuana produced on trespass grows with marijuana from licensed grow operations. As the legal market matures and prices fall, it will divert increasing market share from the trespass grows. And as more states observe the successes of legalization in these eight states and follow suit, demand will no longer sustain trespass grows.

While law enforcement officials advocate for increased funding of enforcement, many also see the potential of legalization. Ed Shemelya of Kentucky HIDTA stated: "I think that the medical and recreational marijuana legalization programs will have a disruptive influence on these trespass grows" (Shemelya 2015). Rather than squeezing the balloon, marijuana legalization can actually deflate it.

ACKNOWLEDGMENTS

The author would like to thank Vera-Jo Kiefer for research assistance and Eric E. Sterling for editorial assistance.

WORKS CITED

Anti-Drug Abuse Act. 1986. Section 6254, PL 100-690, 102 Stat. 4363.

Barr, Robert, and Ken Pease. 1990. "Crime Placement, Displacement, and Deflection." *Crime and Justice* 12: 277–318.

Boehm, Chris. 2014. "Marijuana Cultivation and the Environmental Impacts on Public Lands." Statement to the US Sentencing Commission, March 13. http://www.ussc.gov/sites/default/files/pdf/amendment-process/public-hearings-and-meetings/20140313/Testimony_Boehm.pdf (accessed October 22, 2015).

Bouchard, M. 2007. "A Capture-Recapture Model to Estimate the Size of Criminal Populations and the Risks of Detection in a Marijuana Cultivation Industry." *Journal of Quantitative Criminology* 23: 221–241.

Brecher, Edward M. 1972. "The Consumers Union Report on Licit and Illicit Drugs: Chapter 59." *Consumer Reports Magazine.* http://www.druglibrary.org/schaffer/Library/studies/cu/cu59.html (accessed October 22, 2015).

Calvani, Sandro. 2002. "People's Power against Drugs: Adaptive Changes in Southeast Asia." *Harvard Asia Quarterly,* Summer: 19–27.

Chin, K. 2009. *The Golden Triangle: Inside Southeast Asia's Drug Trade.* Ithaca, NY: Cornell University Press.

Clarke, R. V., and D. Weisburd. 1994. "Diffusion of Crime Control Benefits: Observations on the Reverse of Displacement." In *Crime Prevention Studies,* vol. 2, ed. R. V. Clarke, 165–184. Monsey, NY: Criminal Justice Press.

DEA (Drug Enforcement Administration). 1992. "1992 Domestic Cannabis Eradication/Suppression Program." DEA Cannabis Investigations Section Report, December. http://www.drugscience.org/Archive/DCESP/DEA1992.pdf (accessed October 22, 2015).

Doyle, Kate. 2003. "Operation Intercept: The Perils of Unilateralism." George Washington University National Security Archive. http://nsarchive.gwu.edu/NSAEBB/NSAEBB86/ (accessed October 22, 2015).

Erickson, M. L. 1973. "Group Violations and Official Delinquency: The Group Hazard Hypothesis." *Criminology* 11: 127–160.

Figueroa-Montes, Fredy. 2015a. Phone interview by the author. October 13.

———. 2015b. Phone interview by the author. October 14.

———. 2015c. Phone interview by the author. October 15.

Gallupe, O., M. Bouchard, and J. Caulkins. 2011. "No Change Is a Good Change? Restrictive Deterrence in Illegal Drug Markets." *Journal of Criminal Justice* 39, 1: 81–89.

Huffman, Jared. 2014. "Rep. Huffman Applauds Final Approval of New Guidelines Aimed at Trespass Marijuana Grow Operations." Jared Huffman website press release, November 6. https://huffman.house.gov/media-center/press-releases/rep-huffman-applauds-final-approval-of-new-guidelines-aimed-at-trespass (accessed October 23, 2015).

Kemp, Kym. 2014. "More Penalties Proposed for Marijuana Growers/More Money Spent on Enforcement." *Lost Coast Outpost*, January 20. http://lostcoastoutpost.com/2014/jan/20/more-penalties-marijuana-growers-more-mon (accessed October 23, 2015).

Kramer, T., E. Jensema, M. Jelsma, and T. Blickman. 2014. "Bouncing Back: Relapse in the Golden Triangle." *Transnational Institute*. https://www.tni.org/files/download/tni-2014-bouncingback-web-klein.pdf.

Lee, Charles. 2015. Defense attorney for Heriberto Sicairos-Quintero. Phone interview by the author, October 8.

McCoy, A. 2003. *The Politics of Heroin: CIA Complicity in the Global Drug Trade: Afghanistan, Southeast Asia, Central America, Colombia* (Rev. ed.). Chicago: Lawrence Hill.

Meehan, P. 2011. "Drugs, Insurgency, and State-Building in Burma: Why the Drugs Trade Is Central to Burma's Changing Political Order." *Journal of Southeast Asian Studies* 42, 3: 376–404.

National Drug Intelligence Center. 2001. Pennsylvania Drug Threat Assessment. June. http://www.justice.gov/archive/ndic/pubs0/670/marijuan.htm (accessed October 22, 2015).

Nguyen, H., A. Malm, and M. Bouchard. 2015. "Production, Perceptions, and Punishment: Restrictive Deterrence in the Context of Cannabis Cultivation." *International Journal of Drug Policy* 26, 3: 267–276.

ONDCP. n.d. "Marijuana on Public and Tribal Lands." Office of National Drug Control Policy website. https://www.whitehouse.gov/ondcp/marijuana-on-public-lands (accessed October 22, 2015).

Pollan, Michael. 1995. "How Pot Has Grown." *New Yorker Magazine*, February 19. http://michaelpollan.com/articles-archive/how-pot-has-grown (accessed October 22, 2015).

Robbins, Clyde. 1986. Testimony before the House Committee on Foreign Affairs for the Annual Review of International Narcotics Control Programs and the Impact of Gramm-Rudman on Overseas Narcotics Control Efforts. February 6. http://njlaw.rutgers.edu/collections/gdoc/hearings/8/86602677/86602677.html (accessed October 22, 2015).

Rouse, S., and M. Arce. 2006. "The Drug-Laden Balloon: US Military Assistance and Coca Production in the Central Andes." *Social Science Quarterly* 87, 3: 540–557.

Ruzzamenti, William. 2015. Director of California's Central Valley High-Intensity Drug Trafficking Area (HIDTA). Phone interview by the author, September 25.

Salazar, L., and L. Fierro. 1993. "'Drug Trafficking' and Social and Political Conflicts in Latin America: Some Hypotheses." *Latin American Perspectives* 20, 1: 83–98.

Salisbury, Robert. 2015. Defense attorney for Fredy Figueroa-Montes at second trial. Phone interview by the author, October 7.

Sedgwick, Scott. 2015. Senior deputy sheriff, Ventura County, California. Phone interview by the author, September 28.

Shemelya, Ed. 2015. National Marijuana Initiative Coordinator for Kentucky HIDTA. Phone interview by the author, October 9.

Sterling, Eric E. 2015. Counsel to the House Judiciary Committee from 1980 to 1989. Interview by the author, September 24.

Strack, Ray. 2015. Retired federal agent, Florida. Phone interview by the author, September 30.

Theodore, Nik. 2013. "Insecure Communities: Latino Perceptions of Police Involvement in Immigration Enforcement." PolicyLink Report, May. http://www.policylink.org /sites/default/files/INSECURE_COMMUNITIES_REPORT_FINAL.PDF (accessed October 24, 2015).

Thompson, Craig, Richard Sweitzer, Mourad Gabriel, Kathryn Purcell, Reginald Barrett, and Robert Poppenga. 2013. "Impacts of Rodenticide and Insecticide Toxicants from Marijuana Cultivation Sites on Fisher Survival Rates in the Sierra National Forest, California." *Conservation Letters* 7, 2: 1–12.

Thorsen, Kim. 2012. "Exploring the Problem of Domestic Marijuana Cultivation." Testimony before the US Senate Caucus on International Narcotics Control. https:// www.doi.gov/ocl/hearings/112/MarijuanaCultivation_120711 (accessed October 22, 2015).

USA v. Fredy Figueroa-Montes. 2013a. Transcript: Trial 2, Day 3. Portland, OR, December 12. Case 3:11-cr-00249-MO, document 381.

———. 2013b. Transcript: Trial 2, Day 4. Portland, OR, December 13. Case 3:11-cr -00249-MO, document 382.

USA v. Heriberto Sicairos-Quintero. 2009a. Transcript: Day 1. Fresno, CA, December 10. Case 1:09-cr-00271-AWI, document 72.

———. 2009b. Transcript: Day 2, Afternoon Session. Fresno, CA, December 11. Case 1:09-cr-00271-AWI, document 74.

Walters, Dan. 2014. "California's Illegal Immigrant Population Drops, Still Largest." *Sacramento Bee,* November 18. http://www.sacbee.com/news/politics-government/capitol -alert/article3999037.html (accessed October 23, 2015).

Weisheit, Ralph A. 1992. *Domestic Marijuana: A Neglected Industry.* New York: Greenwood.

Windle, J., and G. Farrell. 2012. "Popping the Balloon Effect: Assessing Drug Law Enforcement in Terms of Displacement, Diffusion, and the Containment Hypothesis." *Substance Use and Misuse* 47, 8–9: 868–876.

CHAPTER **8**

Southern Exposure

Marijuana and Labor in the Appalachians

Hawes Spencer and Char Miller

In Virginia, there is no place more rural or remote than Highland County. Set in the far northwestern portion of the state, Highland is home to a declining population of about 2,300 people, the least populated of the ninety-five counties in the Old Dominion. Its western border fronts the eastern continental divide in the Allegheny Mountains, a rough country of sharp ridges, steep-sloped valleys, and countless creeks, rills, and rivers, a verdant land over which the George Washington and Jefferson National Forests are draped. Well named, this rugged county also deserves its sobriquet: "Virginia's Little Switzerland."

The county's physical features, tiny population, and plentiful precipitation make it potentially fertile ground for the illegal cultivation of marijuana. So too is the large size and tiny staff of the local national forest. "The George Washington National Forest is hundreds of thousands of acres," said Fred Heblich, an attorney who has defended marijuana farmers, "and there's only a few rangers" (Spencer 2016a).

It was this attractive potential that prompted the national forest, which covers nearly 1.8 million mountainous acres running from southwestern Virginia north into portions of Kentucky and West Virginia, to alert the public about the dangers associated with illegal marijuana production on these isolated public lands. While noting that "only a fraction of the National Forest System is affected by illegal marijuana cultivation," the release confirmed that "the Forest Service believes that safety risks are real and visitors and employees should be informed about them." In the words of then deputy forest supervisor Ted Coffman: "The safety of forest visitors and our employees is our top priority. Marijuana cultivation occurs on some National Forests and it's important for visitors and employees to be aware of their surroundings" (George Washington and Jefferson National Forests 2011).

The announcement then detailed the kinds of damage that these trespass grows generated, from the deleterious use of herbicides and pesticides that killed wildlife and habitat and that also compromised water quality to the diversion of water from creeks and streams that could have long-term impacts on forest health. Yet it was with the safety of hikers, hunters, and campers that the announcement was particularly concerned, and it provided a list of clues those recreating in the forests should be alert for:

- A skunk-like odor
- Hoses or drip lines located in unusual or unexpected places
- A well-used trail where there shouldn't be one
- People standing along roads without vehicles present, or in areas where loitering appears unusual
- Grow sites are usually found in isolated locations, in rough steep terrain
- Camps containing cooking and sleeping areas with food, fertilizer, weapons, garbage, rat poison, and/or dead animals
- Small propane bottles, used to avoid the detection of wood smoke
- Individuals armed with rifles out of hunting season

More disturbing still was the scary, if sensible, advice about what, for example, a thru-hiker on the Appalachian Trail should do if she stumbled into an illegal marijuana plantation: "As soon as you become aware that you have come upon a cultivation site, back out immediately. Never engage the growers as these are extremely dangerous people."

The particulars of the cautionary press release are not surprising. Other national forests had issued similar warnings, and with good reason: many of those cultivating these sites are in fact armed, and reports of violence, real or threatened, against those who wound up in the wrong place at the wrong time have become commonplace. They have been most common, however, in the West—not the South. The reason is clear. As many of the chapters in this volume underscore, the largest and most aggressively defended illegal trespass grows are located in the western states, especially in California; the Golden State—and its Emerald Triangle—produce upwards of 60 percent of the domestic crop, a multibillion-dollar, black-market industry.

By contrast, the data on illegal marijuana production on public lands in the South has been hard to come by. No Forest Service scientist working within the Southern Research Station has analyzed marijuana's impact on soil and water quality, or endangered species, as have those operating out of the agency's western stations. Newspaper accounts of raids on or busts of trespass grows also have been considerably more episodic and partial than those emanating each year from California's Mendocino, Three Rivers, or Trinity National Forests, or those arcing around the Los Angeles region—the Los Padres, Angeles, or Cleveland National Forests. In this regard, the South seems a (lucky) backwater.

That caveat notwithstanding, the 2011 press release from the George Washington and Jefferson National Forests was not random. It reflects a no-less-persistent, if smaller-scale, problem for this particular forest and its southern peers in what is designated as Region 8 of the Forest Service; the region covers thirteen states (and Puerto Rico) and manages fourteen national forests, whose land mass totals more than 13 million acres. Many of these forests, like the George Washington in Highland County, protect the forested headwaters of major rivers, a tangled terrain often distant from population centers, little visited, and rarely surveilled.

In the 1980s this seemingly prime territory for trespass grows caught the eye of those who *Washington Post* columnist Jack Anderson called "criminal cultivators." As illegal grows and related drug task force crackdowns were ramping up out West, forest rangers and scientists stationed on the southern forests became aware that large-scale marijuana plantations were being cultivated on the lands they managed. The two events were connected, the *Wilmington* (NC) *Morning Star* asserted in March 1987. "The drive against marijuana planting in the west has escalated in recent years, [and] growers who are concentrated in California are . . . setting up 'franchise' operations in the Southeast." The most heavily impacted at that time were the Nantahala and Pisgah National Forests in western North Carolina. "We are seeing something that was pretty much of a culture of the West Coast that is moving to the Southeast," noted John Gregory, a Forest Service special agent. "We got off to a later start than California. But it is now as much of a problem," an assertion that the land-management agency's statistics for 1987 appeared to confirm. That year, Kentucky alone accounted for one quarter of all marijuana plants uprooted in law enforcement raids on national forests across the country, and seven of the top ten states with the largest confiscations were in Region 8 (Weiss 1987).

To bolster efforts to combat these depredations, and to generate public opinion in support of the new offensive, law enforcement officers gathered at the Ocala National Forest in central Florida in June 1987 for the first meeting explicitly focused on the training they would need to protect the George Washington National Forest, South Carolina's Sumter, the Daniel Boone in Kentucky, and Arkansas's Ozark National Forest, among other sites. As they swapped horror stories about discovering decomposing bodies of growers and dealers on national forests killed by their well-armed competitors; or their flying Forest Service helicopters or driving pickups that were hit by high-powered rifle fire; or de-arming booby traps located on the edges of illegal grows, grisly tales that columnist Anderson publicized nationally, they recognized that the violence wracking western forests was being transplanted to the East. Anderson later internationalized this reference point, arguing that what he heard during his interviews with forest rangers was more "reminiscent of the jungles of Colombia, not the vacation lands of the United States" (Loy 1987; Anderson 1988).

One year later, the "marijuana war," as Anderson dubbed it, heated up in the South and West. Chastising the George H. W. Bush administration for its failure to better underwrite the Forest Service's failing effort to control trespass grows on the national forests, the journalist noted that the federal agency was outgunned and outspent. Yet even as it managed to eradicate many more plants in 1988 than in 1987, this increase in interdiction down south and out west also carried a foreboding message: an internal USDA report revealed that "the more aggressive the Forest Service becomes, the more virulent the drug growers become." Anderson's conclusion was that the agency, "the poor stepchild of the Bush administration," was unable to fulfill one of its key mandates: "The national forests are no longer a pristine place for hikers" (Anderson and Atta, 1989).

However overwrought Anderson's encompassing claim about the widespread threat these illegal grows posed, he was not wrong to zero in on their then-emerging presence in the southern forests. It had seemed an aberration in the late 1980s when the Daniel Boone National Forest topped all others in the amount of marijuana confiscated within its borders. Over the next decade, the forest maintained this dubious distinction, and it has continued to do so. Not only had the production of "green lightning" supplanted moonshine in some areas of Kentucky—notably the back country and high ground set within the Daniel Boone National Forest, but this $4 billion industry had become a more pervasive and lucrative cash crop than tobacco. In 2003, the amount of cannabis eradicated on the Boone amounted to an estimated 29 percent of the national total (Cline 2000; National Drug Intelligence Center, 2005).

Eradicating a larger percentage has proved difficult. For one thing, and in sharp contrast to cartel-operated trespass grows on other national forests across the country, the bulk of illegal cultivation on the Daniel Boone is conducted by local residents; by those "who run family-based, vertical operations (controlling cultivation through distribution) or who deal with a broker as part of a loose confederation of marijuana producers." According to the Forest Service and the DEA, "these groups and individuals typically maintain smaller plots of cannabis than do Mexican DTOs [drug trafficking organizations] and usually travel long distances from their homes to sites scattered throughout remote areas of federal lands in order to tend their plots" (National Drug Intelligence Center 2005).

Keeping tabs on those mobile farmers and their disparate acres has been further complicated as a direct result of the complex patchwork of land ownership inside the Boone and other southern forests. Unlike their western counterparts, which were designated as national forests from preexisting federal lands, national forests east of the Mississippi were almost entirely purchased from willing sellers, a process that was launched in 1911 with the passage of the Weeks Act. Congress and the executive branch then used this legislation in 1937 to establish the Boone's proclamation boundary so that it encompassed roughly 2.1 million acres. Yet when the forest was established, the Forest Service actually owned less than 340,000 acres. It has taken more than sixty years to double that number to its present-day total of 706,000 acres; the rest is privately owned. Similarly, the George Washington National Forest's proclamation boundary is more expansive than the acres it stewards, a pattern consistent across Region 8 of the Forest Service. This entangling of private and public ownership has made it easier for those who want to plant marijuana on public lands—whether these sites are abutting their home ground or are at some remove—to escape detection; this thorny reality has complicated the efforts of law enforcement to locate and break up proliferating trespass grows (Miller 2012a; 2012b).

Drug trafficking organizations like the Mexican cartels have found this situation as irresistible as those who have lived in these hills and hollers for generations. To feed the escalating demand for marijuana in the urban northeastern corridor, they began to set down roots on national forests in the 1980s and flourished despite a series of intensified crackdowns. Shrewd growers like the cartels plant three patches, Knott County (KY) sheriff Wheeler Jacobs told the *New York Times*: "One for us to find, one for his livelihood and the third for his competitors to steal." They also learned to shift their operations in response to enforcement pressures, seeking new terrain that might be safer and that could offer a competitive advantage (Cline 2000). Just as they did in Highland County, Virginia. "They know a good thing when they see it," the county sheriff, Timothy Duff, recounted in 2015. "A good thing being a remote county, a heavily forested county, owned by the feds or the state. Minimal exposure to the public. It's in the South, so you've got enough sunlight, water—it's perfect" (Spencer 2015).

Perfect, that is, until July 2013, when a hunter, making a pre-season terrain check along a south-facing slope that rose up to 3,000 feet in elevation, spotted an illegal grow. He quickly notified authorities, and the Alleghany Highlands Drug Task Force swung into action. Its ranks include officers from Highland and two adjacent counties, as well as from the Virginia State Police, and their first move was to set up an array of cameras. "They knew about the grow, and they were trying to capture more of what was going on," said Duff, who was part of the investigative team. What the search team found was a complex of four gardens connected by a network of well-trodden paths. Before they built up the gardens, the farmers had logged thirty to fifty trees per plot. "This is very open for the National Forest," Duff said, speculating that the workers may have deliberately left some of the larger trees to shield the crop from helicopter patrols. "Just enough trees were left to obscure it from the air, but the sun still penetrates here, here, and here" (Spencer 2015c). Duff's observation squares with what the US Justice Department found in its 2011 Drug Market Analysis of the Appalachia High Intensity Drug Marketing Area. It reported that "some growers are sacrificing crop yield to avoid law enforcement detection by establishing plots in areas with less than favorable growing conditions, such as areas with significant canopy coverage from trees that reduce light necessary for plant growth." This tactic may explain the decline in the number of plants eradicated between 2009 and 2011: the Kentucky State Police advised the US Department of Justice "that this decrease is most likely related to the difficulty in detecting grow operations, particularly largescale Mexican DTO grow operations, and not to a decrease in cannabis cultivation in the region" (Appalachia High Intensity Drug Marketing Area 2011).

This strategy did not help in the Highland County incident, given that it was a random hunter who found the site. Moreover, as the Alleghany Highlands task force approached the well-tended grow, it spotted evidence that also would have been hard to detect from the air: the cultivators indiscriminately used fertilizer, and spread and sprayed insecticides, pesticides, and rat poison, around the area to protect the more than 4,500 marijuana plants they had planted. This highly toxic approach is routinely employed on trespass grows around the country, and in the West to devastating effect on endangered species like the Pacific fisher (discussed in Chapter 3 of this volume), as well as on coyotes, bobcats, and foxes. Although there has been no investigation whether similar devastation is occurring on the southern national forests, Lonnie Murray, a publicly elected director of the Thomas Jefferson Soil and Water Conservation District, would not be surprised if similar depredations were occurring. The Appalachian Mountains are home to many endangered species, such as rare orchids that can take more than fifteen years to get established. These and other endemic plants, and even some animals, exist nowhere else on earth—indeed, the Southeast generally and the Appalachians in particular contain the highest concentration of endemic mammals, birds, and amphibians in the country—so, the prospect of poison-saturated land-clears in Highland and elsewhere makes Murray shudder: "pH changes and nutrient changes can kill something," he argues. "You douse a big area with fertilizer, and you can wipe things out. It wouldn't take much. All it takes is one irresponsible operation and you've lost a species" (Spencer 2016b; Palmer 2015).

As crucial as these ecological concerns are, they were not uppermost in the minds of the well-armed task force stalking the Highland site; their collective safety understandably took precedence. As they converged on the center, they discovered a tent. "One of the officers looked inside the tent and startled two individuals," Duff recalled. Joaquin Gonzalez Vicencio, age thirty, and Joaquin Berumen Cortes, age twenty-four, were promptly arrested. Duff indicated that he had reason to believe that at least one of them may have been a kidnap victim, possibly a slave. His reasoning was based on something he noticed when he checked on the man's handcuffs. "He tried to hide his left hand a little bit with his right hand, and I separated the hands, thinking he may have had something in his hands, and I noticed his ring finger, second digit left hand was cut off." The last time Duff had seen this kind of disfigurement was in the 1990s when he was with the US Coast Guard working drug interdiction in the South American nation of Colombia. He says the finger would be sent home to the family as proof the man was still alive—and a reminder to stay quiet and keep him alive. "When I looked at this individual and mentioned his family, he broke down crying" (Spencer 2015).

Additional evidence of the imprisoned men's low-level role was that they spoke no English, possessed no firearms and no vehicle, and had no American money. Duff observed that in addition to tending the marijuana fields, the two had planted a sizable vegetable garden and had received other necessities from a van making supply runs to a nearby poultry farm—the so-called lunchmen who serve as the workers' only contact with the outside world. These workers' plight bothered Duff: "They're a commodity: just bought, sold, traded. They have no means of getting out of here; they're here until their job is done. And then when the job is done, there's no telling that they're going to make it back to Mexico because they've been here and they've seen what goes on. They could quite easily be eliminated" (Spencer 2015).

Their vulnerability also concerns Sylvia Longmire, the author of *Cartel: The Coming Invasion of Mexico's Drug Wars*. "The cartels either voluntarily recruit or forcibly recruit people from Mexico and bring them into the United States to work on these grows, and they live on these grows for four to five months," she asserts. "They're there living in a tent that entire time. They can get severely punished if they allow the grow to get detected. They pretty much have to follow orders. They're stuck there" (Spencer 2016d, Longmire 2013).

Such insights into these men's plight did not sway the jury empaneled at the US District Court for the Western District of Virginia in Charlottesville. Although Vicencio's and Cortes's lawyer argued that his clients were mere field hands laboring for a shadowy figure known only as Jesus, in December 2013 jurors concurred with the prosecution, convicting each man of conspiracy. The following September the pair were sentenced: Vicencio to 134 months of federal incarceration to be followed by five years of supervised release, and Cortes to 120 months of federal incarceration with five years of supervised release. "The misuse of federal land to cultivate marijuana remains an enforcement priority of the Department of Justice," US Attorney Timothy J. Heaphy declared in a release. "These defendants operated one of the largest outdoor marijuana growing sites we have encountered in this or many other districts, conduct for which they have now been held accountable" (US Department of Justice 2014).

Imprisoning such lower-echelon laborers does nothing to hold the cartels accountable, of course. Cortes, for example, is an undocumented immigrant, and as Amos Irwin notes in Chapter 7 of this volume, his immigrant status would "make it easier to obtain a conviction" and also makes it "harder for law enforcement to squeeze the industry. Investigators cannot rely on tips and would find it difficult to use undercover agents or informants. Prosecutors struggle to charge anyone other than the lowest-level workers apprehended at the grow site." This situation, moreover, does next to nothing to undercut the ability of traffickers to plant, harvest, and distribute marijuana grown on federal lands (or on any other property). Observes Irwin: "No supervisor in the Justice Department even considers whether those prosecutions will have any impact on the appearance of new grow sites the next year."

Locking Vicencio and Cortes away for a decade or more will not shrink the demand-side of the equation, either. Curiously enough, demand for marijuana might be accelerating in the mid-Atlantic region as a result of its legalization in the District of Columbia in November 2014. Although its use has been decriminalized, as of February 2016 selling marijuana within the district remained against the law. To finesse this legal conundrum, those consumers eager to smoke legal weed will have to resort to illegal means to secure cannabis (see Chapter 11). Producers are also feeling the heat from a shifting marketplace. Sylvia Longmire is among those pointing to the increase in decriminalization and support for medical marijuana as two reasons why the drug's street price has fallen. In response, the cartels and other growers may well be putting more acreage into production to compensate for the lower prices, a time-honored practice in agriculture generally. If these factors hold true, then high-volume producers will continue to seek the most hidden, well-watered, and fertile sites close enough to the nation's capital for ready access, but far enough away to avoid easy detection. Fitting that bill perfectly are the George Washington and Jefferson National Forests located deep in the mountains of western Virginia.

WORKS CITED

Anderson, Jack. 1988. "Forest Service Is Fighting Drug War." *Lakeland (FL) Ledger*, June 1, 11A. https://ncws.googlc.com/newspapers?nid=1346&dat=19880601&id=n7wwAA AAIBAJ&sjid=CPwDAAAAIBAJ&pg=4151,54154&hl=en.

Appalachia High Intensity Drug Marketing Area. 2011. Drug Market Analysis. Washington, DC: Department of Justice, 8.

Cline, Francis X. 2000. "Reaping Marijuana in the Hills Emptied of Stills." *New York Times*, June 4. http://www.nytimes.com/2000/06/04/us/reaping-marijuana-in-hills-emptied -of-stills.html.

George Washington and Jefferson National Forests. 2011. Marijuana Awareness on National Forest Lands. May 20. http://www.fs.usda.gov/detail/gwj/news-events/?cid=STEL PRDB5302169.

Longmire, Sylvia. 2013. *Cartel: The Coming Invasion of Mexico's Drug Wars*. New York: St. Martin's.

Loy, Wesley. 1987. "Can't See the Pot for the Trees." *Orlando Sentinel*, June 27. http://ar ticles.orlandosentinel.com/1987-06-27/news/0180060107_1_ocala-forest-florida-for ests-national-forest.

Miller, Char. 2012a. *Public Lands, Public Debates: A Century of Controversy*. Corvallis: Oregon State University Press.

———. 2012b. "Neither Crooked nor Shady: The Weeks Act, Theodore Roosevelt, and the Virtue of Eastern National Forests, 1899–1911." *Theodore Roosevelt Association Journal* 33, 4: 15–24.

National Drug Intelligence Center. 2005. Marijuana. http://www.justice.gov/archive/ndic /pubs10/10402/marijuan.htm.

Palmer, Brian. 2015. "America's Best Idea, Executed Poorly." NRDC: *Onearth*, April. https://www.nrdc.org/onearth/americas-best-idea-executed-poorly.

Spencer, Hawes. 2015. Interview with Timothy Duff. April 23.

———. 2016a. Interview with Fred Heblich. January 6.

———. 2016b. Interview with Lonnie Murray. January 7.

———. 2016c. "Highland County Grow Bears Cartel Hallmarks." WCVE, February 1. http://ideastations.org/radio/news/highland-county marijuana grow bears cartel -hallmarks.

———. 2016d. Interview with Sylvia Longmire. February 3.

US Department of Justice. 2014. "Two Men Sentenced for Growing Marijuana on Federal Land in Highland County." US Attorney's Office, Western District of Virginia, September 11. http://www.justice.gov/usao-wdva/pr/two-area-men-sentenced-growing -marijuana-federal-land-highland-county.

Weiss, Kenneth R. 1987. "South's Latest Fame Claim: Marijuana." *Wilmington Morning Star*, March 16, 1A, 9A. https://news.google.com/newspapers?nid=1454&dat=19870316 &id=gOEyAAAAIBAJ&sjid=DBQEAAAAIBAJ&pg=5643,38391&hl=en.

PART THREE

Regional Varieties

CHAPTER 9

Low, Slow, and in Control

Colorado's Experiment with Legalized Recreational Marijuana

Courtenay W. Daum

On January 1, 2014, Colorado became the first state to allow legal recreational marijuana sales via government licensed dispensaries.* Adults age twenty-one and older are able to purchase and possess one ounce or less of marijuana and may legally consume marijuana and marijuana-infused products in private spaces (Colorado Constitution, Article 18, Section 16). The legalization of recreational marijuana in the state of Colorado resulted from the state's use of the initiative process to place policy and revenue issues on the ballot as an exercise in direct democracy. In November 2012, a majority of Colorado voters approved Amendment 64 on "Use and Regulation of Marijuana" and legalized the sale and consumption of recreational marijuana as well as industrial hemp within the state; local governments retain discretion on allowing retail establishments within their borders as well as the authority to implement time, place, and manner restrictions resulting in variation across the state. In preparation for legal recreational marijuana sales and use, the state passed numerous regulations and revenue laws in advance of the 2014 launch. Even so, new issues and regulatory challenges have arisen on a regular basis, and government regulations continue to be adapted and devised in response to unforeseen developments. Colorado's experience with legalized recreational marijuana and the ensuing developments provide a useful case study given efforts to move forward with legalization in other states—including, most recently, approval by popular referendums in California, Massachusetts, Maine, and Nevada in November 2016.

This chapter begins with a review of the political battle over Colorado's Amendment 64 and its subsequent passage. Next, the discussion proceeds to an assessment of the implementation of Amendment 64, including the initial rules and regulations governing growth/production, sales/distribution, and possession/consumption. Then, attention shifts to an analysis of the political environment and legal developments that have resulted from the legalization of recreational marijuana in Colorado, the economic challenges facing the industry given the complexity of federal banking laws, and ongoing regulatory concerns including health and safety issues. The chapter concludes by looking ahead to the future of legalized recreational marijuana in Colorado as well as the likelihood of federal government intervention moving forward.

THE POLITICS OF AMENDMENT 64

Colorado is one of many states that utilize the initiative process as a form of direct democracy (National Conference of State Legislatures 2012). In Colorado, residents can petition to place constitutional amendments or statutes before the voters of the state (ibid.). For a proposed initiative to qualify for the ballot, individuals and organizations must collect signatures from registered voters within the state. A successful petition requires signatures equal to 5 percent of the number of votes cast for the office of Colorado's secretary of state in the preceding election (Ballotpedia 2015c). Proposed petitions are then subject to a series of reviews to ensure that they comply with a variety of state regulations governing the initiative process, and if all requirements are met, the item will be included on the ballot. In this way, the direct initiative process enables the people of Colorado to introduce and consider policies and laws that elected officials would not consider politically palatable legislation. Colorado's foray into legalized marijuana is the result of this process of direct democracy and likely would have been unthinkable in a state that did not utilize citizen initiatives.

Colorado voters first indicated support for legalized marijuana in 2000 when they approved Amendment 20 to the Colorado Constitution legalizing the growth and sale of medicinal marijuana in the state; it passed by a vote of 53.5 to 46.5 percent (Ballotpedia 2015b). The legalization of medical marijuana in Colorado quickly led to the establishment of the infrastructure and industry necessary to grow, cultivate, and distribute medicinal marijuana, and it was not long before support began to mobilize behind initiatives for legal recreational marijuana in the state. In November 2006 a ballot measure went before the voters that if passed would have legalized recreational marijuana via state statute, but Initiative 44 was defeated 59 to 41 percent (Ballotpedia 2015a). In the aftermath of this defeat, local organizations such as Sensible Colorado joined forces with national interests such as the Marijuana Policy Project to mobilize support for a second attempt at legalizing recreational marijuana. According to Greg Stinson, president of the Front Range chapter of the National Organization for the Reform of Marijuana Laws, supporters were optimistic in 2012: "We've got considerably more manpower this time around, and the climate is a lot more favorable," he said, citing the successful implementation of medical marijuana and the increased institutionalization of medical marijuana grow houses and distribution outlets in the state (Meltzer 2010).

After extensive efforts to secure the necessary signatures to place a recreational marijuana initiative before the voters, in May 2011 supporters of legalized marijuana presented the secretary of state with eight separate initiatives proposing legalized recreational marijuana use in Colorado (Hoover 2011). In June 2011 the state's Ballot Title Setting Board approved the following ballot initiative, now widely known as Amendment 64, on the "Use and Regulation of Marijuana":

> Shall there be an amendment to the Colorado constitution concerning
> marijuana, and, in connection therewith, providing for the regulation of
> marijuana; permitting a person twenty-one years of age or older to consume
> or possess limited amounts of marijuana; providing for the licensing of
> cultivation facilities, product manufacturing facilities, testing facilities, and
> retail stores; permitting local governments to regulate or prohibit such
> facilities; requiring the general assembly to enact an excise tax to be levied
> upon wholesale sales of marijuana; requiring that the first $40 million in
> revenue raised annually by such tax be credited to the public school capital
> construction assistance fund; and requiring the general assembly to enact
> legislation governing the cultivation, processing, and sale of industrial hemp?
> (Ballot Title Setting Board 2011–2012)

Once it was on the ballot, extensive political mobilization occurred among proponents and opponents of Amendment 64. Notably, the overwhelming majority of the money utilized to fund support for and opposition to Amendment 64 came from sources outside of the state, demonstrating the political and financial stakes associated with the legalization of marijuana (Ingold 2012).

The arguments against Amendment 64 were fairly straightforward. Organizations such as Smart Colorado, a group that aggressively opposed the initiative, argued that marijuana is a dangerous and addictive drug (Ingold 2012) and that legalization would increase drug use among Colorado's youth and teens (Moreno 2012). Furthermore, many elected leaders in the state from both political parties opposed legalization, citing federal prohibitions on marijuana (Ferner 2012b). Democratic governor John Hickenlooper stated: "Colorado is known for many great things—marijuana should not be one of them" (Ferner 2012a). He proceeded to cite the risks to children and the conflict with federal law as reasons for opposing Amendment 64 (ibid.). Interestingly, some of the opposition to Amendment 64 came from proponents of legalized marijuana who argued that if Amendment 64 passed, individuals could still be criminally liable for failure to abide by the strict state rules governing recreational marijuana (Cannabis Policy Project 2012). They argued that Amendment 64 did not legalize marijuana but rather regulated marijuana growth, distribution, and consumption via extensive rules that would work in effect to strengthen government oversight of the industry and consumers (ibid.).

The arguments in favor of Amendment 64 were quite diverse, and proponents included individuals from across the political spectrum. One argument in favor of legalizing marijuana for recreational use was that marijuana is similar to and should be regulated like alcohol. As one organization explained: "Regulating marijuana like alcohol will take marijuana sales out of the hands of cartels and criminals, and redirect that money toward legitimate, taxpaying Colorado businesses. It will also reduce youth access to marijuana by requiring that consumers are asked for proof of age prior to purchasing the product" (Campaign to Regulate Marijuana Like Alcohol 2012). As indicated by this comment, another argument in favor of legalization was that it would decrease criminal activity in the state by legalizing the marijuana economy and decreasing the influence of criminal enterprises. Similarly, it was suggested that legalizing marijuana and legitimating the marijuana economy would generate significant revenue for the state via excise and sales taxes. According to a report by the Colorado Center on Law and Policy, Amendment 64 would lead to $60 million in new revenue and savings for the state between implementation and the year 2017 (Stiffler 2012). Amendment 64 also specified that the first $40 million raised via excise taxes would be earmarked for the Public School Capital Construction Assistance Fund—a promise that was attractive to many voters (Amendment 64, Section 5, (d)). Finally, a diverse group of supporters ranging from the NAACP to prominent Republicans within the state, including former US representative Tom Tancredo, favored Amendment 64 because it was a vote against the failed policies of the War on Drugs (Bartels 2012; Ferner 2012a). For example, Republican state senator Shawn Mitchell stated: "It's clear the War on Drugs isn't working, and we need to try different approaches to this in society" (Hoover 2012). On November 6, 2012, the ballot initiative passed. Among voters casting a vote on the amendment, 55.32 percent supported it and 44.68 percent were opposed (Colorado Secretary of State 2012). On December 10, 2012, it was added to the Colorado Constitution.

IMPLEMENTATION OF AMENDMENT 64

The text of Amendment 64 is lengthy and offers numerous specifics, including details on growth/production, sales/distribution, and possession/consumption. For example, with respect to growth/production, the amendment specifically differentiates between marijuana and industrial grade hemp and subjects the two crops to different regulations (Colorado Constitution, Article 18, Section 16, 1.V.c). Amendment 64 also authorizes private individuals—in contrast to industrial grow operations—to grow up to six marijuana plants subject to various rules and regulations (Article 18, Section 16, 3.b).

The amendment's text imposes various restrictions on marijuana sales. Similar to alcohol, Amendment 64 specifies that recreational marijuana may only be purchased by those who are twenty-one years of age or older. The amendment limits purchases and possession to one ounce or less of marijuana (Article 18, Section 16, 3.a) and requires that consumption take place in private locations and not public spaces (Article 18, Section 16, 3.d). Furthermore, it authorizes the state legislature to establish an excise tax of up to 15 percent on marijuana sold from cultivators to retailers, subject to adjustment by the legislature after January 1, 2017 (Article 18, Section 16, 5.II.d). As previously mentioned, the first $40 million raised from the excise tax is designated to pay for school construction costs as specified in Amendment 64.

Despite these specifics, the amendment left it to the state to devise various rules and regulations governing the implementation of legalized recreational marijuana growth/production and sales/distribution. Amendment 64 specified that the state must "adopt regulations necessary for implementation" by July 1, 2013 (Colorado Constitution, Article 18, Section 16, 5.a). As such, immediately following the passage of Amendment 64, both houses of the state legislature began the process of crafting and passing legislation to govern the implementation of the amendment (Colorado Senate Bill 13-283, Colorado House Bill 13-1317). Under the direction of Governor Hickenlooper, the state government convened the Amendment 64 Implementation Task Force to draft regulations for the implementation and regulation of recreational marijuana sales and consumption by the July deadline. Governor Hickenlooper directed the task force "to identify the legal, policy, and procedural issues that must be resolved, and to offer suggestions and proposals for legislative, regulatory, and executive actions that need to be taken, for the effective and efficient implementation of Amendment 64" (Colorado Department of Revenue 2013a, 2).

One of the challenges associated with devising regulations for individual state recreational marijuana industries is that local, state, and federal officials and laws are all implicated in drug policy. As such, different states have crafted different regulatory regimes and licensing mechanisms. In Colorado, the state generates industry-wide rules and regulations, but the referendum reserved to locales the decision to allow retail establishments as well as impose time, place, and manner restrictions on their operations. In practice, this means that local governments decide if they will sanction recreational marijuana operations within their borders and, if so, how many establishments will be allowed. Only then will the state Marijuana Enforcement Division entertain license applications from retail businesses seeking to operate in those jurisdictions (Colorado Department of Revenue 2016). This practice stands in contrast to Washington State, where the state Liquor and Cannabis Board establishes the number of licenses to be issued and their geographic allocation within the state, and then local governments must decide whether to sanction or prohibit these establishments within their borders (MRSC 2016). That being said, Colorado, Alaska, Washington, and Oregon have all empowered local governments to impose time, place, and manner restrictions or prohibitions on retail establishments, consistent with how liquor stores are regulated (Marijuana Policy Project 2016). California's Adult Use of Marijuana Act (2016) similarly gives local governments the authority to pass ordinances banning all local commercial marijuana activity or subject local nonmedical marijuana businesses to local licensing and zoning requirements (Marijuana Policy Project 2017).

In addition to the complex allocation of licensing and regulatory authority within individual states, federal regulations are implicated as well. Notably, Colorado's Amendment 64 directly contradicts the federal Controlled Substances Act, which criminalizes marijuana across all fifty states and US territories. As such, the rulemaking process that followed the passage of Amendment 64 was incredibly complex and involved input from a variety of players, including the public, law enforcement, local and state elected leaders and officials, representatives of the marijuana industry, public health and environment experts, substance abuse experts, child protection advocates, and representatives of the pharmaceutical industry (Colorado Department of Revenue 2013a, 3). In addition, the state solicited input from the Office of the US Attorney General under the Obama administration to evaluate the likelihood of federal government intervention in the state.

Shortly after Colorado voters passed Amendment 64, President Barack Obama was asked how the federal government would respond to this state preemption of the federal Controlled Substances Act. He responded, "We've got bigger fish to fry. . . . It would not make sense for us to see a top priority as going after recreational users in states that have determined that it's legal" (Dwyer 2012). The following year, on August 29, 2013, US Deputy Attorney General James Cole issued a memo (known as the Cole Memo) to all US attorneys "Providing Guidance Regarding Marijuana Enforcement" in response to the legalization of recreational marijuana in Colorado and Washington (Cole 2013). The Cole Memo specified that state laws legalizing marijuana do not negate the federal Controlled Substances Act in those jurisdictions. At the same time, it recognized that the traditional relationships among state and federal actors in the enforcement of drug laws are altered when states such as Colorado begin to devise regulatory schemes governing the production, distribution, and consumption of marijuana within their borders (Cole 2013). That being said, Cole advised federal prosecutors to continue their long practice of deferring to state and local authorities in the investigation and prosecution of marijuana activities within a state as long as those states have enacted "strong and effective regulatory and enforcement systems that will address the threat those state laws could pose to public safety, public health, and other law enforcement interests" (ibid., 2). The memo specified that there are eight areas of paramount concern to federal law enforcement that may justify federal intervention, such as preventing the distribution of marijuana to minors, intervening when marijuana is being grown on public lands, and prohibiting marijuana use on federal property (ibid., 1–2). In a press release issued the same day, the US Justice Department stated that it would defer any legal action against the state of Colorado with the understanding that the state would devise strict regulatory schemes governing marijuana (Office of Public Affairs 2013). The US attorney for the District of Colorado indicated that he intended to comply with the requirements of the Cole Memo, and the proliferation of commercial marijuana dispensaries is evidence that the US Attorney's Office has allowed Amendment 64 to take effect (US Attorney's Office 2013).

That being said, given President Donald Trump's election and his decision to appoint Senator Jeff Sessions (R-AL) as US attorney general, there is uncertainty surrounding the new administration's approach to the growing recreational marijuana industry. As a candidate and as president-elect, Trump sent mixed messages about his support for legalized recreational marijuana in the states (Berke 2016). Senator Sessions was vocal in his opposition to legalized marijuana and criticized the Obama administration for not enforcing the federal prohibition in states such as Colorado; it is not clear what his position will be now that he is serving as US attorney general (Higdon 2016). In his written responses to the Senate Judiciary Committee during his confirmation hearing, Sessions indicated that he would "review and evaluate" the Cole Memo (Berke 2017).

The minimal federal government interference to date likely reflects the fact that the state of Colorado developed an extensive regulatory scheme governing the implementation of Amendment 64 consistent with both the text of the initiative and the recommendations of the Cole Memo. After gathering abundant information, the Colorado task force on implementation provided policy recommendations to the State Licensing Authority within the Colorado Department of Revenue. On September 9, 2013, the Marijuana Enforcement Division of the Colorado

Department of Revenue released a 144-page document titled "Permanent Rules Related to the Colorado Retail Marijuana Code" (Colorado Department of Revenue 2013b). The rules addressed issues ranging from licensing, cultivation, manufacturing, testing, transportation and storage, to record keeping, labeling and packaging, product safety, advertising and marketing, enforcement, and discipline (ibid.). Despite these extensive regulations, numerous unforeseen developments presented shortly after the first recreational stores opened on January 1, 2014, and additional regulations have been forthcoming as a result. The sections that follow examine the political, legal, economic, and ongoing regulatory developments associated with the legalization of recreational marijuana in the state of Colorado.

POLITICAL AND LEGAL DEVELOPMENTS IN COLORADO POST-AMENDMENT 64

At this time, there appears to be little political momentum within the state to overturn Amendment 64. Outspoken opponents such as Governor Hickenlooper have gone from calling Amendment 64 "reckless" (Nelson 2014) to stating:

> If you look back it's turned out to not be as vexing as some of the people like myself [thought]—I opposed the original vote, didn't think it was a good idea. Now the voters spoke so we're trying to make it work, and I think we are . . . I think we are slowly, through hard work, building a regulatory system, making sure we keep it out of the hands of kids, making sure we keep our streets and roads safe, making sure we kill that illegal black market—drug dealers don't care who they sell to. And we're getting there. (Baca 2015a)

Instead, internal political activity continues to focus on refining the rules and regulations governing the recreational marijuana industry.

There is also evidence to suggest that the marijuana industry may be making positive contributions to the Colorado economy that have the potential to undermine political opposition. For example, according to the Marijuana Policy Project, the marijuana industry has created over 20,000 jobs and generated new work for a variety of related industries, ranging from legal professionals to accountants to security (Marijuana Policy Project 2015a). Given the taxing scheme devised by the state—"When purchasing retail marijuana, the purchase is subject to the 10% state marijuana, 2.9% state sales tax and a 15% excise plus any local sales taxes" (Colorado Department of Revenue Tax Division 2015)—marijuana taxes have translated into a significant revenue stream for the state. In the twelve-month period ending in May 2015, the state collected approximately $88 million in marijuana tax transfers and distributions and approximately $102 million in all marijuana taxes, licenses, and fees (Colorado Department of Revenue 2015a). A large portion of this money is then allocated to the Marijuana Tax Cash Fund to cover the costs of implementing and enforcing marijuana regulations in the state (Colorado Office and State Planning and Budgeting 2015, 32). In November 2015, Colorado voters authorized the state to retain approximately $66 million in collected marijuana revenue to be used for a variety of public projects including $40 million for school construction; $12 million for various state programs including marijuana education, bullying prevention, dropout prevention, youth mentoring services, and poison control; with the remaining $14 million to be allocated at a future date (*Denver Post* Editorial Board 2015). Revenue reports for 2016 indicate that the state brought in $199 million in taxes and fees on $1.3 billion in combined recreational and medical marijuana sales (Wallace 2017a). In a state like Colorado, where legislative complexities have limited the state's ability to collect revenue and appropriate funds (Straayer 2011), the influx of revenue from marijuana sales provides a cushion that may be difficult for the state to abandon in the future.

Despite majority support for legalizing recreational marijuana, according to an April 2015 poll, "Only 18 percent of Colorado voters say they've tried marijuana since it became legal January 1, 2014. That includes 39 percent of voters 18 to 34 years old, 16 percent of voters 35 to 54 years old and 10 percent of voters over 55 years old" (Quinnipiac University 2015). As such, many individuals who support the legalization of recreational marijuana in Colorado are not interested in purchasing or consuming marijuana products. The passage of Amendment 64 has not caused Colorado to go "up in smoke," and residents have not turned into a bunch of potheads.

Likewise, the fear that Colorado would become a draw for "stoners" across the United States does not appear to be true, as there is little evidence at this time to suggest that the state is experiencing an influx of new residents as a result of Amendment 64. Yet, one of the more interesting developments in Colorado is the relocation to the state of some families calling themselves "marijuana refugees" (Healy 2013). These families are seeking easy and legal access to cannabidiol oils that are used to treat children suffering from seizures (ibid.). This limited number of families seeking access to health care for their children does not conform to stereotypes about "stoners" and "pot culture."

While industrious companies—see, for example, My 420 Tours, Travel THC, and 420 Layover Solutions (Weed 2015)—are venturing into "pot tourism" to lure tourists interested in visiting and sampling Colorado's marijuana market, it does not appear that droves of people are opting to vacation in Colorado to gain access to legal marijuana. In fact, the Colorado Tourism Office reported that 2016 "represented a return to the more usual Colorado traveler," indicating that the nascent pot tourism industry may already be waning in the state (Wallace 2017a).

Concerted efforts to educate individuals visiting Colorado about the ins and outs of purchasing and consuming marijuana are prevalent in ski resort towns, a reflection that these tourist destinations receive an influx of out-of-state visitors during the winter ski season and, increasingly, during the summer season (Wyatt 2013). These education efforts focus on the fact that many ski resorts are located on federal lands where marijuana use is still prohibited by federal law.

While Coloradans may be taking a wait-and-see approach to legalized marijuana, neighboring states have taken legal action in the federal courts. Although the Obama administration declined to initiate legal action against Colorado for preempting the Controlled Substances Act, in December 2014 the states of Nebraska and Oklahoma sued Colorado and filed a complaint at the US Supreme Court arguing that Amendment 64 creates a dangerous gap in US drug policy resulting in the trafficking of marijuana out of Colorado into neighboring states thereby placing immense and costly burdens on the criminal justice systems and law enforcement agencies in those jurisdictions where marijuana is illegal (Bruning and Pruitt et al. 2014, 3–4). The two states argue that Amendment 64 undermines the solvency of the federal Controlled Substances Act as well as several of the US government's treaty obligations—the Single Convention, the 1971 Convention, and the 1988 Convention (ibid., 22–23)—and in doing so violates the US Constitution's supremacy clause (ibid., 23). As such, Nebraska and Oklahoma believe that the rules and regulations promulgated to govern the production and distribution of recreational marijuana in Colorado should be preempted. Colorado responded in May 2015 with a brief in opposition, arguing that preempting the state's regulatory scheme would create numerous problems and shift the burden of enforcement to the federal government (Coffman 2015). That month, the US Supreme Court asked the solicitor general to submit a brief articulating the US government's position on the issues raised by Nebraska and Oklahoma (US Supreme Court 2015). In December 2015, Solicitor General Donald B. Verrilli Jr. filed an amicus curiae brief at the US Supreme Court that urged the justices to deny the states' motion "because this is not an appropriate case for the exercise of this Court's original jurisdiction. Entertaining the type of dispute at issue here— essentially that one State's laws make it more likely that third parties will violate federal and state law in another State—would represent a substantial and unwarranted expansion of this Court's original jurisdiction" (Office of the US Solicitor General 2015, 8).

Essentially, the solicitor general's argument is that the dispute at hand does not directly implicate the state of Colorado, but rather involves the actions of third-party actors who are allegedly bringing marijuana into Nebraska and Oklahoma in violation of state and federal laws. As such, Colorado has not inflicted a direct injury on either state, which is a necessary requirement for a case involving a dispute among states to go directly to the US Supreme Court as an exercise of its original jurisdiction (Office of the US Solicitor General 2015, 14). In March 2016 the US Supreme Court declined to intervene in the case, suggesting that the judicial branch is inclined to defer to the executive branch for the time being (Liptak 2016).

The solicitor general's brief in this case is consistent with the executive branch's tacit acceptance of Colorado's marijuana laws and markets under the Obama administration. To date, the US attorney for the state of Colorado has followed the guidelines of the 2013 Cole Memo and allowed Amendment 64 to take effect with limited interference. In fact, the federal government's greatest legal intervention in the state appears to be focused on the illegal growth of marijuana on federal lands, which seems to be increasing post–Amendment 64 (Gurman 2015). On October 8, 2015, the US Attorney's Office for the District of Colorado announced that it had arrested thirty-two individuals, nearly all of whom are foreign nationals or residents of other states, who will be charged with drug trafficking in violation of federal law (US Attorney's Office 2015). According to the press release, federal, state, and local officials worked together to identify and dismantle illegal marijuana grow operations throughout the state including multiple grow sites on federal lands such as the Pike, Routt, and San Isabel National Forests and Bureau of Land Management lands (ibid.). These operations netted nearly 20,000 marijuana plants, the majority of which were intended for out-of-state markets and over 300 kilograms of dried marijuana (ibid.). In addition to being in violation of federal law, these operations were not licensed by the state of Colorado and are illegal under state law as well. Consistent with the Cole Memo, US Attorney John Walsh explained that his office is focused on investigating and prosecuting drug traffickers operating outside of the bounds of Colorado's regulatory system; those charged "were making no effort to comply with the regulatory system. . . . This is good-old, traditional marijuana growing, the illegal way" (Gurman 2015).

ECONOMIC CHALLENGES: FEDERAL BANKING LAWS

Marijuana is big business. In 2014 marijuana sales in Colorado totaled $699,198,805, of which the 2014 recreational total was $313,226,353 (Baca 2015b), and by 2016 annual marijuana sales totaled $1.3 billion in the state, $875 million of which came from recreational sales (Wallace 2017a). Yet, due to a variety of federal statutes including prohibitions on money laundering (18 USC §§ 1956 and 1957), the unlicensed money transmitter statute (18 USC § 1960), and the Banking Secrecy Act, businesses profiting from marijuana sales in the state have been denied access to banking services because federally licensed banks fear running afoul of these laws (Cole 2014). Notably, banks worry that accepting and recirculating marijuana proceeds may lead federal prosecutors to charge them with violating federal banking laws, thereby exposing banks to severe criminal and civil penalties (Richtel 2015, B4).

It is estimated that approximately 5 percent of Colorado's marijuana businesses utilize banks, which means that the bulk of marijuana proceeds are being held and circulated throughout Colorado in cash (Richtel 2015, B4). Desperate to gain access to banks, some marijuana businesses have taken to laundering their cash in air freshener to remove the strong smell of marijuana that accrues to dollar bills and obfuscate the actual nature of their enterprises (Daum 2014). Many business owners report that they opened accounts only to have them shut down once a bank deduced that their transactions involve marijuana proceeds. Kristi Kelly, the owner of a medicinal marijuana dispensary in Colorado, reported to the *New York Times* that she opened and then had canceled a total of twenty-three bank accounts since 2009 (Richtel 2015, B4). As such, she has resorted to operating as her own bank and stores cash proceeds in a safe, which are then hand delivered to employees, state revenue officials, utility operators, trade associations, and so on (ibid.). In some instances, marijuana businesses and banks enter into covert relationships, as exemplified by the following comment from a retailer in Colorado: "We actually have strong banking relationships . . . [but w]e don't talk about them. Asking someone about their banking is like asking them what they wear to bed at night. It's an intensely personal question, even within the industry" (Sullum 2014). Clearly, however, this model is not sustainable for the long term because it exposes individuals and businesses to extreme safety and financial risks and increases opportunities for criminal activity.

Recognizing that the lack of access to FDIC-insured banks is creating havoc in the state's economy, in February 2014 the US Department of Justice issued additional guidance to prosecutors regarding the treatment of banks for alleged violations of the Banking Secrecy Act (BSA) and money laundering statutes (Cole 2014). Simultaneously, the US Department of the Treasury's Financial Crimes Enforcement Network (FinCEN) issued guidance to the banking industry that was intended to clarify "how financial institutions can provide services to marijuana-related businesses consistent with their BSA obligations, and aligns the information provided by financial institutions in BSA reports with federal and state law enforcement priorities. This FinCEN guidance should enhance the availability of financial services for, and the financial transparency of, marijuana-related businesses" (Financial Crimes Enforcement Network 2014, 1).

While the intent of these memos was to alleviate the banking industry's concerns, the FinCEN guidelines reiterated that banks are required under the BSA to file a Suspicious Activity Report for activities involving any marijuana-related businesses including those licensed under state law because marijuana is prohibited under federal law (ibid., 3). FinCEN, however, advised banks that they could distinguish between those marijuana-related businesses that were operating in accordance with the original US Justice Department memo on "Marijuana Enforcement Policy" and those that were operating illegally or outside of the parameters of the Justice Department enforcement priorities (ibid., 3–4).

Although these two sets of guidelines were intended to ease the banking industry's concerns about doing business with licensed marijuana businesses, they did not have the intended effect. This is because banks still shoulder the burden of distinguishing between legitimate and illegitimate marijuana businesses and assume the risks associated with misidentifying a customer. As such, from the banking industry's perspective, being subject to prosecution outweighs the benefits of this new business. As Don Childears, president of the Colorado Bankers Association, explained, "After a series of red lights, we expected this guidance to be a yellow one. This isn't close to that. At best, this amounts to 'serve these customers at your own risk' and it emphasizes all of the risks. This light is red" (Colorado Bankers Association 2014). As such, marijuana businesses continue to struggle to gain access to financial institutions.

In response to this void, a group of entrepreneurs has been working to establish a credit union for the industry. The Fourth Corner Credit Union was licensed by the state of Colorado and in November 2014 applied to the Federal Reserve Bank for a "master account" that would link the credit union to other financial institutions (Richtel 2015, B1, B4). This request had the backing of Governor Hickenlooper as well as US Senator Michael Bennet, who wrote a letter to the chair of the Federal Reserve asking her to guide the regional office to work with Fourth Corner to satisfy all requirements necessary in order to gain a "master account" (Mason 2015a, 32). In his letter, Senator Bennet explained that the all-cash model undermined public safety and the state's ability to exercise oversight of the industry (Mason 2015a, 32). In July 2015 the Federal Reserve rejected Fourth Corner's application, and the latter promptly filed a lawsuit in federal district court to gain "equal access" to the US financial system (Popper 2015). In January 2016 the Fourth Corner Credit Union's request for an injunction ordering the Federal Reserve Bank of Kansas to issue a "master account" was dismissed by a federal district court judge (*Fourth Corner Credit Union v. Federal Reserve Bank of Kansas City* 2016). In his opinion, Judge R. Brooke Jackson explained that a federal court cannot "issue an order that would facilitate criminal activity" (ibid., 6). Referencing the Cole Memo and FinCEN guidelines, Judge Jackson stated that these guidelines do not change the law but rather "suggest that prosecutors and bank regulators might 'look the other way' if financial institutions don't mind violating the law. A federal court cannot look the other way. I regard the situation as untenable and hope that it will soon be addressed and resolved by Congress" (ibid., 8–9). Undeterred, Fourth Corner Credit Union has appealed to the Tenth Circuit Court of Appeals. In the meantime, Judge Jackson's opinion suggests that congressional action may be necessary in order for marijuana-related businesses to gain equal access to the banking industry.

To date, congressional efforts have not gone very far. For example, Representative Ed Perlmutter (D-CO, 7th Dist.) introduced a bill in the US House of Representatives with extensive cosponsorship, including three other representatives from Colorado, called the Marijuana Businesses Access to Banking Act of 2015, which was intended to insulate banks from the threat of federal prosecution if they agree to accept deposits from marijuana businesses (HR 2076). A few months later a similar bill was introduced in the Senate, with both Colorado senators as cosponsors (S.1726). Both bills have languished in committees, with no sign that they will be taken up by either chamber. Until they are, lack of access to financial institutions will continue to be a major impediment for the marijuana industry in Colorado.

That said, Mark Mason, legal counsel for the Fourth Corner Credit Union, believes that while Congress is unlikely to pass so-called Safe Harbor legislation, Colorado may be able to develop regulatory policies that will enhance the likelihood of banks working with marijuana-related businesses (Mason 2015b). Pointing to Washington State as a model, Mason explains that it is possible for states to gather and report financial information and statistics on different marijuana-related businesses to the banking industry in order to substantiate that the businesses are legitimate and operating consistent with state rules and regulations (ibid.). This verification process may alleviate some of the perceived risks within the banking industry and enhance the likelihood that banks will work with the cannabis industry moving forward. Mason explains that licensed marijuana-related businesses "want to play by the rules as they evolve," and he remains optimistic that "a solution can be crafted short of changes to the Controlled Substances Act and short of a congressional statute providing 'safe harbor' to banks" (ibid.). In the meantime, marijuana-related businesses will continue to devise workaround solutions to deal with the banking situation (ibid.).

ONGOING REGULATORY ISSUES RELATED TO HEALTH AND SAFETY

Regulatory issues as they relate to health and safety matters also remain of concern. For example, one issue that is proving complicated in Colorado is how to address marijuana use and influence in a variety of venues ranging from driving under the influence to workplace protocols on drug testing. Amendment 64 addresses both of the issues and specifies that "Nothing in this section is intended to allow driving under the influence of marijuana or to supersede statutory laws related to driving under the influence of marijuana" (Colorado Constitution, Article 18, Section 16, 6.b). Furthermore, the state has made it abundantly clear that it is against the law to drive under the influence of marijuana and went so far as to launch a public service campaign—"Drive High Get a DUI"—to educate drivers (Colorado Department of Transportation 2015). Similar to alcohol, the state established a blood threshold limit for marijuana (Colorado House Bill 13-1325). Individuals found to have five or more nanograms of active tetrahydrocannabinol (THC) per millimeter of whole blood will be charged with driving under the influence (Colorado Department of Transportation 2015). Yet, some have argued that marijuana is different from alcohol because it dissipates through the blood in less predictable patterns; an individual may test over the 5 nanogram per millimeter limit but actually be fit to drive (Markus 2014). Or, an individual who is impaired and should not be driving may fail to reach the 5 nanogram limit (Elinson 2013). Recognizing that the correlation between blood concentration and impairment is more complicated in cases dealing with marijuana than in alcohol, R. Andrew Sewell, an assistant professor of psychiatry at Yale School of Medicine, told the *Wall Street Journal* that the new limit "is going to cause a lot of impaired drivers to be missed and it's going to cause a lot of innocent people to get arrested" because THC exits the blood stream fairly quickly and individuals who regularly consume marijuana are able to build up a tolerance over time which may mean that they are not impaired even if their THC levels exceed the legal limits (ibid.). In addition to blood testing, many Colorado law enforcement officers have been trained as "drug recognition experts" to recognize the signs of drug impairment during roadside assessments (ibid.).

Another issue is whether employers may terminate employees who utilize marijuana on their personal time but in doing so violate workplace prohibitions on drug use. Disagreements about whether Colorado employers can legally fire employees for marijuana use arose because Colorado has a statute that prohibits the termination of employees for engaging in lawful activities outside of work (see 24-34-402.5, CRS. [2014]). Upon passage of Amendment 64, recreational marijuana use became a lawful activity in the state, raising new questions about employer prohibitions on marijuana use. At the same time, however, the amendment clearly specified that "Nothing in this section is intended . . . to affect the ability of employers to have policies restricting the use of marijuana by employees" (Colorado Constitution, Article 18, Section 16, 6.a). Nevertheless, in June 2015 the Colorado Supreme Court was forced to address these issues in the case *Coats v. Dish Network, LLC.* The court ruled that the lawful activities statute does not extend to marijuana use because marijuana is prohibited by federal law and its use

Figure 9.1. An educational leaflet with guidelines for
safe marijuana consumption. *Courtesy of Amendment 64
Collection, Agricultural and Natural Resources Archive, Colorado
State University*

remains an unlawful activity even though state law has exempted marijuana users
from prosecution for limited marijuana possession and consumption (*Coats v. Dish
Network, LLC* 2015). As such, individuals may be terminated from their jobs for
failure to comply with workplace prohibitions on drug use.

Demanding additional attention are the regulations and standards governing
the edibles market. Edible marijuana products have proven to be very popular in
Colorado. These include candies, baked goods, and beverages that contain concentrated THC—the psychoactive chemical in marijuana—and are available for
purchase at licensed marijuana dispensaries. These products have created numerous unforeseen developments, forcing legislators to revisit regulations on edibles.

Two of the biggest issues related to edibles are individuals inadvertently consuming marijuana-infused products and individuals consuming excessive amounts of THC via edibles.

Reports of children and adults mistakenly consuming marijuana-infused edibles led Colorado to seek more explicit labeling for marijuana products to differentiate these products from traditional candies and baked goods. There was discussion of mandating labels with a red stop sign stating "THC Inside," but that has been replaced with a more modest proposal requiring a universal symbol on all edibles and cannabis products identifying them as THC products followed by the statement "Contains marijuana. Keep out of reach of children" in addition to language about health and safety risks (Colorado Department of Revenue 2015b, 114). The universal symbol and language must be included on each and every single standardized serving of edible marijuana products (Wallace 2016). Furthermore, according to the new rules, edibles may not be labeled as "candy" (Colorado Department of Revenue 2015b, 105) and must be packaged in child-resistant containers that maintain their integrity after repeated openings (ibid., 113–114).

The confusion about the appropriate dosage for edible marijuana products as well as the delayed onset of edibles as compared to the more rapid effects induced by smoking or vaping marijuana have led to some serious problems as individuals overdose by consuming excessive quantities of edible THC. "The results of edible overdoses may be catastrophic as exemplified by the death of a young man who leapt from the roof of a building in downtown Denver after consuming an entire marijuana cookie that contained approximately 6.5 servings of THC" (Daum 2014). In response, producers and distributors have taken action to educate people about appropriate dosage amounts. Edible producers began to manufacture "rookie cookies" and other products that include a single dose of THC per product so that individuals may safely consume an entire cookie or candy bar (ibid.). In addition, the industry has launched a public-service campaign to educate the public about edible consumption predicated on the mantra "Low and Slow," which encourages individuals to consume only 5 milligrams of THC at a time (a low dose) and to wait to consume another 5 milligrams until they have felt and evaluated the effects of the first dose (slow consumption) (Marijuana Policy Project 2014). These education campaigns combined with the new regulations seem to be having the intended effect, but moving forward, an ongoing regulatory concern is likely to be keeping edible marijuana products away from children and teens. The state will continue to tweak regulations and rules governing child safety until regulators are convinced that all means have been exhausted to prevent children from accessing marijuana.

Finally, a new area where Colorado is promulgating regulations is workplace safety for individuals employed within the state's marijuana industry. In January 2017 the Colorado Department of Public Health and Environment published the

"Guide to Worker Safety and Health in the Marijuana Industry." This guide addresses general workplace health and safety issues as well as areas of concern that are specific to the marijuana industry. As Alicia Wallace reported: "'Slips, trips and falls are hazards common to every industry, but the marijuana industry has special considerations,' Roberta Smith, manager of CDPHE's Occupational Health Program, said in a statement. 'For example, fires and explosions can occur during production of marijuana extracts and lead to fatal injuries'" (Wallace 2017b). The time and effort that the Colorado Marijuana Occupational Health and Safety Work Group—composed of professionals from a variety of industries across the state, including "epidemiologists, medical doctors, industrial hygienists, safety professionals, and regulatory specialists"—invested in devising these workplace standards reflects the extent to which the industry is being normalized within and by the state (Marijuana Occupational Health and Safety Work Group 2017).

LOOKING AHEAD: THE FUTURE OF LEGALIZED RECREATIONAL MARIJUANA IN COLORADO

Barring aggressive federal intervention, recreational marijuana is likely to remain legal in Colorado. While regulatory challenges exist and legal questions and challenges remain, there appears to be growing acceptance within the state that this is a viable and profitable industry. According to an April 2015 Quinnipiac University poll, Colorado voters back legalized marijuana 62 to 34 percent; these numbers suggest that support for recreational marijuana has increased post-legalization (Quinnipiac University 2015). This increased support for legalized recreational marijuana is significant because the only way to repeal a popular initiative in Colorado is to return the issue to the voters and have a majority vote in favor of repeal (Ballotpedia 2015c). In light of the growing popular support for legalized recreational marijuana, it seems unlikely that Amendment 64 will be repealed in the near future.

There are various explanations for why public support of legalized recreational marijuana is growing in the state. Most likely, the fact that the marijuana industry has been subject to strict state regulations and has demonstrated compliance while working to establish itself as a legitimate enterprise may have assuaged a lot of people's concerns about the consequences of Amendment 64. As Ron Kammerzell, deputy senior director of enforcement for the Colorado Department of Revenue, the agency charged with marijuana regulation, stated: "I would say that the rollout was extremely smooth, the sky hasn't fallen like some had predicted, and we're moving forward and trying to fine tune this regulatory model" (Marijuana Policy Project 2015a).

The fiscal benefit for a state that has limited opportunities to generate revenue may be attractive to many residents as well. As of September 2015, Colorado had collected more than $76 million in taxes and fees and the state was on its way to raising the $40 million promised for school construction during the 2012 ratification campaign (Baca 2015b), and that number only increased in 2016 (Wallace 2017a). Furthermore, in November 2015, Colorado residents voted on Proposition BB and authorized the state to retain more than $60 million in marijuana revenue to be spent on various public projects and services.

There remain two major obstacles that may derail legalized recreational marijuana in the state. First, the fact that a multimillion-dollar industry continues to operate as a de facto cash-only business is problematic. Chris Myklebust, the commissioner of Colorado's financial services division, told the *New York Times* that "Without banking, the industry is not sustainable in the long run" (Richtel 2015, 4). Second, while the Obama administration deferred legal action against the state and limited federal intervention in the Colorado marijuana industry, all of that is subject to change now that a new president has taken office. As additional states continue to legalize recreational marijuana—including the ramifications of California's decision to move forward with legalization in November 2016—there may be increased pressure on President Trump and Attorney General Sessions to reconcile the current practice of allowing states to act as laboratories of democracy with federal prohibitions on marijuana. Notably, as the number of states allowing legalized recreational marijuana increases, the solvency of the federal Controlled Substances Act is undermined. In addition, the United States is party to three international drug-control treaties that mandate prohibitions on recreational marijuana use (Bennett and Walsh 2014, 2). Absent congressional action on the Controlled Substances Act or a judicial ruling, the president and the executive branch will have to decide if state laws should be preempted to bring them in alignment with federal laws or if states should be allowed to continue with the federal marijuana experiment.

While Colorado continues to revise and issue new regulations for the recreational marijuana industry in the state, to date, the development of a well-specified regulatory system has enabled the industry to grow and prosper. Although some may argue that the industry is overregulated (Cannabis Policy Project 2012), the benefit of an exhaustive regulatory scheme is that it enables businesses and consumers to operate with certainty at the state level, and other states appear to be emulating Colorado's approach to legalizing marijuana and then continuing to draft and refine rules as part of an ongoing regulatory process (Crombie 2016, Hegg 2014).

In addition, a solid regulatory system is necessary not only to avoid potential problems within the state but also to hold off federal intervention. Because Colorado has been able to devise strict regulations, it has met the requirements of the US

Department of Justice's Cole Memo, which in turn has limited the opportunities for federal investigations and prosecutions. Given the successful implementation of legalized marijuana in Colorado, voters in other states may be more inclined to support legalization in their states, as exemplified by the fact that four of the five state recreational marijuana initiatives passed in November 2016, and legislators may be less fearful of the political consequences of voting in favor of it. The Marijuana Policy Project—a leading advocate for legalization and a major supporter of Amendment 64—not only is working to legalize marijuana in states with citizen initiatives but also is beginning to dedicate time and resources to states that do not have the initiative process. This suggests that advocates believe legislators are becoming more receptive to drafting and voting for legislation legalizing marijuana.

As more states follow Colorado's lead there will be increased pressure on the federal government to reconcile the conflicts between federal and state laws. This may take the form of amplified lobbying of Congress to modify the Controlled Substances Act to exempt marijuana from the list of prohibited drugs, enhanced pressure on the executive branch to take action and enforce federal laws in the states, or a judicial decision resulting from ongoing or future litigation challenging state preemption of federal laws and treaties. It seems likely that the recent addition of California—with its massive economy and large population—to the list of states legalizing recreational marijuana is likely to inform these calculations as well. For the time being, Colorado is likely to continue fine-tuning regulations within the state, investing in public service campaigns to raise awareness of the ins and outs of legalized recreational marijuana and the health and safety risks, and working to find a solution to the ongoing financial crisis that exists when marijuana-related businesses are unable to gain access to the banking industry. As Andrew Freedman, Colorado's first director of marijuana coordination, recently wrote in the *Harvard Law and Policy Review*, maybe the conversation has started to shift from asking "'should we legalize marijuana?' to asking 'how would we legalize marijuana?' Can we create a regulated market that more effectively keeps marijuana out of the hands of children than the status quo? Or will we create a system where commercialization and availability creates more substance abuse? What are the proper roles and responsibilities for cities, states, and the federal government? How will we define and measure success? And what will we do if things go wrong?" (Freedman 2016).

WORKS CITED

Baca, Ricardo. 2015a. "Colo. Gov.: Pot Is 'Not as Vexing as We Thought It Was Going to Be.'" *Cannabist,* April 29. http://www.thecannabist.co/2015/04/29/hickenlooper-col orado-pot-marijuana-vexing-video/34193/.

———. 2015b. "Colorado's Pot Tax for Schools Sets Record in May, Crushes 2014 Totals." *Cannabist*, July 13. http://www.thecannabist.co/2015/07/13/may-colorado-pot -school-tax-marijuana/37839/?_ga=1.198316588.2097438102.1410976611.

Ballotpedia. 2015a. Colorado Marijuana Possession, Initiative 44 (2006). http://ballotpe dia.org/Colorado_Marijuana_Possession,_Initiative_44_%282006%29.

———. 2015b. Colorado Medical Use of Marijuana Initiative 20 (2000). http://ballotpe dia.org/Colorado_Medical_Use_of_Marijuana,_Initiative_20_%282000%29.

———. 2015c. Laws Governing the Initiative Process in Colorado. http://ballotpedia .org/Laws_governing_the_initiative_process_in_Colorado.

Ballot Title Setting Board, 2011–2012. "Results for Proposed Initiative 30." Office of Colorado Secretary of State. http://www.sos.state.co.us/pubs/elections/Initiatives/title Board/results/2011-2012/30Results.html.

Bartels, Lynn. 2012. "Tom Tancredo Backs Marijuana Measure." *Denver Post*, September 21. http://blogs.denverpost.com/thespot/2012/09/21/tom-tancredo-backs-marijuana -ballot-measure/82193/.

Bennett, Wells, and John Walsh. 2014. *Marijuana Legalization Is an Opportunity to Modernize International Drug Treaties*. Washington, DC: Center for Effective Public Management at the Brookings Institute. http://www.brookings.edu/~/media/research/files/reports /2014/10/15-marijuana-legalization-modernize-drug-treaties-bennett-walsh/cepm mjlegalizationv4.pdf.

Berke, Jeremy. 2016. "Here's Where President-Elect Donald Trump Stands on Marijuana Legalization." *Business Insider*, November 9. http://www.businessinsider.com/where -donald-trump-stands-on-weed-legalization-2016-11.

———. 2017. "Here's Where Attorney General Jeff Sessions Stands on Legal Marijuana." *Business Insider*, February 8. http://www.businessinsider.com/attorney-general-jeff-ses sions-legal-weed-2017-2.

Bruning, Jon, and E. Scott Pruitt, et al. 2014. "Motion for Leave to File Complaint, Complaint and Brief in Support." *Nebraska and Oklahoma v. Colorado*, US Supreme Court. http://www.scribd.com/doc/250506006/Nebraska-Oklahoma-lawsuit.

Campaign to Regulate Marijuana Like Alcohol. 2012. Overview of Amendment 64. http://www.regulatemarijuana.org/about.

Cannabis Policy Project. 2012. "Amendment 64 Is Not Legalization." Cannabis Policy Project Blog, September 27. https://cannabispolicy.wordpress.com/a64-is-not-legal ization/.

Coats v. Dish Network, LLC. 2015. Colorado Supreme Court, CO 44. No. 13SC394. http:// www.cobar.org/opinions/opinion.cfm?opinionid=9809&courtid=2.

Coffman, Cynthia H., et al. 2015. "Colorado's Brief in Opposition to Motion for Leave to File a Complaint." *Nebraska and Oklahoma v. Colorado*, US Supreme Court. http://www .coloradoattorneygeneral.gov/sites/default/files/press_releases/2015/03/27/032715 _colorados_scotus_brief_opposition_ne_ok.pdf.

Cole, James. 2013. "Memorandum for all US Attorneys: Guidance Regarding Marijuana Enforcement." US Department of Justice: Office of the Deputy Attorney General, August 29. http://www.justice.gov/iso/opa/resources/3052013829132756857467.pdf.

————. 2014. "Memo: Guidance Regarding Marijuana Related Financial Crimes." US Department of Justice: Office of the Deputy Attorney General, February 14. http:// www.dfi.wa.gov/documents/banks/dept-of-justice-memo.pdf.

Colorado Bankers Association. 2014. "CMA Statement Regarding DOJ and Treasury Guidance on Marijuana and Banking." http://www.coloradobankers.org/?60.

Colorado Department of Revenue. 2013a. "Permanent Rules Related to the Colorado Medical Marijuana Code." https://www.colorado.gov/pacific/sites/default/files/Med ical%20Marijuana%20Rules%20-%20ADOPTED%20090913,%20Effective%20 10152013_0.pdf.

————. 2013b. "Permanent Rules Related to the Colorado Retail Marijuana Code." https://www.colorado.gov/pacific/sites/default/files/Retail%20Marijuana%20 Rules,%20Adopted%20090913,%20Effective%20101513%5B1%5D_0.pdf.

————. 2015a. "Total Marijuana Tax, Licenses and Fees Transfers and Distribution, May 2015." https://www.colorado.gov/pacific/sites/default/files/0515%20Marijuana%20 Tax%2C%20License%2C%20and%20Fees%20Report.pdf.

————. 2015b. "Retail Marijuana Proposed Rules." https://www.colorado.gov/pacific /sites/default/files/20150826_RetailRuleRedlines.pdf.

————. 2016. "Business License Application Process: Retail Marijuana." https://www .colorado.gov/pacific/enforcement/business-license-application-process-retail-mari juana.

Colorado Department of Revenue Tax Division. 2015. "Marijuana Taxes: Quick Answers." https://www.colorado.gov/pacific/tax/marijuana-taxes-quick-answers.

Colorado Department of Transportation. 2015. Safety: Drugged Driving. https://www .codot.gov/safety/alcohol-and-impaired-driving/druggeddriving.

Colorado House Bill 13-1317. 2013. "Concerning the Recommendations Made in the Public Process for the Purpose of Implementing Retail Marijuana Legalized by Section 16 of Article XVIII of the Colorado Constitution, and, in Connection therewith, Making an Appropriation." http://www.leg.state.co.us/clics/clics2013a/csl.nsf/fsbill cont2/807A035CD583C95E87257B1F005CDB59/$FILE/1317_enr.pdf.

Colorado House Bill 13-1325. 2013. "Reintroduced Driving under the Influence of Drugs Bill." http://www.scribd.com/doc/139736085/HB-13-1325-Reintroduced-Driving -Under-the-Influence-of-Drugs-Bill.

Colorado Office and State Planning and Budgeting. 2015. "The Colorado Economic Outlook: Economic and Fiscal Review." https://drive.google.com/file/d/0B0TNL0Ct D9wXa2FvM3ExVEtZZW8/view?pli=1.

Colorado Secretary of State. 2012. Election Results: Amendments and Propositions. http://www.sos.state.co.us/pubs/elections/Results/Abstract/2012/general/amend Prop.html.

Colorado Senate Bill 13-283. 2013. "Concerning Implementation of Amendment 64, and, in Connection Therewith, Making and Reducing an Appropriation." http://www .leg.state.co.us/clics/clics2013a/csl.nsf/fsbillcont3/4B75534D3719DBD687257 B490074E195/$FILE/283_enr.pdf.

Colorado State Constitution, Article 18, Section 16. "Personal Use and Regulation of Mari-

juana."https://www.sos.state.co.us/pubs/elections/LawsRules/files/Colorado_US_Con
stitutions.pdf.

Crombie, Noelle. 2016. "Oregon's Draft Rules Would Cap Serving Sizes of Marijuana-Infused Edibles." *Oregonian*, February 1. http://www.oregonlive.com/marijuana/index
.ssf/2015/10/oregond_draft_rules_limit_serv.html.

Daum, Courtenay W. 2014. "The New Wild West: Colorado and Legalized Recreational
Marijuana." *The New West: The Official Blog of the Western Political Science Association*, October 14. https://thewpsa.wordpress.com/2014/10/21/the-new-wild-west-colorado-and
-legalized-recreational-marijuana/.

Denver Post Editorial Board. 2015. "Vote 'Yes' on Colorado Proposition BB." *Denver Post*,
October 5. http://www.denverpost.com/marijuana/ci_28924422/vote-yes-colorado
-proposition-bb.

Dwyer, Devin. 2012. "Marijuana Not High Obama Priority." *ABC News*, December 14.
http://abcnews.go.com/Politics/OTUS/president-obama-marijuana-users-high-pri
ority-drug-war/story?id=17946783.

Elinson, Zusha. 2013. "Blurry Line on Pot-DUI Cases." *Wall Street Journal*, May 19. http://
www.wsj.com/articles/SB10001424127887324031404578481223036526686.

Ferner, Matt. 2012a. "Gov. John Hickenlooper Opposes Legal Weed. 'Colorado Is Known
for Many Great Things, Marijuana Should Not Be One of Them.'" *Huffington Post*,
September 12. http://www.huffingtonpost.com/2012/09/12/gov-john-hickenlooper
-opp_n_1879248.html.

———. 2012b. "Amendment 64 Opponents Speak out on Legal Weed: Hickenlooper
Says 'Don't Break out the Cheetos' Yet; AG Suthers Calls out the DOJ." *Huffington
Post*, November 7. http://www.huffingtonpost.com/2012/11/07/hickenlooper-federal
-law-_n_2088989.html.

Financial Crimes Enforcement Network. 2014. "BSA Expectations Regarding Marijuana
Related Businesses." US Department of the Treasury, February 14. http://extras.mngin
teractive.com/live/media/site36/2014/0214/20140214_113553_Guidance-Marijua
na-Related-Businesses.pdf.

Fourth Corner Credit Union v. Federal Reserve Bank of Kansas City. 2016. US District Court for
the District of Colorado. Civil Action No. 15-cv-01633—RBJ. https://docs.justia.com
/cases/federal/district-courts/colorado/codce/1:2015cv01633/157376/46.

Freedman, Andrew. 2016. "Let's Stop Asking 'Should We Legalize Marijuana?'" *Harvard
Law and Policy Review*, January 13. http://harvardlpr.com/2016/01/13/lets-stop-ask
ing-should-we-legalize-marijuana/.

Gurman, Sadie. 2015. "Authorities Crack down on Illegal Colorado Pot Grows." *Fort Collins
Coloradoan*, October 9, 2A.

Healy, Jack. 2013. "Families See Colorado as New Frontier on Medical Marijuana." *New
York Times*, December 5. http://www.nytimes.com/2013/12/06/us/families-see-colo
rado-as-new-frontier-on-medical-marijuana.html?pagewanted=all&_r=1.

Hegg, Stephen. 2014. "State Regulates Edible Marijuana Products." *Inquisitv KCTS 9*, October 2. https://kcts9.org/programs/in-close/news/legalized-marijuana/state-regulates
-edible-marijuana-products.

Higdon, James. 2016. "Jeff Sessions' Coming War on Legal Marijuana." *Politico*, December 5. http://www.politico.com/magazine/story/2016/12/jeff-sessions-coming-war-on-legal-marijuana-214501.

Hoover, Tim. 2011. "Colorado Pot Backers Aim for Legalization in Vote in 2012." *Denver Post*, May 19. http://www.denverpost.com/breakingnews/ci_18099454.

———. 2012. "State Sen. Shawn Mitchell Comes out in Favor of Ballot Measure Legalizing Pot." *Denver Post*, October 1. http://blogs.denverpost.com/thespot/2012/10/01/state-sen-shawn-mitchell-favor-ballot-measure-legalizing-pot/82939/.

HR 2076. 2015. "Marijuana Businesses Access to Banking Act of 2015." Congress.gov. https://www.congress.gov/bill/114th-congress/house-bill/2076/all-info#cosponsors.

Ingold, John. 2012. "Colorado Marijuana Measure's Backers, Foes Buoyed by Out of State Support." *Denver Post*, June 11. http://www.denverpost.com/recommended/ci_20828371.

Liptak, Adam. 2016. "Supreme Court Declines to Hear Challenge to Colorado's Marijuana Laws." *New York Times*, March 21. https://www.nytimes.com/2016/03/22/us/politics/supreme-court-declines-to-hear-challenge-to-colorados-marijuana-laws.html.

Marijuana Occupational Health and Safety Work Group. 2017. "Guide to Worker Safety and Health in the Marijuana Industry." Colorado Department of Public Health and Environment. https://drive.google.com/file/d/0ByonCYTyaB73Y0gtclJwamtGaDQ/view.

Marijuana Policy Project. 2014. Consume Responsibly Campaign. www.consumeresponsibly.org.

———. 2015. "Colorado and Washington: Life after Legalization." https://www.mpp.org/issues/legalization/colorado-and-washington-life-after-legalization-and-regulation/.

———. 2016. "State Policy." https://www.mpp.org/states/.

———. 2017. "Executive Summary: Adult Use of Marijuana Act." Retrieved: https://www.regulatecalifornia.com/about/executive-summary/.

Markus, Ben. 2014. "Without a Marijuana Breathalyzer, How to Curb Stoned Driving?" *NPR*, May 21. http://www.npr.org/2014/05/21/314279711/without-a-marijuana-breathalyzer-how-to-curb-stoned-driving.

Mason, Mark. 2015a. "Complaint." *The Fourth Corner Credit Union v. Federal Reserve Bank of Kansas City*, US District Court for the District of Colorado. https://consumermediallc.files.wordpress.com/2015/07/fourthcorner.pdf.

———. 2015b. Interview with the author, November 4.

Meltzer, Erica. 2010. "Colorado Pot Advocates Plan 2012 Legalization Push." ColoradoDaily.com, June 11. http://www.coloradodaily.com/cu-boulder/ci_15281752#axzz0qwLyO8Yz.

Moreno, Ivan. 2012. "Colorado Lawmakers Warn About Constitutional Hazards of Marijuana Legalization." *Daily Camera* (Boulder, CO), September 5. http://www.dailycamera.com/state-west-news/ci_21477445/colorado-lawmakers-warn-about-constitutional-hazards-marijuana-legalization.

MRSC. 2016. "Recreational Marijuana: A Guide for Local Governments." http://

mrsc.org/Home/Explore-Topics/Legal/Regulation/Recreational-Marijuana-A -Guide-for-Local-Governmen.aspx.

National Conference of State Legislatures. 2012. Initiative and Referendum States. http:// www.ncsl.org/research/elections-and-campaigns/chart-of-the-initiative-states.aspx.

Nelson, Steven. 2014. "Colorado Governor Calls Pot Legalization 'Reckless.'" *U.S. News and World Report*, October 7. http://www.usnews.com/news/articles/2014/10/07/colorado -governor-calls-pot-legalization-reckless.

Office of Public Affairs. 2013. "Justice Department Announces Update to Marijuana Enforcement Policy." US Department of Justice, August 29. http://www.justice.gov/opa /pr/justice-department-announces-update-marijuana-enforcement-policy.

Office of the US Solicitor General. 2015. "Brief for the United States as Amicus Curiae." *Nebraska and Oklahoma v. Colorado, in the Supreme Court of the United States.* http://www.jus tice.gov/sites/default/files/osg/briefs/2015/12/22/original_no._144_us_cvsg_br.pdf.

Popper, Nathaniel. 2015. "Banking for Pot Industry Hits a Roadblock." *New York Times*, July 30. http://www.nytimes.com/2015/07/31/business/dealbook/federal-reserve-denies -credit-union-for-cannabis.html?_r=0.

Quinnipiac University. 2015. "With Big Age, Party Gaps, Iowa Voters Split on Marijuana, Quinnipiac University Swing State Poll Finds; Colorado, Virginia Voters Back Recreational Pot." http://www.quinnipiac.edu/news-and-events/quinnipiac-university-poll /2016-presidential-swing-state-polls/release-detail?ReleaseID=2186.

Richtel, Matt. 2015. "The First Bank of Bud." *New York Times*, February 8, B1.

S.1726. 2015. "Marijuana Businesses Access to Banking Act of 2015." Congress.gov. https://www.congress.gov/bill/114th-congress/senate-bill/1726/all-info#cosponsors.

Stiffler, Christopher. 2012. "Amendment 64 Would Produce $60 Million in New Revenue and Savings for Colorado." Colorado Center on Law and Policy Report, August 16. http://cclponline.org/wp-content/uploads/2013/11/amendment_64_analysis_final .pdf.

Straayer, John. 2011. "One Thing after Another: Layers of Policy and Colorado's Fiscal Train Wreck." In *State of Change: Colorado Politics in the Twenty-First Century*, ed. Courtenay W. Daum, Robert J. Duffy, and John A. Straayer, 195–216. Boulder: University Press of Colorado.

Sullum, Jacob. 2014. "Marijuana Money Is Still a Pot of Trouble for Banks." *Forbes*, September 18. http://www.forbes.com/sites/jacobsullum/2014/09/18/local-banks-terri fied-by-friendly-neighborhood-marijuana-merchants/.

US Attorney's Office. 2013. "Statement by US Attorney John Walsh Regarding Marijuana Enforcement in Colorado." District of Colorado, US Department of Justice, August 29. http://www.justice.gov/usao-co/pr/statement-us-attorney-john-walsh-regarding-mar ijuana-enforcement-colorado.

———. 2015. "Confronting Wave of Illicit Marijuana Cultivation, Federal State and Local Authorities Discover and Destroy Major Marijuana Grows in Locations across Colorado." District of Colorado, US Department of Justice, October 8. http://www.justice .gov/usao-co/pr/confronting-wave-illicit-marijuana-cultivation-federal-state-and-lo cal-authorities.

US Supreme Court. 2015. *Nebraska and Oklahoma v. Colorado.* Docket: Proceedings and Orders. http://www.supremecourt.gov/Search.aspx?FileName=/docketfiles/22o144.htm.

Wallace, Alicia. 2016. "Marijuana Edibles Will Look Different in Colorado Starting October 1, among Many New State Rules." *Cannabist*, September 29. http://www.thecanna bist.co/2016/09/29/marijuana-edibles-colorado-thc-symbol/64093/.

———. 2017a. "Colorado Sold $1.3 Billion Worth of Marijuana in 2016." *Cannabist*, February 9. http://www.thecannabist.co/2017/02/09/colorado-marijuana-sales-2016/73415/.

———. 2017b. "Colorado Puts New Focus on Worker Safety in Cannabis Industry." *Cannabist*, February 7. http://www.thecannabist.co/2017/02/07/colorado-marijuana -safety-jobs-workplace/73208/.

Weed, Julie. 2015. "Book Your 'Bud and Breakfast': Marijuana Tourism Is Growing in Colorado and Washington." *Forbes*, March 17. http://www.forbes.com/sites/julieweed /2015/03/17/book-your-bud-and-breakfast-marijuana-tourism-is-growing-in-colora do-and-washington/.

Wyatt, Kristen. 2013. "Effect of Recreational Weed on Ski Resorts Remains Hazy." *Summit Daily*, December 31. http://www.summitdaily.com/opinion/9105834-113/ski-colorado -marijuana-resorts.

NOTE

*"Low, Slow, and in Control" is part of the Consume Responsibly Campaign launched by the Marijuana Policy Project to promote legal, safe, and responsible marijuana consumption in Colorado and Washington State.

CHAPTER 10

Legalized, Regulated, and Taxed

How Oregon's Marijuana Measure Went Mainstream

Anthony Johnson

Here is a state that is not afraid to plow new ground in an area where there's a lot of hysteria. It's not going to be very widely understood, but I think as you look back over the handling of drugs, if you can keep it in for a few years, you'll see it was landmark legislation.
—Tom McCall, governor of Oregon (1967–1975)

Oregon has had a long history as a liberal state with a progressive attitude toward cannabis. The Beaver State was the first to decriminalize marijuana in 1973 and allow medical marijuana beginning in 1998. Yet proposals to legalize recreational marijuana failed at the ballot in 1986 and 2012, and the state voted down medical cannabis dispensaries in 2004 and 2010. Advocates persevered, and in 2014 Measure 91, which legalized marijuana, secured the largest margin of victory in any state that year; this victory came despite the fact that 2014 was an off-year election, a seemingly tough time to pass a progressive marijuana measure.

Measure 91 secured a bit more than 56 percent of the vote, thanks to a broad coalition of cannabis law reform proponents who were able to set aside past differences and egos to create a ballot measure that could be supported by patients, activists, and the state's Democratic Party establishment. While the campaign was not without difficulties (it almost never left the ground and was nearly scuttled a couple of times), a formidable campaign team was formed that was able to weather many storms and to achieve an unlikely but decisive victory.

The 2014 campaign to legalize marijuana in Oregon actually started before the 2012 election had concluded and its marijuana-legalization initiative—dubbed Measure 80—had gone down in defeat. Early polling had indicated that Measure 80 would lose, in large part because it contained a provision that would have sanctioned an unlimited amount of marijuana for personal possession and cultivation; this would prove too radical even for progressive Oregonians. Still, Measure 80, despite this and a few other politically problematic provisions, garnered 47 percent of all ballots, a respectable showing that signaled a more carefully crafted measure could win. Developing that winning formula was a committed group of activists and hired professionals who not only wrote a measure that resolved its predecessor's contentious elements but also organized a successful campaign strategy. They did so despite cautionary advice from prominent local and national legalization activists that the Oregon campaign would have much greater chance of success if delayed until the 2016 presidential election (Belville 2012). For those who ultimately decided to press ahead, there were two key reasons: two more years of thousands of arrests and citations for marijuana use (Crombie 2014) was unacceptable, and polling showed that a path to victory existed in 2014 (Belville 2013).

The gamble succeeded in good measure because Oregon's Vote Yes on 91 campaign combined rigorous attention to data, considerable discipline, lots of hard work, and a bit of luck—all that was necessary to pass cannabis legalization with a greater margin of victory than any other state, including Colorado and Washington, which were aided by a larger presidential election voter turnout. While many look back on the 56.1 percent vote to legalize and think that victory was inevitable, in reality Measure 91 almost did not make the ballot. The difficulty of acquiring the necessary funding, a couple of challenges to the language of the ballot title, and thousands of signatures being discounted due to signature-gatherers' errors put the 2014 legalization measure at risk.

After (barely) qualifying for the ballot with roughly 1,000 signatures to spare, the Vote Yes on 91 campaign team utilized a shotgun approach to the campaign, demonstrating that there are many reasons to regulate, legalize, and tax marijuana. Oregon voters were principally concerned with whether the proposition would generate tax revenue for public schools and other important social services. The fact that law enforcement resources could be better prioritized appealed to others. The activist community wanted to ensure that no penalties would be made worse, as had happened with California's Proposition 19, a failed 2010 legalization effort; it would have increased penalties for providing marijuana to a minor, even unwittingly passing a joint to a twenty-year-old at a concert. The Oregon organizers also wanted to make sure that the Oregon Medical Marijuana Program would not be harmed. That thousands of new jobs would be created by the burgeoning cannabis industry brought additional support to the cause.

The Vote Yes on 91 campaign was unlike any other marijuana campaign in Oregon history. It was a professional effort that fought everyday as if it were 100 votes shy of victory and it was every staffer's responsibility to earn those 100 votes. Its advocates spoke at Lion's Club meetings and town halls, participated in City Club debates, and worked the media assiduously. Even as the campaign fought for "mainstream" moderate votes, it did not take the base for granted, working with allies to best communicate with the cannabis community why it should enthusiastically support Measure 91. This all-around effort, which searched for votes among all constituencies and communities, produced a remarkable victory that its proponents believe will be good for Oregon, and might also serve as a model for the rest of the country.

1973: THE YEAR OREGON BLAZED A PATH TO CANNABIS SANITY

In 1972 a commission appointed by Richard Nixon produced what became known as the Shaffer Report—a proposal that called for the decriminalization of marijuana because the harms of the drug did not warrant the human and fiscal resources employed to enforce laws against cannabis possession, distribution, and consumption. Richard Nixon and Congress did not abide by the report, but soon thereafter Oregon would start the nation down a path away from "reefer madness" anxieties and a fixation on harsh punishment and toward a more sensible, less punitive policy; a policy that recognized that many people were going to utilize a substance less lethal than alcohol and tobacco and that they should not be penalized for doing so.

An Oregon representative named Earl Blumenauer, then in his early twenties, was one of the legislators who in 1973 voted to make Oregon the first state to decriminalize personal amounts of cannabis (Crombie 2014). Blumenauer, as his legislative career progressed, would remain a staunch advocate of legalization at the state and federal levels. After Blumenauer and his colleagues passed that decriminalization measure, which made possession of less than an ounce a ticketable offense—like a (rather expensive) traffic violation—several other states followed suit, including Alaska, California, Colorado, Ohio, and Nebraska (Stroup 2001). NORML, the National Organization for the Reform of Marijuana Laws, was the driving force behind many of these legislative efforts, and it seemed that the battle to end cannabis prohibition was moving forward effectively and with great momentum (Warner 2015).

President Jimmy Carter endorsed the Shafer Commission's findings: "Penalties against possession of a drug should not be more damaging to an individual as the use of the drug itself." By 1981 ten more states followed Oregon's lead in decriminalizing the personal use of cannabis, but the momentum halted as Ronald Reagan escalated the War on Drugs and Nancy Reagan's Just Say No campaign took off across the country (Graham 2014). Despite this retreat, a group of Oregon activists continued to press for the end of cannabis prohibition during the tough War on Drugs of the 1980s.

THE OREGON MARIJUANA INITIATIVE OF 1986

John Sajo, Paul Stanford, Doug McVay, and Jack Herer were just a few of the advocates who put the Oregon Marijuana Initiative (OMI) on the 1986 ballot. Activists campaigning for OMI emphasized that the initiative was fundamentally about "freedom" and "liberty." After turning in more than 87,000 signatures to qualify for that year's ballot, the organizers and their supporters gathered on the steps of the Oregon state capitol in Salem and released green balloons emblazoned with a single word—"Freedom!" (RestoreHemp, 2011). For all the appeal this term might have held for voters, it was not enough to attract broad support; the 1986 initiative garnered just over 26 percent of the vote. In their postmortem analysis, advocates believed that voters had been turned off by OMI's failure to establish a system of regulated sales that would have generated tax revenue for the state; voters were also concerned that the measure contained a provision that would have allowed unlimited possession of marijuana. Ultimately, it would seem that the voters were not ready for marijuana legalization, as support for marijuana legalization hovered around 25 percent at the time (Jones 2015).

While not successful, the OMI campaign of 1986 nonetheless laid the foundation for future initiative efforts, including Measure 91, which would be on the ballot twenty-eight years later. Its core supporters went on to inspire, train, and employ future activists, a cross-generational cadre of activists that placed subsequent measures on the Oregon ballot. Although these efforts did not always succeed, they kept the issue in front of the voters, helping move the marijuana reform movement forward. John Sajo, who directed the 1986 campaign, would go on to start a nonprofit called Voter Power that would become a force in Oregon marijuana politics in future decades (Melton 2010); Paul Stanford would go on to establish, under the auspices of The Hemp and Cannabis Foundation (THCF), clinics to register medical marijuana patients in several states and serve as chief petitioner and author of Measure 80 (Bacca 2015); Doug McVay became editor of *Drug War Facts* and a board member of Students for a Sensible Drug Policy (Common Sense for Drug Policy 2014); and Jack Herer, author of *The Emperor*

Wears No Clothes (1985), a sharp critique of federal- and state-level marijuana prohibition, would become known as the "Hemperer," the godfather of the cannabis hemp legalization movement, not only in Oregon but across the globe (King 2010).

1998: MEDICAL MARIJUANA COMES TO THE GREAT NORTHWEST

Oregon and its neighbor to the north, Washington, joined California in legalizing medical cannabis in 1998. The Oregon Medical Marijuana Act passed with over 54 percent of the vote (Oregon Blue Book 2016) and eventually would lead to more than 70,000 registered medical marijuana patients (Oregon Medical Marijuana Program 2016); its success at the polls and in communities would help launch marijuana law reform. The Oregon Medical Marijuana Program, in addition to legalizing tens of thousands of patients, subsequently generated millions of dollars for other state programs through state licensing fees (Crombie 2015).

Medical cannabis would fight for legitimacy over the years but would eventually become very much a part of mainstream Oregon society, with the exception of in some rural counties, which proved hostile to regulated marijuana businesses; this left some patients without easy access to a dispensary (Selsky 2016). An example of this struggle for legitimacy was a 2010 protest at the headquarters of the Portland *Oregonian*, the Northwest's largest newspaper, after medical cannabis patients and advocates took exception to its slanted coverage of medical marijuana. Particularly irksome was the newspaper's use of quotation marks around *medical marijuana,* as in this editorial: "Let the charades begin: Another 'medical marijuana' measure is coming to the fall ballot," the *Oregonian* editorial board scoffed (*Oregonian* Editorial Board 2010). This delegitimizing angered those who depended on the drug for their health and sparked their public protest. The protest was effective, leading to a meeting between advocates and the *Oregonian*'s editorial board, one key result of which was that the newspaper changed how it referred to medical marijuana. Four years later, in another turnaround, the *Oregonian*, long opposed to legitimization, endorsed Measure 91 (*Oregonian* Editorial Board 2014).

Marijuana advocates also demonstrated their power to organize when in 1998 they quashed legislation that recriminalized marijuana. Members of the Republican-controlled legislature, with strong support from the Oregon Police Chiefs for Safer Communities, argued that charging a misdemeanor for an ounce or less of marijuana was necessary to "send a clear message to Oregon's children" (Oregon Police Chiefs for Safer Communities 1998). The bill passed, and Democratic governor John Kitzhaber signed it into law. Oregon activists, led by John Sajo and Voter Power, collected the necessary signatures to place a referendum on the ballot, giving Oregon voters an opportunity to overturn the recriminalizing legislation. More than 66 percent of voters chose to keep the possession of less an ounce of cannabis a civil infraction (Oregon Blue Book 2016). By their work and votes, that era's energized activists and sympathetic voters kept alive Governor Tom Mc-Call's hope that if the original legislation decriminalizing marijuana survived the predictable early challenges to it, the law would become "landmark legislation."

2004 AND 2010: TWO INITIATIVES TO LEGALIZE MEDICAL MARIJUANA DISPENSARIES

The Oregon Medical Marijuana Act, following its passage in 1998, is a unique law that depended upon the compassion of growers to supply medical cannabis to patients because the act did not establish a system for licensing and regulating supply. The proposal, known as Measure 67, was promoted as a moderate ballot measure centered on patients' rights; it was not touted as a revenue generator (Bayer 1998). Since then, thousands of patients have been able to acquire medical cannabis from a grower, at times even free of charge; those patients without a compassionate grower have been out of luck. To resolve this inequity was the driving force behind a pair of initiatives, the first in 2004 and the second in 2010. The 2004 attempt, Measure 33, would have required dispensaries to provide free cannabis to low-income patients, increased the amount of marijuana that patients could possess to 6 pounds, and compelled county health departments to open up medical dispensaries if there was not a privately operated dispensary within its jurisdiction. Measure 33 garnered just under 43 percent of the vote. The 2010 attempt, Measure 74, would have established a system of licensed producers and dispensaries and a fund to provide assistance to low-income patients. Measure 74 earned just over 44 percent of the vote. That it secured even that many votes is striking, given that that particular election heralded the emergence of the so-called Tea Party in Oregon and across the nation. I was coauthor and co–chief petitioner of Measure 74, along with medical cannabis patient advocates, Alice Ivany, and the late Jim Klahr. While Measure 74 did not succeed, we learned what it took to mount a successful statewide political campaign; it provided as well great training for the 2014 legalization effort.

2012: OREGON DOESN'T QUITE JOIN COLORADO AND WASHINGTON STATE

The Oregon Cannabis Tax Act (OCTA), also known as Measure 80, was the brainchild of long-time activist Paul Stanford, one of the advocates who helped put the 1986 OMI measure on the ballot. When it qualified for the 2012 ballot, it thus joined legalization measures in Colorado and Washington. Like its peer legislation in those two states, OCTA was an ambitious effort, not least because it did not put a limit on the amount of marijuana that Oregon adults could possess or cultivate; instead, the measure would "fully replace and supersede" most marijuana penalties (Oregon Secretary of State 2012). The certified ballot title—with its emphasis on taxes—is revelatory of the strategy its advocates pursued:

> Allows personal marijuana, hemp cultivation/use without license; commission to regulate commercial marijuana cultivation/sale.
>
> Result of a "Yes" Vote: "Yes" vote allows commercial marijuana (cannabis) cultivation/sale to adults through state-licensed stores; allows unlicensed adult personal cultivation/use; prohibits restrictions on hemp (defined).
>
> Result of a "No" Vote: "No" vote retains existing civil and criminal laws prohibiting cultivation, possession, and delivery of marijuana; retains current statutes that permit regulated medical use of marijuana.
>
> Summary: Currently, marijuana cultivation, possession, and delivery are prohibited; regulated medical marijuana use is permitted. Measure replaces state, local marijuana laws except medical marijuana and driving under the influence laws; distinguishes "hemp" from "marijuana"; prohibits regulation of hemp. Creates commission to license marijuana cultivation by qualified persons and to purchase entire crop. Commission sells marijuana at cost to pharmacies, medical research facilities, and to qualified adults for profit through state-licensed stores. Ninety percent of net goes to state general fund, remainder to drug education, treatment, hemp promotion. Bans sales to, possession by minors. Bans public consumption except where signs permit, minors barred. Commission regulates use, sets prices, other duties; Attorney General to defend against federal challenges/prosecutions. Provides penalties. Effective January 1, 2013. . . . (Oregon Secretary of State 2012)

Note the qualifications this text contained and the positive revenue stream it predicted would be one of the results of the passage of Measure 80. Additionally, the initiative would have created a new government agency, a cannabis commission that would buy all of the marijuana produced by licensed growers and then resell it—at a profit to consumers, at cost to patients.

The *Oregonian* and most other mainstream media outlets opposed Measure 80. "Vote no on Measure 80, Oregon's marijuana manifesto," the newspaper's editorial board wrote (*Oregonian* Editorial Board 2012). The campaign also suffered from a lack of fiscal and logistical support from organizations like the Marijuana Policy Project (MPP) and Drug Policy Alliance. They channeled their dollars and energies into the campaigns in Colorado and Washington, which polls suggested might be more winnable than Oregon. That calculation may have been the result, too, of how the media portrayed the three campaigns. In Oregon, Measure 80 was described as a pro-marijuana measure while Amendment 64 in Colorado and I-502 in Washington were considered regulatory proposals; the difference was a result of the stricter limits on the amounts of cannabis that could be possessed and cultivated in Washington and Colorado. In the end, while Oregon's Measure 80 earned a respectable 47 percent of the vote, the initiatives in Colorado and Washington became law with 54 percent of the vote.

2013: LEGISLATIVE SUCCESSES

In 2013 cannabis advocates, led by Geoff Sugerman and Sam Chapman, spearheaded an effort to pass House Bill 3460, landmark legislation that finally legalized medical marijuana dispensaries in Oregon. Compared to Measure 33 and Measure 74, House Bill 3460 was a relatively conservative measure that merely licensed and regulated medical marijuana dispensaries under the Oregon Health Authority—the same agency (although the name had since changed) that had regulated the Oregon Medical Marijuana Program since its establishment in 1999. House Bill 3460 did not establish any fund for low-income patients, allowed localities to place a moratorium on dispensaries, and mandated that dispensaries must be 1,000 feet apart. The concept of the 1,000-foot barrier was greatly influenced by the consequences of video lottery machines, which had generated the ire of some neighborhood associations after the establishment of so-called lottery rows (Parks 2012).

The passage of House Bill 3460 was important not only for patients who would be able to acquire cannabis through a regulated establishment but also for the Measure 91 legalization effort in 2014, as it lay the foundation for licensed and regulated cannabis commerce, demonstrating that the sky would not fall if the state inspected and audited establishments that sold cannabis to adults.

House Bill 3460 worked in conjunction with House Bill 3371, a precursor to Measure 91 that would have legalized marijuana for all adults over the age of twenty-one. House Bill 3371, sponsored by New Approach Oregon, the political action committee that would lead the Vote Yes on 91 campaign to legalize cannabis the following year, was the first marijuana legalization measure to be provided a hearing at the Oregon legislature and to pass out of a committee; it did not gain enough support from the legislature, though. Organizers knew that any effort to legalize marijuana through the legislative process was going to be a long shot, but the process provided the New Approach team the opportunity to hone its arguments, messaging, and strategies and to learn the varied concerns of legislators and opponents.

2014: OREGON BECOMES THE THIRD STATE TO LEGALIZE

Although the majority of Beaver State voters did not support Measure 80, cannabis activists were encouraged—so much so, that they immediately began to debate when the next initiative should be placed on the ballot. Some believed that delaying until 2016 would allow for a longer organizing process that might produce a progressive measure with larger home cultivation and possession limits. Others wanted to capitalize on the 2012 results, confident that a 2014 vote would lead to victory. Still others, including me, leaned toward waiting until 2016 but were fine with an earlier campaign so long as polling of likely 2014 voters showed strong support and—crucially—if the campaign could raise the necessary funding. To mount an even bare-bones campaign operation was estimated to cost at least $1 million; a more robust one would cost upward of $5 million, which, in the end, was how much the Measure 91 campaign would raise.

With these concerns and questions in mind, shortly after Measure 80's defeat more than thirty advocates from across Oregon met to discuss whether to move forward in 2014 or 2016; out of the intense dialogue emerged a consensus to test a 2014 campaign through statewide polling. If the numbers were not there, or funding would be short, then we would wait until 2016. There was considerable pressure to do so, when there would be greater voter turnout due to the presidential election and, it was said, a reasonable legalization measure would be sure to pass. The Marijuana Policy Project, one of the national leaders of the legalization movement since 1996, weighed in in favor of delaying until 2016 (Crombie 2012). A key voice in this regard was Rob Kampia, MPP's executive director. He had blogged about the electoral success in Colorado in the *Huffington Post*, and his postelection analysis offered considerable insight into what made the Colorado campaign successful, including its inclusive legislation-drafting process, years of groundwork, and the increased turnout that in this instance came with a presidential election. Believing that what had happened in the Centennial State would hold true for the Beaver State, Kampia cautioned Oregon marijuana advocates against ignoring what he asserted was the crucial first step for a successful legalization campaign: placing legalization measures on the ballot during a presidential election, "which always attracts a larger proportion of young voters, who are more supportive" (Kampia 2012).

"To that point, there are already well-meaning activists in Oregon and other states who aren't remembering the efforts of well-meaning activists in California, who ignored the lesson of step #1 and pushed a risky initiative during a non-presidential election in 2010, which I'm sure felt good but succeeded at failing" (Kampia 2012). Kampia then followed up his *Huffington Post* blog with a private memo to several Oregon activists that laid out why he believed waiting until 2016 made more political sense. The *Oregonian* reported on the memo that December: "Much more work needs to be done to build public support" for legalization to be successful in the state, Kampia wrote in a memo obtained by the *Oregonian*, "and this cannot happen quickly."

> Kampia's memo underscores how far the national conversation on marijuana has moved since Oregonians approved marijuana as medicine. Some advocates say it is time to move beyond laws that make marijuana available only with a doctor's approval. Some key policymakers say when legalization comes to Oregon, medical marijuana will become irrelevant.
>
> But the Kampia memo also highlights the uncertainties involved. Oregon's views of marijuana are quirky but consistent. Voters twice rejected efforts to expand access to medical marijuana before defeating legalization this year. (Crombie 2012)

In his memo, Kampia pointed to recent losses in midterm elections for marijuana legalization in California (Proposition 19 in 2010) as well as two MPP-led measures in Nevada in 2002 and 2006. He inferred from these losses that an Oregon initiative would also need the boost that could come from a presidential campaign. He projected that in 2016 a legalization measure would secure a 3 percent increase in support over the 2012 results, and then he broke this increase down into its constituent parts: 2 percent would come from a spike in advertising and 1 percent from a well-crafted initiative designed to appeal to a broad spectrum of voters. If Oregon moved ahead with a legalization measure in 2014, Kampia predicted, the effort would earn the same: just 47 percent of the vote as in 2012, even with "better drafting" of the measure and a significant advertising edge. Kampia recommended a multiyear campaign to increase support for a 2016 measure. The Colorado measure had great success with the so-called Safer Campaign to educate voters and policymakers about the fact that marijuana is safer than alcohol. MPP pledged to make contributions and devote staff time to the 2016 Safer Campaign in Oregon, a contribution totaling $700,000. If Oregon decided to move forward with a 2014 effort, then the "initiative would almost be certain to lose," he asserted, and the state would "fall by the wayside" in 2016, just as California did in 2012, after losing at the ballot box in 2010.

Two months later, MPP's then-director of government affairs, Steve Fox, hosted a town hall for Oregon legalization advocates. He provided a detailed analysis of how Oregon could legalize in 2016 by utilizing the "marijuana is safer" message. As the *Oregonian* noted, not all Oregon activists wanted to wait:

Fox said the extra two years gives voters the chance to see how legalization has worked in Colorado and Washington. But his advice to wait another three years for another legalization initiative was a tough sell for some Oregon activists. They cite Oregon's proximity to Washington and the relatively narrow defeat of Measure 80, Oregon's legalization ballot measure, as reasons for pursuing an initiative sooner.

"There is a lot of pressure right now," said Russ Belville, a Portland marijuana legalization activist and host of a radio show dedicated to cannabis news and culture. "There is a part of me that says strike while the iron is hot." (Crombie 2013)

The idea of taking quick advantage of the 2012 momentum persuaded a large contingent of Oregon activists to move forward in 2014; they committed themselves to writing a measure more palatable to voters than Measure 80 proved to be. What they were uncertain about is whether the requisite funds to launch an effective campaign would be available. To secure the millions of dollars necessary for such a campaign, polling would need to show that legalization was viable in a midterm election cycle. New Approach Oregon commissioned polls by DHM Research and Greenberg Quinlan Rosner, and they revealed that 54 percent of Oregon voters now favored marijuana legalization. While normally 54 percent is a good polling number, initiative campaigns are usually expected to decrease in support over time. This normal decline in the polls seems tied to that fact that while a majority of voters support legalization, many people may be concerned about admitting to a stranger on the phone that they support legalizing a federally illegal substance. In a pre-2012 election poll that SurveyUSA conducted, Measure 80 was supported by only 37 percent of likely voters, yet it had earned 47 percent approval by those who voted in that election (SurveyUSA 2012). Washington's I-502 polled at 47 percent among likely voters in a KCTS Washington Poll, before securing a strong majority (Washington Poll 2012).

With polling in Oregon showing that legalization could win in 2014, there was another hurdle: to draft a measure that was progressive enough to keep the Oregon cannabis community on board but conservative enough to satisfy national funders and potential establishment endorsers. Attorney David Kopilak was the primary drafter of the measure, taking input from local and national advocates.

The likely funders for an Oregon legalization measure were many of the same people and organizations who underwrote Washington's successful I-502 legalization campaign. Washington's measure has been considered very conservative: the ballot summary for the Washington I-502 noted that possession would be legalized but did not mention personal cultivation (as that remained prohibited); it also established a THC driving limit:

This measure removes state-law prohibitions against producing, processing, and selling marijuana, subject to licensing and regulation by the liquor control board; allow[s] limited possession of marijuana by persons aged twenty-one and over; and impose[s] 25% excise taxes on wholesale and retail sales of marijuana, earmarking revenue for purposes that include substance-abuse prevention, research, education, and healthcare. Laws prohibiting driving under the influence would be amended to include maximum thresholds for THC blood concentration. (McKenna 2011)

Initially, many Oregon advocates pushed for a progressive measure that would allow individuals to cultivate twenty-four total plants (although only six could be mature plants over a foot tall). After much heated debate and compromise, four marijuana plants and no DUI provisions were selected. The four plants were per household, not per adult, and the Oregon Liquor Control Commission, the regulatory body for the legalization regime, would study driving under the influence and would report to the Oregon legislature on the issue. Driving under the influence of marijuana remained a crime under the legalization provision, and a new violation prohibiting using marijuana while driving was added to what would become Measure 91.

After more than thirty-some drafts of the measure, the next step was to gather the 1,000 valid signatures required to secure a ballot title and move the initiative process forward. My wife, Sarah Duff, herself a longtime activist with experience collecting signatures for marijuana decriminalization and medical cannabis measures in Missouri, volunteered to collect most of the initial signatures. She succeeded, and after the Oregon secretary of state verified the first 1,000 signatures, the process was then opened to public comment on the title. At that point, an unexpected roadblock emerged: local attorney Michael McNichols, who claimed to be a supporter of legalization, indicated that he preferred other legalization measures that were gathering signatures (VanderHart 2014). While the ballot title was being challenged, our campaign filed another measure, changing the definition of industrial hemp to ensure that the Oregon Liquor Control Commission would not regulate hemp products. Otherwise, the measures were identical.

McNichols commented on the second draft of the measure to the Oregon secretary of state, preserving his right to challenge the ballot title before the Oregon Supreme Court; this delayed our ability to gather signatures and could have scuttled the legalization effort altogether. Several concerned citizens and advocates contacted McNichols and urged him to refrain from challenging our ballot title. Eventually, he decided against a challenge, and the signature gathering could proceed.

That process was not challenge-free, either. To gather the necessary 87,213 valid signatures to place a statutory measure on the ballot required a paid signature-gathering effort and a volunteer signature effort. It gathered more than 145,000 bulk signatures that were then submitted to the state on June 26, 2014, a few weeks ahead of the July 3 deadline. Advocates were extremely confident of making the ballot, even though more than 7,000 signatures were invalidated immediately due to signature gatherer error. Ultimately, 88,500 signatures were declared valid, more than the 87,213 required. After certification, the initiative petition was named Measure 91 and the campaign was on. It was led by veteran campaign director Liz Kaufman, and the day-to-day campaign manager was Dan Maher, a veteran of Democratic and union organizing efforts. Peter Zuckerman led the communications department; Zuckerman, a former investigative journalist, had been working on a marriage equality campaign. Fundraising was led by Ellen Flenniken, who had raised money for the marriage equality campaign as well as for US Representative Susan Bonamicci. The outreach director was Dominic Lopez, also fresh off of Oregon's marriage equality campaign. Eventually, journalist Brad Reed was added to the communications department. I was somewhat of a jack-of-all-trades in the campaign, working with all of the various departments. I had worked on a couple of marijuana law reform campaigns in the past, and while I was considered savvy about campaign politics these organizers taught me what it was like to really work hard on a political campaign.

There are many reasons to support legalizing, regulating, and taxing marijuana, and our campaign made sure to discuss those reasons at every opportunity. Some voters supported legalization because of the social justice impact, particularly the fact that people of color are more likely to be arrested and cited for marijuana possession. Others appreciated the initiative's ability to generate new jobs and tax revenue. Overwhelmingly, voters felt that law enforcement faced much more pressing challenges and that its limited resources would be better spent on more significant crimes. This calculation found support in our internal polls: around 70 percent of Oregon voters agreed that legalizing marijuana would free up time and resources for law enforcement to combat other crimes. So while we focused on the debate over arrests versus citations throughout the campaign, we were also able to pivot to a key reason why some voters supported legalizing marijuana: that Measure 91 would generate tax revenue in support of public safety and other state programs.

One of the most, if not the most, egregious social-justice implications of marijuana prohibition has been the disproportionate impact criminalization of marijuana has had on people of color, in particular black communities. The American Civil Liberties Union (ACLU) conducted an extensive study of marijuana arrests, finding that nationwide African Americans were much more likely to be arrested for marijuana offenses (ACLU 2013). Oregon followed these national trends:

Figure 10.1. The tax revenues that legalizing marijuana would generate helped sell voters on Measure 91. *Courtesy of New Approach Oregon*

across the state, blacks were more than twice as likely to be arrested and cited for marijuana offenses; those numbers were even higher in urban Multnomah and Lane Counties, where blacks were three times as likely to be arrested (ACLU-Oregon 2013).

A policy with such uneven racial consequences is tough to defend, and our opponents did not effectively counter this point, other than to state that marijuana offenses are not such a big deal. However, we countered that marijuana offenses, however minor, could have severe consequences, especially for individuals on probation and parole, and as proof, we pointed to an Oregon school district that prohibited anyone from working or volunteering for the district with a minor possession charge.

Creating jobs and generating revenue would be another positive development from legalizing marijuana. Likely 2014 voters very strongly supported sending millions of dollars to schools and mental health programs. Measure 91 allocated 40 percent of tax revenue to schools, 25 percent to mental health and substance abuse treatment programs, and 35 percent to local and state police.

The state's financial impact statement, mailed with every voter pamphlet, estimated that marijuana sales would generate between $17 million and $40 million once the program was implemented. In retrospect, we now know that the upper range of the state's projection was accurate: in the first two months of taxed revenue, Oregon collected nearly $7 million, an amount that would equal $42 million in the first year (Crombie 2016a). However, the tax revenue is likely to be even more substantial, as the state has only taxed the flowers (or buds) of the plant;

this revenue will increase once the state starts selling and taxing other marijuana products, such as marijuana-infused edibles.

These projected financial benefits dovetailed with broad, mainstream support for Measure 91. A slew of newspapers endorsed the measure, including the *Oregonian*, which editorialized: "Measure 91 would move Oregon from a hazy condition of almost-legalization to one of rational access guided by straightforward regulations and subject to sensible taxation" (*Oregonian* Editorial Board 2014). The Eugene *Register-Guard*, the Pendleton *East Oregonian*, and the Medford *Mail Tribune* followed suit, as did alternative weeklies, such as the *Willamette Week* and the *Portland Mercury*. The campaign was also boosted by the national endorsement of the *New York Times*, which agreed with the *Oregonian* that Measure 91 would "be worth supporting for reasons of honesty and convenience alone" (*New York Times* Editorial Board 2014). Public officials also lined up behind the measure. As expected, US Representative Earl Blumenauer, a longtime supporter of marijuana law reform, endorsed it, and even stepped up to debate Clatsop County district attorney Josh Marquis, the opposition's main spokesperson, before the Salem City Club. Joining Blumenauer were former US attorney Kris Olson and William Riggs, a retired Oregon Supreme Court judge. Toward the end of the campaign, the effort received a significant endorsement from King County (Washington) sheriff John Urquhart, who had experienced legalization firsthand. Sheriff Urquhart even filmed a commercial supporting Measure 91, and polls found that he was the figure most associated with the campaign.

The opposition, under the banner of Vote No on 91, tried to undercut the broad support that Measure 91 enjoyed by featuring cannabis-infused edibles and products heavily in their media campaign, arguing that these products would fall into the hands of too many children. Its organizers also flew in mothers from Colorado to speak out against legalization in Oregon. Our counter was simple: the campaign put together our own mothers group, featuring then–Clackamas County Commissioner Ann Lininger and a collection of local mothers advocating for regulating all marijuana sales as a way to shut down the unregulated, illicit market.

Our strategies gained their final, and most important, confirmation on election eve. Within minutes of the polls closing, we knew that we had secured an impressive victory. The early returns, usually consisting of older and more rural voters, came in at just over 50 percent "yes" votes. That percentage kept climbing throughout the night and was boosted over the next few days as votes in our campaign's stronghold, Multnomah County, were finally tabulated. Not only had Measure 91 locked in 56.1 percent of the vote, but that level of support represented the largest margin of victory for any of the four states to have legalized cannabis thus far. Yet those other states' successes were among the reasons that

Beaver State voters were so supportive of Measure 91. The results in Oregon, in turn, likely helped propel other states' legalization campaigns, not least in neighboring California, which, with the world's sixth-largest economy (Respaut 2016), is also the world's largest cannabis market.

Following legalization in Oregon, the Oregon legislature got to work passing legislation to implement the new regulated system. Some changes, such as reducing the number of plants that medical marijuana growers could cultivate per address, were opposed by many Measure 91 campaign members and supporters, including myself. Legislators also passed some historic, progressive provisions that pleased advocates, including further reductions of criminal penalties for marijuana offenses and the ability of previous offenders to retroactively expunge their old legal transgressions. The progressive criminal justice reforms garnered national attention (Rivero 2015), led to the introduction of marijuana expungement federal legislation by Representative Blumenauer (Holley 2015), and certainly didn't hurt (Holmes 2016), setting the stage for California's 2016 legalization measure, Proposition 64, to include similar provisions (Steinmetz 2016).

Oregon advocates like myself, with an eye toward national politics, were certainly cognizant that Oregon's implementation of marijuana regulations could impact the states voting to end prohibition in 2016 (California, Nevada, Arizona, Massachusetts, and Maine), with the California Proposition 64 election looming as a potential major turning point in the national fight against the War on Drugs (Margolin 2016). Like Colorado and Washington before the Oregon vote, the news out of Oregon could sway undecided Golden State voters, although Colorado was still likely to have the most influence (Tvert 2015).

California's top marijuana regulator, Lori Ajax, stated that other states' experiences provide some lessons for her state, but that California would forge its own path on marijuana, when she spoke at the International Cannabis Business Conference in San Francisco on February 17, 2017 (Krieger 2017). Oregon and California, as West Coast neighbors, will continue to impact each other, with California's massive economy casting a large sphere of influence over the Beaver State and the entire nation. It will be interesting to see how Oregon's strict cannabis testing standards, making the state's regulated marijuana "safer than food," will influence California's testing regime. Conversely, California's Proposition 64 provision that allows localities to permit on-site cannabis consumption (Associated Press 2017) will likely influence the ongoing cannabis consumption debate in Oregon (Ditzler 2017).

A cooperative relationship between the two states is already evident as Oregon Democrat Earl Blumenauer joined forces with California Republican Dana Rohrabacher to found the Congressional Cannabis Caucus (Green 2016) to work on sensible cannabis policies at the federal level. As Rohrabacher, Blumenauer, and their allies in Congress work to pass sensible cannabis legislation, California and Oregon advocates will be natural allies to improve banking access for state-regulated marijuana businesses, reform the 280e tax code as it applies to state-licensed cannabis business expenses, and eventually end federal prohibition altogether (Matthews and Wallace 2017). With marijuana legalization experiencing majority support in national polling (Swift 2016) and in states like Oregon (Crombie 2016b) that have legalized marijuana, the future of the cannabis community in Oregon, California, and the rest of the nation should be very bright in the coming years.

WORKS CITED

ACLU. 2013. "The War on Marijuana in Black and White." American Civil Liberties Union. https://www.aclu.org/report/war-marijuana-black-and-white.

ACLU of Oregon. 2013. "Marijuana Arrests and Citations on the Rise in Oregon." American Civil Liberties Union of Oregon. http://www.aclu-or.org/content/marijuana-arrests-and-citations-rise-oregon.

Associated Press. 2017. "Most Legal States Don't Allow Cannabis Consumption in Designated Public Places." *Civilized*, February 3. https://www.civilized.life/articles/most-legal-states-still-dont-allow-cannabis-consumption-in-public-places/ (accessed February 20, 2017).

Bacca, A. 2015. "Paul Stanford: 40-Year Cannabis Activist Reflects on Legalization." *Cannabis Now Magazine*, December 6. http://cannabisnowmagazine.com/current-events/legal/paul-stanford-40-year-cannabis-activist-reflects-on-legalization.

Bayer, R. 1998. Oregon Secretary of State archives. *Library of the Oregon Secretary of State*. http://library.state.or.us/repository/2010/201003011350161/ORVPGenMari1998m.pdf.

Belville, R. 2012. "MPP's Rob Kampia Warns Oregon Not to Try Marijuana Legalization in 2014." *Huffington Post*, November 29. http://www.huffingtonpost.com/russ-belville/oregon-marijuana-legalization_b_2201395.html.

———. 2013. "Only One-Third of Likely 2014 Oregon Voters Oppose Marijuana Legalization." *Huffington Post*, May 22. http://www.huffingtonpost.com/russ-belville/voters-oppose-marijuana-legalization_b_3322137.html.

Common Sense for Drug Policy. 2014. "Doug McVay, Director of Research and Editor of Drug War Facts." Common Sense for Drug Policy. http://www.csdp.org/cms/doug_mcvay#sthash.fZFYT4T9.dpbs.

Crombie, N. 2012. "What's Next for Oregon Medical Marijuana in an Era of Legalization?" *Oregonian: Oregonlive*, December 30. http://www.oregonlive.com/health/index.ssf/2012/12/whats_next_for_oregon_medical.html.

———. 2013. "Oregon Seen as Next Battleground for Marijuana Legalization." *Oregonian: Oregonlive*, January 27. http://www.oregonlive.com/politics/index.ssf/2013/01/oregon_seen_as_next_battlegrou.html.

————. 2014. "Marijuana News: Oregon's Proposed Recreational Pot Measure Starkly Different from Washington's Law." *Oregonian: Oregonlive,* October 6. http://www.oregon live.com/marijuana/index.ssf/2014/10/marijuana_news_oregons_propose.html.

————. 2015. "Oregon Proposes Higher Medical Marijuana Fees." *Oregonian: Oregonlive,* December 15. http://www.oregonlive.com/marijuana/index.ssf/2015/12/oregon_pro poses_higher_fees_fo.html.

————. 2016a. "Oregon Has Collected $6.84 Million in Recreational Pot Taxes since January." *Oregonian: Oregonlive,* April 20. http://www.oregonlive.com/marijuana/index .ssf/2016/04/oregon_collects_684_million_in.html.

————. 2016b. "Poll: Most Oregonians View Legal Pot Favorably 2 Years after Vote." *Oregonian: Oregonlive,* September 16. http://www.oregonlive.com/marijuana/index .ssf/2016/09/poll_most_oregonians_view_lega.html (accessed February 20, 2017).

Ditzler, Joseph. 2017. "Cannabis Clubs Could Be Coming." *Bend Bulletin,* February 16. http:// www.bendbulletin.com/business/5076150-151/story.html (accessed February 20, 2017).

Graham, D. 2014. "Are Pot Reformers Too Optimistic? The View from 1977." *Atlantic,* April 14. http://www.theatlantic.com/politics/archive/2014/04/are-pot-reformers -too-optimistic-the-view-from-1977/360441.

Green, Johnny. 2016. "Congressional Cannabis Caucus to Be Launched with Bipartisan Support in 2017." *Weed News,* December 10. http://www.weednews.co/congressional -cannabis-caucus-to-be-launched-with-bipartisan-support-in-2017/ (accessed February 20, 2017).

Holley, Claire. 2015. "US Rep. Earl Blumenauer Wants to Take Oregon's Weed-Crime Expungement National." *Willamette Week,* July 17. http://www.wweek.com/portland /blog-33481-u-s-rep-earl-blumenauer-wants-to-take-oregons-weed-crime-expunge ment-national.html (accessed February 20, 2017).

Holmes, Steve. 2016. "Stigma Follows Those Convicted of Cannabis Crimes, but New Laws Offer Some Hope." *Source Weekly,* August 31. http://www.bendsource.com/bend /stigma-follows-those-convicted-of-cannabis-crimes-but-new-laws-offer-some-hope /Content?oid=2754188 (accessed February 20, 2017).

Jones, J. 2015. "In US, 58% Back Legal Marijuana Use." *Gallup,* October 21. http://www .gallup.com/poll/186260/back-legal-marijuana.aspx.

Kampia, R. 2012. "The 10 Things That Led to Legalized Marijuana in Colorado." *Huffington Post,* November 26. http://www.huffingtonpost.com/rob-kampia/colorado-mar ijuana_b_2139163.html.

King, B. 2010. "The Hemperor, Jack Herer, Has Died." *Salem News,* April 15. http://www .salem-news.com/articles/april152010/jack_herer_died.php.

Krieger, Lisa M. 2017. "Six New Things We Learned from California's Cannabis Czar." San Jose, CA, *Mercury News,* February 17. http://www.mercurynews.com/2017/02/17/6 -new-things-we-learned-from-californias-cannabis-czar/ (accessed February 20, 2017).

Margolin, Madison. 2016. "The Pot Law That Could Be 'Deal-Breaker for the Drug War.'" *Rolling Stone,* July 5. http://www.rollingstone.com/politics/news/the-pot-law -that-could-be-deal-breaker-for-the-drug-war-20160705 (accessed February 20, 2017).

Matthews, Mark K., and Alicia Wallace. 2017. "Cannabis Caucus Ready to Roll in Con-

gress." *Cannabist,* February 16. http://www.thecannabist.co/2017/02/16/cannabis
-caucus-congressional-colleagues-legalized-states-join-forces/73784/ (accessed February 20, 2017).

McKenna, R. 2011. Letter re: Initiative #502. *New Approach Washington,* July 15. http://
www.newapproachwa.org/sites/newapproachwa.org/files/I-502%20%28mari
juana%29%20BT%20and%20Summary.pdf.

Melton, K. 2010. "Measure 74 Would Allow Medical Marijuana to Be Sold Legally in
Oregon and Create More Regulation." *Oregonian: Oregonlive,* October 5. http://www
.oregonlive.com/politics/index.ssf/2010/10/measure_74_would_make_medical.html.

New York Times Editorial Board. 2014. "Yes to Marijuana Ballot Measures: Alaska, Oregon,
and the District of Colombia Should Legalize Pot." *New York Times,* October 5. http://
www.nytimes.com/2014/10/06/opinion/alaska-oregon-and-the-district-of-columbia
-should-legalize-pot.html?_r=0.

Oregon Blue Book. 2016. Initiative, Referendum, and Recall: 1996–1999. http://blue
book.state.or.us/state/elections/elections22.htm.

Oregonian Editorial Board. 2010. "Another Dance around Marijuana." *Oregonian: Oregonlive,* July 25. http://www.oregonlive.com/opinion/index.ssf/2010/07/another_dance
_around_marijuana.html.

———. 2012. "Vote No on Measure 80, Oregon's Marijuana Manifesto: Editorial Endorsement." *Oregonian: Oregonlive,* September 22. http://www.oregonlive.com/opinion
/index.ssf/2012/09/measure_80_vote_no_on_oregons.html.

———. 2014. "It's Time to Legalize Recreational Marijuana: Editorial Endorsement." *Oregonian: Oregonlive,* August 23. http://www.oregonlive.com/opinion/index.ssf/2014/08
/its_time_to_legalize_recreatio.html.

Oregon Medical Marijuana Program. 2016. Oregon Medical Marijuana Program Statistics. Oregon Health Authority. https://public.health.oregon.gov/diseasesconditions
/chronicdisease/medicalmarijuanaprogram/pages/data.aspx.

Oregon Police Chiefs for Safer Communities. 1998. *Oregon Voters Pamphlet, Arguments in Favor
of Measure 57.* http://library.state.or.us/repository/2010/201003011350161/ORVP
GenMari1998m.pdf.

Oregon Secretary of State. 2012. Initiative 9 text. OregonVotes.org. http://oregonvotes.
org/irr/2012/009text.pdf.

Parks, C. 2012. "Jantzen Beach's 'Lottery Row' Will Remain after Oregon Lottery Commission Pulls Proposed Limits." *Oregonian: Oregonlive,* August 5. http://www.oregonlive
.com/portland/index.ssf/2012/08/jantzen_beachs_lottery_row_wil.html.

Respaut, Robin. 2016. "California Surpasses France as World's Sixth-Largest Economy." Reuters, June 17. http://www.reuters.com/article/us-california-economy-idUS
KCN0Z32K2 (accessed February 20, 2017).

RestoreHemp. 2011. "Moment in History: 1985 Oregon Marijuana Initiative Petition Signature Turn-in." YouTube. https://www.youtube.com/watch?v=MTrN_uVev3k.

Rivero, Daniel. 2015. "Pot Legalization in Oregon May Come with a Big Perk." *Fusion,*
July 14. http://fusion.net/story/166376/oregon-marijuana-legalization-perk (accessed
February 20, 2017).

Selsky, A. 2016. "More Than a Year after Oregon Voters Approved Marijuana for Recreational Use, the Ground Is Still Shifting on Pot." *U.S. News & World Report,* May 14. http://www.usnews.com/news/us/articles/2016-05-14/marijuana-legalization-still-contentious-in-oregon-counties.

Steinmetz, Katie. 2016. "What to Know about Marijuana Legalization in California." *Time,* November 9. http://time.com/4565438/california-marijuana-faq-rules-prop-64/ (accessed February 20, 2017).

Stroup, K. 2001. "Which States Have Decriminalized Marijuana Possession?" *Slate,* February 14. http://www.slate.com/articles/news_and_politics/explainer/2001/02/which _states_have_decriminalized_marijuana_possession.html.

SurveyUSA. 2012. Results of SurveyUSA Election Poll #19677. SurveyUSA, September 13. http://www.surveyusa.com/client/PollReport.aspx?g=f35f6734-8377-4585-bb0e -a1a5fc418199.

Swift, Art. 2016. "Support for Legal Marijuana Use Up to 60% in US" Gallup, October 19. http://www.gallup.com/poll/196550/support-legal-marijuana.aspx (accessed February 20, 2017).

Tvert, Mason. 2015. "Five Lessons for California on Marijuana Legalization." *San Francisco Chronicle,* April 24. http://www.sfchronicle.com/opinion/openforum/article/5-lessons-for-California-on-marijuana-legalization-6220242.php (accessed February 20, 2017).

VanderHart, D. 2014. "Slow Burn: A Pot Supporter Is Stymieing Our Best Shot at Legal Weed." *Portland Mercury,* March 12. http://www.portlandmercury.com/portland/slow -burn/Content?oid=11946670.

Warner, J. 2015. "Marijuana Legalization 2015: As Legal Pot Spreads, NORML, the Nation's Oldest Marijuana Advocacy Group, Faces Uncertainty." *International Business Times,* June 3. http://www.ibtimes.com/marijuana-legalization-2015-legal-pot-spreads-norml-na tions-oldest-marijuana-advocacy-1940478.

Washington Poll. 2012. KCTS 9 Washington Poll. WashingtonPoll.com, October 16. http://www.washingtonpoll.org/results/kcts9wapoll_oct18.pdf.

CHAPTER 11

"This Is Democracy Held Hostage"

Cannabis in the Capital

Karen D. August and Char Miller

The District of Columbia (DC) is a long way from the Emerald Triangle of Northern California. The three counties that constitute the triangle—Mendocino, Humboldt, and Trinity—are thought to be the single largest marijuana producing region in the United States and home to some of the nation's earliest advocates for legalization of the drug. The district is also distant from those sites of political contest where powerful grassroots and national reform organizations—some of which are featured in this book—fought first to secure ill patients access to marijuana's medicinal qualities and then successfully battled to decriminalize recreational use in four western states: Colorado, Washington, Oregon, and Alaska.

Although the West may drive the national narrative about the processes and politics of legalization, the District of Columbia has not been removed from these struggles. Indeed, medical marijuana is legal in DC, as is recreational use. Yet how activists there achieved these two victories in the face of overwhelming odds depends on an understanding of DC's peculiar and fraught relationship with Congress, its colony-like status in the heart of the republic, a subordination that led the American Civil Liberties Union—which has played a key role in some of the court challenges that paved the way for decriminalizing marijuana in the capital—to declare the district the "Last American Plantation" (ACLU 2000). The ACLU's rhetorical jab was a calculated response to Congress's effort in 1998 to suppress the results of Initiative 59, the district's first attempt to legalize medical marijuana. Dubbing Congress's interference an example of "tinpot democracy," it alleged that this marked "the first time in this nation's history [that] an election was canceled for fear of its outcome" (ACLU 2000). While this was not the first time that voters' rights had been suppressed in DC or elsewhere, this particular incident in 1998—along with other episodes that this chapter probes—makes clear that securing the legal right to use marijuana in DC has imposed a level of difficulty no other similar movement in the United States has had to confront. DC campaigners have also forged a very different set of strategies than those routinely deployed around the country. Not surprisingly, the drive to legalize marijuana in the district has been bound up with a larger demand for political rights and social justice.

THE DISTRICT OF COLUMBIA: A BRIEF HISTORY

The need to establish a national capital was a key feature in the debates surrounding the crafting of the US Constitution and was formally incorporated in that foundational text in Article I, Section 8:

> To exercise exclusive Legislation in all Cases whatsoever, over such District (not exceeding ten Miles square) as may, by Cession of particular States, and the Acceptance of Congress, become the Seat of the Government of the United States, and to exercise like Authority over all Places purchased by the Consent of the Legislature of the State in which the Same shall be, for the Erection of Forts, Magazines, Arsenals, dock-Yards, and other needful Buildings.

Much about this original text was open for negotiation. The new states of Maryland and Virginia ceded land for the creation of the new federal district, to be called Columbia, and the city, to be named Washington. The District of Columbia Organic Act of 1801 would set the boundaries using the ceded land and formally established federal control over the entire region—the citizens became District of Columbia constituents as they were no longer citizens of either Virginia or Maryland; ultimately the land from Virginia was returned to that state in 1846. In 1871 Congress developed a local governance scheme for the district that it then revised three years later, establishing a three-member board of commissioners that was responsible for governing the district. A century later, in 1973, Congress enacted the District of Columbia Home Rule Act, which gave a limited range of power to the district government. Since then, the district governmental structure has included a mayor, a thirteen-member council, and an attorney general specific to the district, each of whom is an elected official. The district is represented by a nonvoting at-large congressional delegate to the US House of Representatives but has no representation in the US Senate. In 1961 the Twenty-Third Amendment granted three electoral votes to the district, giving the residents representation in the presidential election process. Despite these many alterations in its physical space and political governance, DC's subordinate status to Congress has not changed since the founders wrote Article I, Section 8 of the US Constitution. Not only has Congress maintained its exclusive jurisdiction over the district but its purview is comprehensive—extending from budgets and policing to lawmaking. One troubling consequence of this relationship is that residents of the District of Columbia, who have no voting representation in either the US Senate or the US House of Representatives, are nonetheless "represented" by politicians with absolute, unchecked oversight of district policies and politics. A pointed reference to this discriminatory situation, and a phrase that amounts to the district's unofficial motto, is embossed on local license plates: Taxation without Representation.

These inequities are underscored when set within the context of the city of Washington, DC. Home to just over 672,000 residents, as of 2014 it was the twenty-second-largest city in the United States. Daily commuters increase its population to nearly a million during the workweek. It is also a strikingly diverse community. In 2014, African Americans constituted 46 percent of the population, non-Hispanic whites were roughly 30 percent, Hispanics were a bit more than 10 percent, and Asians were 3 percent. Like most other American cities, beginning in the 1960s DC's central core lost population, a consequence of white flight to the suburbs. One result was that in the 1970s, African American residents constituted nearly 70 percent of the population; that percentage declined in the succeeding decades in part because more African Americans moved to nearby suburbs within commuting distance. Since 2010 the district's population has slowly rebounded—also like most US cities. One reason for this is gentrification, a process that has also altered some of the city's demographic percentages, bringing with it increases in those identifying as white and declines in those identifying as African American. What has remained unchanged is that the federal government is DC's largest employer; as of 2016 it provided 29 percent of district jobs. That federal presence is made manifest in the fact that the twenty-second-largest city is the ninth-largest media market in the United States. Surely this outsize presence is a reflection of its status as the national capital and the site of its three iconic and photogenic structures—the White House, the Capitol, and the Supreme Court.

Because Congress maintains full authority over DC, district law-making processes are quite different there than in most cities or states, as has been evident in matters routine and controversial. To start, bills that are brought to the DC council are assigned to a council committee with expertise to review the bill. There is no obligation to consider the bill, and if no action is taken for a period of two years the bill dies. If the bill is reviewed favorably it then moves to public hearings where residents and officials may comment. If the committee continues to support the proposed legislation, it moves forward to the Committee of the Whole—comprised of all thirteen council members. At this point, if supported, it will move to a council agenda to be reviewed at a council meeting. If the bill survives this meeting, it is put on the agenda one last time at least fourteen days after the first meeting and if approved is then forwarded for mayoral approval. Once the mayor approves, the bill is given an act number and is sent to Congress for its approval. An act must be reviewed by the US Senate and the House of Representatives within thirty days before becoming codified. This congressional review period may extend as long as sixty days if the legislation is criminal in nature. If Congress objects to the act, a joint resolution may be enacted and upon presidential approval would effectively bar that act from becoming law. This joint-resolution disapproval may come about regardless of election outcomes in the district or official positions taken by district officials. Time and again, Congress has used its oversight authorities to strike down, frustrate, or squelch the will of district voters concerning marijuana legalization—medical or recreational.

INITIATIVE 59 AND THE BARR AMENDMENT

In November 1998 district residents voted on Initiative 59, the Legalization of Marijuana for Medical Treatment Initiative of 1998. In language similar to that of other states that earlier had passed such legislation (Arizona and California), and of those states such as Oregon and Washington that succeeded in legalizing medical marijuana that same year, the DC initiative would permit

> all seriously ill individuals to obtain and use marijuana for medical purposes when a licensed physician has found the use of marijuana to be medically necessary and has recommended the use of marijuana for the treatment (or to mitigate the side effects of other treatments) of diseases and conditions such as HIV/AIDS, cancer, glaucoma and any other serious or chronic illnesses for which the recommending physician reasonably believes that marijuana has demonstrated utility.

Even before the election was held, however, Congress pushed back. That October, Representative Bob Barr (R-GA) slipped into the annual congressional omnibus appropriations legislation a stealth provision that read: "None of the funds contained in the [DC Budget Act] may be used to conduct any ballot initiative which seeks to legalize or otherwise reduce the penalties associated with the possession, use or distribution of any Schedule I substance under the Controlled Substances Act of any tetrahydrocannabinols (THC) derivative."

The provision passed both houses of Congress, leading Wayne Turner, who directed the Initiative 59 campaign, to fume: "This is democracy held hostage" (Lee 2012, 275). Congress's actions immediately prompted a lawsuit from the initiative's backers and the ACLU that was heard in US District Court in December. The ACLU attorneys argued that Barr's amendment was a clear violation of the First Amendment, launching, in its words, "a preemptive strike against the DC electorate: if voters are intent on enacting these laws, the Barr Amendment simply cancels voters' ability even to consider such laws" (ACLU 2000). While awaiting a ruling, the DC ballots were not counted and would not be until September, when Circuit Court Judge Richard Roberts concurred with the plaintiffs. In a ruling released in September 1999, Roberts concluded that to "cast a lawful vote only to be told that that vote will not be counted or released is to rob the vote of any communicative meaning whatsoever; the vote would be a muzzled expression and a meaningless right." Not surprisingly, when finally tabulated, Initiative 59 had received 69 percent of the vote—a high level of support, similar to the margins of victory achieved in other states where voters had approved medical marijuana laws.

This victory was short-lived. In the summer of 1999, as Congress drafted a new omnibus appropriations bill, Representative Barr once again placed language in its text that prohibited the expenditure of federal and local funds to "enact and carry out" Initiative 59 in the district. Twice President Bill Clinton vetoed the appropriations legislation due to its excessive interference in DC's affairs; but to avoid a fiscal crisis, the president signed a third such bill, which also contained Barr's provisions undercutting Initiative 59 (Rubens 2014).

INITIATIVE 63: ROUND TWO

In hopes of forcing the issue, in July 2001 the Marijuana Policy Project (MPP) submitted a new medical marijuana initiative to the District of Columbia council that would become Initiative 63: the Medical Marijuana Initiative of 2002. The MPP is a grassroots organization based in Washington, DC, dedicated to the decriminalization of marijuana; it has helped to spearhead campaigns for medical marijuana in a number of the twenty-five states where medical marijuana has been approved and in those where recreational marijuana has been legalized. Its successes elsewhere did not immediately translate into getting Initiative 63 on the ballot. The DC council rejected the proposal based on the congressional marijuana ban embedded in the 2000 omnibus appropriations legislation. In response, the MPP brought suit against the federal and district governments, claiming that Barr's amendment was a direct violation of First Amendment rights. Arguments were heard in federal court in February 2002, and the court's ruling, siding with the MPP, came the following month. By June 2002 over 39,000 signatures had been collected, a sufficient number to have placed Initiative 63 on the November ballot. The US Court of Appeals for the DC Circuit, however, reiterated the provisions within Barr's amendment, successfully preventing Initiative 63 from moving forward. To keep this or any other similar proposal off the DC ballot, Representative Barr and his successors continued to insert his amendment in every appropriations bill until 2009; that year, following the election of Barack Obama, the House and Senate stopped employing this text to keep the district under its control. In so doing, Congress effectively lifted the ban on medical marijuana development in the district; however, it was not until 2013 that the first patient purchased marijuana as medicine at a local dispensary.

INITIATIVE 71: ONCE MORE INTO THE VOID

Proponents of recreational marijuana had not been idle as the fight over medical marijuana unfolded. In January 2014 the homegrown DC Cannabis Campaign, with considerable support for national marijuana-reform organizations, submitted what would become Initiative 71 to the DC Board of Elections and Ethics. After two months of public hearings, the board finalized its short title—"Legalization of Possession of Minimal Amounts of Marijuana for Personal Use Act of 2014"— and published its summary statement that demonstrated the legislation's careful crafting: if passed, the law would enable a person twenty-one years or older to

- possess up to two ounces of marijuana for personal use;
- grow no more than six cannabis plants, with three or fewer being mature, flowering plants, within the person's principal residence;
- transfer without payment (but not sell) up to one ounce of marijuana to another person 21 years of age or older; and
- use or sell drug paraphernalia for the use, growing, or processing of marijuana or cannabis.

Among its most noteworthy provisions, wrote *Slate* commentator Mark Kleiman on the day of the vote, was a potentially new way to regulate and manage sales of legal marijuana. Initiative 71 "embodies a different—and perhaps better—approach to cannabis legalization than the laws already in effect in Colorado and Washington State, or the similar laws that Oregon and Alaska voters might adopt," he argued. Unlike these other entities, which had drafted legislation similar to those governing the sale and distribution of alcohol and tobacco, and which privileged "private, for-profit production and sale, regulated and taxed by the state," Initiative 71 would not allow or foster the growth of commercial production or sales. "District residents will be able to grow a limited number of plants, possess a limited amount of the resulting cannabis, and give away—but not sell—whatever they don't want to smoke themselves. The system is called 'grow and give'" (Kleiman 2014a). DC voters supported this proposed system in large numbers; Initiative 71 gained roughly 70 percent of the vote.

Once again, Congress undercut DC voters' will. This time, Representative Andy Harris (R-MD) successfully introduced a congressional rider that prohibited the District of Columbia from using city funds to "enact any law, rule, or regulation" to legalize recreational use of marijuana. At the time, Eleanor Holmes Norton, the district's nonvoting delegate to the House of Representatives, complained that she had been locked out of the decision-making process completely (Davis and O'Keefe 2014). Her complaints fell on deaf ears, as did the trenchant comments of DC council representative David Grasso: "It's been the same thing over and over and over," he told National Public Radio. "Congress thinks that they can meddle in our business and basically use us as a sort of petri dish where they do things to us that they could never possibly do in their own jurisdiction—they'd be thrown out." Their hypocrisy was galling, he asserted: "Most Republicans want less federal government, they want less intrusion, yet here they are, every single day of the year, thinking about how they can mess with us. They're just purely hypocritical, but that's no surprise" (Austermuhle 2015).

What happened next was unprecedented. Delegate Norton and other DC politicians argued that the congressional rider's language—and the timing of its passage—provided the district with a loophole that they then exploited. Taking her cue from Democratic negotiators who had pared down the omnibus rider's original prohibition from "enact and carry out" to "enact," Norton noted that district voters had already "enacted" Initiative 71 when they voted for it on November 4; moreover, the congressional prohibition did not occur until after the election's results had been certified (Norton, n.d.). In early January 2015, DC council chairman Phil Mendelsohn dispatched the Initiative 71 legislation to Congress as required by the Home Rule Charter, which started the clock on the national legislature's thirty-day review period (Davis 2015). He dismissed suggestions that his action was provocative—"I'm not trying to defy anybody," he assured reporters. "I have a very clear requirement in the Home Rule Act to transmit the legislation" (Bowman 2014). Despite Republican threats to take legal action against the city, in fact Congress did not reject the initiative, as it could have done. At 12:01 a.m. on February 26, 2015, the provisions of Initiative 71 became law. In this rare case, the murky machinations that have enabled Congress to dominate the District of Columbia worked to its advantage, a startling turnaround.

RACE AND POT

One critical reason for the local success of Initiatives 56, 63, and 71 was their advocates' recognition of the inequities embedded in the criminal justice system and their desire to shift those dynamics as best they could through their efforts to decriminalize marijuana. Historically the District of Columbia has been home to a large number of African Americans. US Department of Justice statistics demonstrate that African Americans living in DC serve prison time for property, drug, and weapons offenses at three times the national average (Wilkins 1998). More chilling, African Americans are incarcerated at thirty-six times the rate of whites, and the result is that 50 percent of African American males aged eighteen to thirty-five in the district are either in prison or under the supervision of the criminal justice system (ibid.). These dispiriting data have helped frame the enduring fight over marijuana legalization in the district. A 2013 ACLU report cited the District of Columbia as having the highest arrest rates for marijuana—higher than in all fifty states (Nelson 2013). District residents were arrested at a rate of 846 per 100,000, considerably higher than the 535 per 100,000 in the next highest state, New York. Every state has had higher arrest rates for blacks than whites, and the difference between them increased in thirty-eight states and in DC in the decade between 2000 and 2010. In fact, more than 90 percent of those arrested nationally for marijuana offenses were black (Nelson 2014).

Although these rates are reflective of targeted law enforcement efforts, they also show that the Nixon-era War on Drugs remains formative in shaping how many law-enforcement agencies—local, state, and national—secure funding and pursue their agenda. As Mason Tvert, the MPP's director of communications, told *U.S. News & World Report*: "Discrimination against communities of color played a role in [marijuana prohibition laws] and it continues to play a role in their enforcement" (Nelson 2013). Malik Burnett of the Drug Policy Alliance said of congressional efforts to block legalization in the district: "By attempting to keep in place the criminal penalties for possession of marijuana, Congress is saying that they want more people of color to go to jail" (PR Newswire 2014). By stressing these issues to DC voters, particularly the "outsized number of arrests of African Americans on minor drug charges," the local campaign pursued a strategy different from that in Colorado, Oregon, and Washington, where questions of racial justice proved less central to legalization; in those states, the Associated Press noted, "voters are mostly white and their campaigns focused more on other issues" whereas the "race factor hits closer to many more homes in the District, where nearly half the population is black." This facet of the successful Initiative 71 campaign, mused Bill Piper, director of national affairs at the Drug Policy Alliance, might "set off a chain of events in which communities of color generally

Figure 11.1. Artist Mike Flugennock produced this image for the DC Cannabis Campaign in 2014, and it served as the campaign's website masthead; its subject and location demonstrate the campaign's conviction that legalization would help lessen the racial inequities embedded in the criminal justice system.

and cities in particular take on the issue of legalization as a racial justice, social justice issue in a much stronger way than they have so far" (Associated Press 2014).

THE BODY POLITIC SHIFTS

Like peer campaigns in the western states, the DC initiatives and their organizers also have benefited from a long-term evolution in the public's perception of drug enforcement. To understand this shift, as many of the chapters in this volume indicate, the Nixon era was particularly important because it established a baseline against which to judge the transformation in attitudes toward legalization of marijuana. In 1970 Congress passed the Controlled Substances Act. As a result of this legislation, five categories of drugs were created based on medical application, side effects, and the potential for abuse. The most restricted category is Schedule 1, which includes heroin, LSD, and marijuana. The scheduling of marijuana as a Schedule 1 drug means there is no accepted medical use and there is a high propensity for abuse. The scheduling also prevents medical research from being conducted that would empirically prove the efficacy or its lack for clinical applications. Several amendments have been passed to the Controlled Substances Act, but none has changed the current listing of marijuana as a Schedule 1 substance (Rubens 2014). As a result, marijuana possession, sales, and cultivation can garner the most severe penalties in federal court (Titus 2016).

The political environment, if not the law, has been changing. Cracks in what had amounted to a rigid opposition to marijuana—medical or recreational— began to appear in the first decades of the twenty-first century. None was more startling than former Representative Bob Barr's change of heart. In 2008 he ran as the Libertarian Party's presidential candidate, and as part of his conversion he renounced his earlier steadfast opposition to legalizing marijuana. "Today, I can reflect on my efforts and see no progress in stopping the widespread use of drugs," he declared in a *Huffington Post* commentary. "I'll even argue that America's drug problem is larger today than it was when Richard Nixon first coined the phrase, 'War on Drugs,' in 1972" (Barr 2008).

Successful state initiatives in Colorado, Washington, Oregon, and Alaska even more powerfully altered the situation on the ground and in Washington, DC. Most noteworthy perhaps is that these states' election results forced the Obama administration to reconsider its approach to drug-law enforcement. In October 2009, Eric Holder, then the US attorney general, established the foundation for a more hands-off approach to medical marijuana. This was expressed in the October 2009 "Ogden memo" that set up formal guidelines for federal prosecutors in states that had enacted laws authorizing medical marijuana: "Rather than developing different guidelines for every possible variant of state and local law, this memorandum provides uniform guidance to focus federal investigations and prosecutions in these States on core federal enforcement priorities" (Ogden 2009). Holder clarified the memorandum's significance, assuring the *New York Times*: "It will not be a priority to use federal resources to prosecute patients with serious illnesses or their caregivers who are complying with state laws on medical marijuana. But we will not tolerate drug traffickers who hide behind claims of compliance with state law to mask activities that are clearly illegal" (Stout and Moore 2009). Even though Holder's successor, Loretta Lynch, opposed marijuana legalization during her confirmation hearings held in January 2015, she also indicated that she would follow the Ogden memo's guidelines (Glenza 2015). As a result, variation in federal enforcement of particular aspects of marijuana production, distribution, and use will continue until such time as the drug's Schedule 1 status is revised (Titus 2016). For Paul Armentano, deputy director of the National Organization for the Reform of Marijuana Laws, that alteration may come sooner rather than later: "The genie is already out of the bottle, and it cannot be put back in" (Gwynne 2013).

IS GRASS A CASH COW?

Another driver in legalization campaigns across the United States is the potential for high revenues from taxation, licensing, and regulation of the new industry. In 2015 Colorado hauled in $135 million in revenues from the green rush, triple the amount generated in the preceding year (Baum 2016; Vaida 2015). These revenues have been dedicated to underwriting pensions, school construction, law enforcement, and health-care initiatives, among others. In its first three years, Washington State's excise tax on marijuana brought in $250 million (Washington State i502 Recreational Marijuana Sales 2016), and Oregon, which was projected to bring in a modest $2–$3 million in 2016, took in $10.5 million in the first three months alone; state economists there offered a revised prediction that the 2016 total might reach $43 million (Crombie 2016), funding destinations that have been short-changed of late in many states. These real-time figures, and the (perhaps) inflated claims that nationwide legalization and resulting taxation might generate $20 billion annually, make clear why some states are taking a very close look at the revenue potential of decriminalizing the drug. "To those real gains," observes Mark Kleiman, a professor of public policy at New York University, "must be added the political lure that comes without raising taxes on currently legal products or incomes"—an almost irresistible combination (Kleiman 2014b).

This tantalizing greenback allure has not yet been realized in the District of Columbia. Because of Initiative 71's "grow and give" provision, there was no mechanism for the commercial growing and sales of marijuana in the city, and thus no means by which the often cash-strapped jurisdiction can raise funds through its taxation. As of summer 2016, this situation had not changed, though that spring four councilmembers introduced legislation to create the regulatory framework that would enable the district "to register and regulate marijuana cultivators, product manufacturers, retail stores, and testing labs and to impose taxes on the sale of marijuana to adults 21 and older." Advocates were exploring other mechanisms that would allow the city to secure the power to tax marijuana while working around congressional prohibitions (Marijuana Policy Project 2016). This approach received a major boost in March 2016, when a Superior Court judge upheld the district's 2013 Budget Autonomy Act, which granted the city the power to spend local funds without congressional oversight (Kurzius 2016a); the ruling, one activist asserted, is "a positive step for cannabis. The taxing and licensing of marijuana social clubs seems like the next logical step, and that would be based on budget autonomy" (Kurzius 2016b).

MARIJUANA, POLITICAL IDENTITY, AND STATEHOOD

Given the peculiarities of the District's constitutionally mandated relationship with Congress, which has done so much to complicate the efforts of residents of the district to legalize marijuana, DC's history provides no sustained roadmap for other jurisdictions seeking to make pot legal. That said, there are two important lessons to be drawn from DC's experience. By making the legalization of marijuana a matter of social justice, the DC campaign built a larger and more inclusive movement. One of the intended consequences of its success is reflected in the 93 percent decline in arrests for marijuana, which fell from 5,756 in 2011 to a mere 266 in 2015. The data is not yet available to determine whether this dramatic drop also rectified the overwhelming racial disparities evident in the disproportionate number of African Americans who in the past police have busted for distribution and possession; but if so, this would signal a vital transformation in law enforcement that other legalization campaigns might well adopt in their strategic appeal to voters (Kurzius 2016b). By also tying Initiative 71 to local demands for greater political enfranchisement, marijuana advocates in DC may have done something even more important than simply legalizing recreational use. They may have opened the eyes of their fellow Americans who live in states that their compatriots residing under the shadow of the gleaming Capitol do not share in the full blessings of democracy, a disturbing realization that in time might spark another movement—statehood for the district. "Without it," argued legal scholar Jamin B. Raskin in 1989, "the citizens of the District cannot be fully incorporated into the national community" (Raskin 1990, 434). Surely there is no little irony that the fight to legalize marijuana has raised anew his concluding query: "The real question to be posed is not whether the citizens of the District are committed to democracy, but whether the rest of the country is in fact committed to democracy for the citizens of the District" (ibid., 440).

WORKS CITED

ACLU (American Civil Liberties Union). 2000. *Democracy Held Hostage.* https://www.aclu
.org/democracy-held-hostage.
Associated Press. 2014. "Race Turns DC Pot-Legalization Debate into Social Justice Issue."
SFGate, October 13. http://www.sfgate.com/news/article/Race-turns-D-C-pot-legal
ization-debate-into-5819983.php.
Austermuhle, M. 2015. "Voters Said Yes, But DC and Congress Continue to Spar over
Pot." National Public Radio, January 21. http://www.npr.org/2015/01/21/378844795
/voters-said-yes-but-d-c-and-congress-continue-to-spar-over-pot.
Barr, Bob. 2008. "I Was Wrong about the War on Drugs—It's a Failure." *Huffington Post,* June
18. http://www.huffingtonpost.com/bob-barr/i-was-wrong-about-the-war_b_106249
.html.
Baum, D. 2016. "Legalize It All: How to Win the War on Drugs." *Harper's Magazine,* April.
http://harpers.org/archive/2016/04/legalize-it-all/.
Bowman, B. 2014. "DC Council Chairman: Marijuana Rider Doesn't Block Transmittal to
Congress." *Roll Call,* December 16. http://www.rollcall.com/news/home/d-c-council
-chairman-pot-rider-does-not-block-transmittal-to-congress.
Crombie, N. 2016. "Oregon on Track to Collect $43 Million in Pot Taxes This Year." *Or-*

egonian: Oregonlive, May 23. http://www.oregonlive.com/marijuana/index.ssf/2016/05 /oregon_collected_105_million_i.html.

Davis, A. C. 2015. "Obama Budget Would Clear Path for Legal Sales of Recreational Marijuana in DC." *Washington Post*, February 2. https://www.washingtonpost.com /local/dc-politics/obama-budget-would-allow-recreational-pot-use-in-dc/2015/02 /02/93461e52-ab06-11e4-ad71-7b9eba0f87d6_story.html?tid=a_inl.

Davis, A. C., and E. O'Keefe. 2014. "Congressional Spending Deal Blocks Pot Legalization in DC." *Washington Post*, December 9. https://www.washingtonpost.com/local/dc-pol itics/congressional-budget-deal-may-upend-marijuana-legalization-in-dc/2014/12/09 /6dff94f6-7f2e-11e4-8882-03cf08410beb_story.html.

Glenza, J. 2015. "Attorney General Nominee Loretta Lynch Opposes Marijuana Legalisation." *Guardian*, January 28. https://www.theguardian.com/us-news/2015/jan/28 /attorney-general-nominee-loretta-lynch-opposes-marijuana-legalisation.

Gwynne, K. 2013. "Legalization's Biggest Enemies." *Rolling Stone*, January 17. http://www .rollingstone.com/politics/news/legalizations-biggest-enemies-20130117.

Kleiman, M. 2014a. "How Not to Make a Hash out of Cannabis Legalization." *Washington Monthly*, March/April/May. http://washingtonmonthly.com/magazine/marchapril may-2014/how-not-to-make-a-hash-out-of-cannabis-legalization.

———. 2014b. "The Other Way to Legalize Marijuana." *Slate*, November 14. http:// www.slate.com/articles/news_and_politics/politics/2014/11/d_c_marijuana_legal ization_initiative_71_is_going_to_pass_and_could_show.html.

Kurzius, R. 2016a. "Court Rules the District Should Control Its Own Damn Money." *DCist*, March 21. http://dcist.com/2016/03/superior_court_says_dc_council_shou .php.

———. 2016b. "Report: If Weed Sales Become Legal in DC, Recreational Market Could Reach Nearly $100 million in 2020." *DCist*, March 29. http://dcist.com/2016/03/re port_dc_marijuana_market_100_million.php.

Lee, Martin. 2012. *Smoke Signals: A Social History of Marijuana—Medical, Recreational, and Scientific*. New York: Scribner.

Marijuana Policy Project. 2016. District of Columbia. May 8. https://www.mpp.org /states/district-of-columbia/.

Nelson, S. 2013. "ACLU Marijuana Study: Blacks More Likely to Be Busted." *U.S. News & World Report*, June 4. http://www.usnews.com/news/newsgram/articles/2013/06/04 /aclu-marijuana-study-blacks-more-likely-to-be-busted.

———. 2014. "DC Votes to Legalize Marijuana." *U.S. News & World Report*, November 5. http://www.usnews.com/news/articles/2014/11/05/dc-votes-to-legalize-marijuana.

Norton, E. H. n.d. Frequently Asked Questions on Implementing DC's Marijuana Legalization Initiative. http://norton.house.gov/initiative71.

Ogden, D. W. 2009. Memorandum for Selected United States Attorneys on Investigations and Prosecutions in States Authorizing the Medical Use of Marijuana. US Department of Justice, October 19. https://www.justice.gov/opa/blog/memorandum-select ed-united-state-attorneys-investigations-and-prosecutions-states.

PR Newswire. 2014. "DC Cannabis Campaign Collects over 55,000 Signatures to Place Marijuana Legalization on the Ballot." *TheStreet*, June 30. https://www.thestreet.com /story/12760897/1/dc-cannabis-campaign-collects-over-55000-signatures-to-place -marijuana-legalization-on-the-ballot.html.

Raskin, J. B. 1990. "Domination, Democracy, and the District: The Statehood Position." *Catholic University Law Review* 39: 417–440.

Rubens, M. 2014. "Political and Medical Views on Medical Marijuana and Its Future." *Social Work in Public Health* 29: 121–131.

Stout, D., and S. Moore. 2009. "US Won't Prosecute in States That Allow Medical Marijuana." *New York Times*, October 19. http://www.nytimes.com/2009/10/20/us/20can nabis.html?_r=1.

Titus, D. 2016. "Puff, Puff, Pass . . . That Law: The Changing Legislative Environment of Medical Marijuana Policy." *Harvard Journal on Legislation* 53: 39–58.

Vaida, J. H. 2015. "The Altered State of American Drug Taxes." *Tax Lawyer* 68: 761–793.

Washington State i502 Recreational Marijuana Sales. 2016. Washington Marijuana. http://www.502data.com/.

Wilkins, R. L. 1998. "Federal Influence on Sentencing Policy in the District of Columbia: An Oppressive and Dangerous Experiment." *Federal Sentencing Reporter* 11: 143–148.

CHAPTER 12

Cannabis Legalization in California

A Long and Winding Road

Amanda Reiman

Many people assumed that the approval of cannabis use in California was a given, mostly due to the 1960s hippie movement that overtook the San Francisco Bay Area, and the hazy aura that seemed to envelop that moment. However, cannabis legalization in the Golden State has never been a sure thing. From decriminalization and medical cannabis access to marijuana becoming viewed as a legal infraction similar to a parking ticket, Californians have been inching closer to legal weed for upwards of forty years. This chapter will explore the history of the cannabis movement in California, with a focus on the period from 1996 to the present. It was in 1996, after all, that California, via voter initiative, became the first state to implement the medical use of cannabis, effectively ending the federal government's forty-year prohibition of the plant. This was just the beginning. A legislature that refused to act and create a state-level regulatory system, combined with an already burgeoning cannabis industry subject to piecemeal regulations, left cannabis policy in California as ambiguous as ever. A failed attempt at legalization in 2010 had many asking, "Will cannabis ever be legal in California?" An answer came in November 2016, with the passage of Proposition 64, the Adult Use of Marijuana Act. Yet its passage comes with additional questions, not least whether this state—and others—will be forced to respond to a more aggressive Trump administration's eagerness to enforce the still-extant federal laws that have criminalized the use and possession of marijuana.

THE LANDSCAPE LEADING TO THE PASSAGE OF PROPOSITION 215

Cannabis became decriminalized in California in 1975 via SB 95, the Moscone Act, making possession of less than an ounce a nonarrestable offense for adults (Aldrich and Mikuriya 1988). This was partially due to the overt, widespread use of cannabis in the state in the 1960s by otherwise law-abiding citizens (i.e., white suburban teenagers). As the Free Love movement slowly dissipated into the more party-intensive and risky disco culture of the 1970s and the early 1980s, another community was becoming more visible in San Francisco: HIV-positive gay men (Katz 1997). The incorrect beliefs surrounding the illness (that you could get it from hugging, breathing the same air, etc.) often meant that those with the disease experienced social isolation, even from those closest to them. Even in the hospital, HIV patients were quarantined and allowed little social interaction. There was, however, one woman who volunteered in the AIDS ward at San Francisco General Hospital who made it her mission to care for those left to die. Her brand of care was unique. Relying on a medical treatment for nausea and lack of appetite thousands of years old, "Brownie" Mary Rathburn regularly delivered cannabis-laced brownies to AIDS patients at San Francisco General, until she was arrested for a third time in 1992 (Pimsleur 1999).

The optics of an elderly hospital volunteer being arrested for baking brownies for terminally ill patients was moving. However, the softening and empathy infused into the social perception of cannabis would not have evolved into policy change had it not been for another San Francisco resident, Dennis Peron. Peron's partner was one of the many struggling with the symptoms of HIV in San Francisco in the early 1990s. Akin to a scene in the *Dallas Buyers Club,* Dennis opened up his home to those with HIV as a place to use a substance that many found to be life-saving: cannabis. Peron's home was more than a makeshift pharmacy; it was the beginning of a movement melding the healing aspects of cannabis with the empowering aspects of community. Individuals who had been marginalized due to their sexual orientation and health status came together and became a political force in the city of San Francisco. (It is a force that can still be felt today, as San Francisco continues to be one of the most progressive cities in the state on the issue of medical cannabis and LGBTQ rights.) To ensure that his community was not subject to arrest—specifically those suffering from AIDS who used marijuana for pain relief—Peron placed Proposition P on the ballot in San Francisco in 1991, a nonbinding declaration that urged the city to support the use of marijuana for medical purposes (Peron and Entwistle 2012). The public agreed, and Proposition P passed in November 1991 with 79 percent of the vote (Californians for Compassionate Use 1991).

Emboldened by the move in San Francisco and cities that followed, such as Santa Cruz, advocates for the use of cannabis began discussing how to make medical cannabis a statewide issue. The first strategy was to pass a bill through the legislature. Bills were introduced during legislative sessions by State Senator Milton Marks and Assemblyman John Vasconcellos, but they were eventually vetoed by Governor Pete Wilson at the close of the session (Bailey 1997). Unable to make progress in the state legislature, activists such as psychiatrist Tod Mikuriya and Dale Gieringer from the California chapter of the National Organization to Reform Cannabis Laws (NORML) in 1995 started Californians for Compassionate Use, a political action committee developed for the purpose of bringing a proposition legalizing medical cannabis to the voters. To secure the signatures needed to make the ballot, the campaign was given financial support from a group of philanthropists including George Soros. After a contested election in 1996, voters approved Proposition 215. This partnership of activism and philanthropy succeeded in achieving, by a vote of 55.6 percent, the first state-level medical cannabis law. The proposition was simple. It added Section 11362.5, which included three provisions, to the California Health and Safety Code: First, that people who were using, possessing, or cultivating cannabis would be exempt from cannabis prohibition if they had a recommendation from a physician. Second, that physicians could not be punished for recommending cannabis; and third, that the new law did not override cannabis prohibition in terms of diversion or public protection. What the proposition did not do was establish a state-level system for licensing commercial cannabis activities or a state registry for patients.

THE STRUGGLE TO REGULATE POST–PROPOSITION 215

Given that Proposition 215 did not establish a regulatory system, legislators in Sacramento (California's capital) were tasked with developing one. Cannabis voters passed Proposition 215 with the assumption that in the months following its passage, rules would be developed about who could grow and distribute medical cannabis, how patients would be able to identify themselves, and how law enforcement was to treat this activity that was now in conflict with federal law. However, given that this was the first time any state legislature was asked to develop rules such as these, there was much disagreement on what this program should look like. Since the beginning of this task, localities, law enforcement, and the cannabis industry itself have been consistent barriers to regulation at the state level.

Localities in California that were not in favor of medical cannabis wanted the ability to ban activity within their borders, a right that was not afforded in Proposition 215 and, patients argued, would in fact violate the access that the initiative assured to them. Some localities were proactive in their medical cannabis regulations. San Francisco, Oakland, and Berkeley developed local regulations regarding the number and placement of cannabis distribution almost immediately (Drug Policy Alliance, n.d.). As a result, the longer the legislature stalled on passing regulations, the more these cities wanted the regulations to be compatible with their already established frameworks. Another twist in the road came in 2013 when Los Angeles, which had largely turned a blind eye to the thousands of dispensaries that had opened in the absence of local regulation, passed Measure D, allowing limited immunity to the dispensaries open before 2007. This left the city with the nearly insurmountable task of shutting down the thousands that are no longer allowed to operate under this new measure (Associated Press 2013). Given that immunity is not the same as licensure, Los Angeles demanded that any state regulatory bill include a carve-out for the largest city in the state. Law enforcement also stalled the process by refusing to participate in the development of regulations and adamantly opposing whatever was brought to them under the grounds that cannabis is federally illegal (Hecht 2014). Another barrier to regulation was a direct result of the inaction in Sacramento; the burgeoning cannabis industry proved a hindrance, too. Had the legislature acted in 1997, its ability to regulate the industry would have been exponentially easier than it is twenty years later. Companies that have been in operation for two decades are not nearly as malleable now because they have political power and capital in their own right, including lobbyists. Furthermore, only certain cannabis activities have been the subject of regulation at the local level; to date, local regulation has focused almost exclusively on distribution, with little (if any) attention paid to cultivation and manufacturing. Twenty years ago, farmers and manufacturers were not politically active. Now, organizations like the California Growers Association and the California Cannabis Industry Association spend a lot of time in the state capitol ensuring that their interests are reflected in any legislation being considered. On top of these pressure-groups' influence is the fact that California politics makes passing even the blandest legislation a challenge due to the vast diversity and size of the population. Over twenty years after the passage of Proposition 215, California still has not implemented a state-level regulatory system for medical cannabis.

That does not mean that California is completely devoid of medical-cannabis regulation at the state level. In 2003, Senate Bill 420 was signed into law (State of California 2003), thereby clarifying a legal question that Proposition 215 had not resolved. Although Proposition 215 gave doctors the ability to recommend medical cannabis and patients the right to grow their own medicine and to collectively cultivate that medicine with immunity from state-level cannabis laws, it was not clear whether patients were required to actively participate in the cultivation of the cannabis or could instead become members of a collective. Some localities had already decided that collectives were permissible, and storefront dispensaries had been licensed in Oakland, Berkeley, and San Francisco. Senate Bill 420 codified that belief into law, and storefront dispensaries began to proliferate throughout the state. Many localities, overwhelmed with the challenge of regulating them without any help from the state and on cash-strapped local budgets, banned dispensaries entirely. This furthered the divide on the issue in Sacramento and made consensus on state-level regulations even more difficult.

A kind of consensus appears to have emerged in the run-up to the 2016 elections. Figures such as Lieutenant Governor Gavin Newsom are leading the charge for full legalization, and there has been a renewed fervor in the capital and among medical cannabis advocates to establish a state-level regulatory system. Newsom, along with the ACLU, has convened a blue-ribbon commission for the purpose of studying the best policies for regulating cannabis in California (ACLU 2013; Mehta 2015). From the regulatory perspective, reining in medical cannabis before full-blown legalization is implemented made sense because it allowed regulators to test strategies on a smaller, more contained market and has even brought law enforcement to the table for the first time on this issue (Leff 2015). Furthermore, keeping medical and adult-use programs separate may have helped to address the differing needs of the public and patient populations. There are several reasons for this. First, states that pass adult-use laws might not require testing and product standards at the level considered necessary for medical use by those with serious illnesses. There is concern that the adult-use market will cap potency per package and the high-potency concentrates that seriously ill patients rely on. Patient activists also worry that a combined program will not make the financial allowances necessary to ensure access for economically vulnerable patients. They argue that those who are most in need, with expensive medical treatments and an inability to work, will be most impacted by having to purchase their medicine in a combined market, even with a patient tax break, due to the high rate at which adult-use cannabis is taxed (Ruke 2014).

Of the four states (and the District of Columbia) that had legalized cannabis for adult use prior to November 2016, two of these entities—Oregon and Washington—did not have state-level medical cannabis regulatory programs when their adult use laws passed in 2014 and 2012. This resulted in a combining of the two programs. Colorado already had a robust state level medical-cannabis regulatory system when its voters passed adult use in 2012, therefore Colorado's medical and adult-use programs operate in tandem (National Conference on State Legislators, 2015). In Oregon and Washington, similar to California, in the absence of state regulation, informal networks of cultivation and distribution arose; also like California, regulation only existed in some localities and was largely focused on distribution. As the programs in Washington and Oregon meld into one, informal networks are required to become formal, licensed entities. Sometimes the move is seamless, such as a dispensary that has been operating with a license from their locality. For others, such as cultivators and patient collectives, the move to legitimacy has been far more difficult resulting in, according to some, a large disruption in access for patients in those states (Ruke 2014).

The lessons from Oregon and Washington, along with impending legalization in California, had Sacramento buzzing in 2015. The dilemmas were on display during that year's legislative session in California, during which three medical cannabis regulatory bills were introduced: two comprehensive bills (one in the Assembly and one in the Senate) and a cultivation-tax-and-regulation bill. Unlike years past, and perhaps due to what many assumed would be a successful campaign to legalize marijuana in 2016, law enforcement and the League of California Cities (an association of most of the state's 482 cities) supported medical cannabis regulations for the first time since Proposition 215 passed. Recognizing the importance of regulating medical cannabis, myriad interests participated in crafting the legislation, including the unions, farmers, cannabis business owners, and localities. In the end, the three bills were combined into one. The governor's office gutted that legislation and rewrote it behind closed doors so that none of the folks who originally had been at the table had an opportunity to see the bill's final language (Downs 2015a). In the end, on October 9, 2015, Governor Brown signed the legislation (McGreevy 2015). After nineteen years of "gray area" confusion, these regulations finally provide much-needed guidance to localities, law enforcement, and businesses around the provision of medical cannabis. It was also possible that the state regulatory system would embolden localities to move forward with regulations or overturn bans that were in place. However, concerns remained about discrimination against persons with prior convictions for cultivation of cannabis, and possession for sale, as these penalties fall overwhelmingly on low-income people of color.

LEGAL CANNABIS IN CALIFORNIA

Back in 2010, nearly fifteen years after the passage of Proposition 215, Californians received another chance to weigh in on the issue when Proposition 19, the Marijuana Legalization Initiative appeared on the ballot. The initiative was funded largely by Richard Lee from Oakland. Lee, confined to a wheelchair after a skiing accident, relied on medical cannabis and opened some of the first dispensaries in the country along with founding Oaksterdam University, the first cannabis trade school, also located in Oakland. Lee contributed $1 million of his own money to gather enough signatures to put the proposition on the ballot (McKinley 2009). The campaign was not funded enough to make much noise after achieving ballot status and was hindered by its presence in a nonpresidential election year, which tends to draw older, more conservative voters. It was also apparent that the public was still very wary of legalization, as some of the antiquated "reefer madness" arguments about youth and public safety dominated the discourse. The final nail in the coffin for Proposition 19 came when Governor Arnold Schwarzenegger made possession of less than an ounce of cannabis an infraction, punishable by a traffic ticket, in the months leading up to the election (Condon 2010). This took the wind out of the sails of the campaign, as many voters felt this went far enough. However, the Proposition 19 campaign offered some important priming for the legalization efforts to come. The fact that the issue was discussed in venues such as parent-teacher association meetings and by groups such as the League of Women Voters and Young Republicans as a viable policy shift, did much to lay the groundwork for Colorado and Washington in future years (Hoeffel 2010). In the end, Proposition 19 garnered 46.5 percent of the vote (Secretary of State's Office 2011).

Proposition 19 was also a very important organizing opportunity for California's cannabis advocates. The proposition of legalization forced many groups to think about their place in a regulated market. Cannabis farmers, who had long stayed out of the spotlight and preferred anonymity, began to organize into groups like the California Growers Association. Dispensaries and product manufacturers realized that, in a legal market, they are just like any other industry and, in an effort to protect their interests and encourage self-regulation and standards within the industry, organized as the California Cannabis Industry Association. The unions saw the potential for an enormous newly legal workforce and started a medical cannabis division within the United Food and Commercial Workers Union with the website cannabisworkers.org. Venture capital firms such as ArcView started entertaining questions and interest from investors about the impending green rush, and CEOs of California cannabis companies in operation since shortly after Proposition 215 passed began exerting their power as shapers of policy and the future industry. Meanwhile, activists and advocates who had spent decades trying to eliminate policies that criminalize cannabis activities, used to empty rooms and lack of attention, were suddenly finding themselves at a very crowded table.

PLAYERS IN THE LEGAL CANNABIS MOVEMENT

The impending legalization of cannabis in California was like blood in water to some people and threatened the way of life for countless others. These two sides exist in the context of a racist and classist war on drugs that has been the method of regulating cannabis up until now. Besides the cannabis-related interests described earlier, groups that have remained silent or on the periphery of the conversation began asserting themselves as 2016 moved closer. California is well known for its wine-growing regions. It is also well known for its cannabis growing regions, namely, the area in Northern California known as the Emerald Triangle. The cannabis produced in this region is regarded by many as the finest in the world. However, cannabis prohibition has had an impact on how this cultivation interacts with the environment. The Justice Assistance Grant (JAG) at the federal level provides funds for cannabis eradication in the Emerald Triangle, including helicopters and SWAT teams (US Department of Justice, n.d.). This legal response has pushed cultivation into public, tribal, and protected lands, encouraged hazardous practices such as the use of rodenticides and the diversion of rivers and streams, and has helped ensure that those unwilling to produce cannabis in these conditions are left out of the equation while those more than willing to cause harm are encouraged to exist. The emergence of the Emerald Grower's Association, which morphed into the California Growers Association, was important because it allowed those farmers wanting to work in harmony with the land, including transparent practices, to gain visibility. It also brought environmental advocacy groups and local regulators to the table to inform the conservation conversation. These groups understand that prohibition is a barrier to good environmental farming practices. They also understand that their best chance of funding the restoration of lands ravaged by unregulated cannabis farming could lie in the revenues collected under legalization (Harkinson 2014).

In the first six months of legalization, Colorado added 10,000 jobs to the market (Lopez 2014). Indeed, the already thriving cannabis industry in California employs millions of people, many of them young people. The opportunity for a new workforce complete with good wages and benefits has unions and labor groups excited. However, the continued disparity between state and federal law leaves the extent to which regulations can mandate union activity in question. Organizations that represent typically underemployed populations are eyeing the cannabis industry with great interest, as are communities that have been most impacted by the war on drugs.

Who will run the legal cannabis market? This is a question that is gaining steam, as the early market seems to be dominated by the status quo of well-financed white men. While this is not atypical of industry in America, it is a far cry from the demographic of those who typically work in the illicit cannabis market. As cannabis is not a new drug, cannabis production and sales is not new either. Until recently, cannabis has been solely controlled underground. And while it is no doubt that well-financed white men played a major role in financing this as well, the difference is that under prohibition, the young person of color selling cannabis on their behalf stood to be arrested, while under legalization this transaction would happen in a regulated store environment. But is this replication of the prevailing power dynamic something that we should accept? Many who work in the area of racial justice feel that those targeted by the War on Drugs should be first in line to run the new industry, not just find employment in it. So far, high application fees in medical cannabis and adult-use states have been barriers to equity within the industry, but this pattern can be disrupted. Groups like the Minority Cannabis Business Association and the California chapter of the NAACP have spoken out about the need to make a place for their communities at the forefront of the green rush (Downs 2015b). From the perspective of criminal justice reform organizations like the ACLU and the Drug Policy Alliance, this means fighting against regulations that bar those with criminal histories from obtaining licenses and advocating for regulatory language that reduces or eliminates criminal sanctions for cannabis activity.

While groups like environmentalists and labor advocates are fairly new to the table, one group that has been a consistent presence are the cannabis advocates themselves. Groups such as NORML, the Marijuana Policy Project (MPP), and Americans for Safe Access (ASA) have spent their organizational careers fighting for cannabis access and the elimination of penalties. But, as is common in the advocacy world, their strategies do not always align with each other. This is expected and understood at the organizational leadership level, but their constituencies often dramatize these differences and beliefs about what "good" legalization looks like to the point that the cannabis base is sometimes its own worst enemy.

IS UNITY POSSIBLE?

As the November 2016 election loomed, other states were closely watching whether California would legalize. If it did, the California cannabis market would dwarf the markets in the four currently legal states combined. It would also likely create a domino effect among other states considering legalization. Legalization in California also has enormous international implications. Currently, a 1961 treaty prohibits countries from legalizing illicit drugs except for research and medical purposes. Uruguay became the first country to break the treaty when it legalized cannabis for adult use in 2013. When the federal government decided to allow Colorado and Washington to implement their adult-use laws, the decision was defended to the United Nations as not being in violation of the treaty because the legalization happened at the state and not the federal level (Reuters 2014). Several countries, especially in South and Central America, would like to consider legalization in light of the horrific violence that has befallen their communities at the hands of prohibition (*Economist* 2012). If the US government allows legalization to be implemented, it will be hard to deny the right of other, smaller, international jurisdictions to legalize cannabis. The United Nations discussed this issue at its meeting in the fall of 2016 (International Drug Policy Consortium, n.d.).

The potential globalization of the California cannabis market as well as its sheer size has elicited the usual politicking from those who currently have the most to gain and/or lose from how the program is eventually structured—those who run cannabis businesses in California right now. The gray market has resulted in confusion but has also allowed many companies to grow, uninhibited by the usual regulations that are designed to slow growth and ensure a level playing field. Many first out of the gate in California's cannabis industry took on great risks, and now they are looking for their great reward in the form of priority licensing and control over the market via structures like vertical integration. The importance of this evolution of a high-risk cannabis industry in California was not lost on support- ers or opponents of legalization. In 2010, Proposition 19 saw very little funded opposition. Law enforcement has remained staunchly opposed to legalization but had very little capital to carry out its message. In fact, funded opposition stayed largely out of the game until Florida tried to pass a medical cannabis initiative in 2014. Then, Sheldon Adelson, gaming and substance-abuse-treatment billionaire, contributed $2.5 million to defeat the Florida initiative (Klas 2014). Given the impact that California would have on the discredited War on Drugs if it legalized marijuana, some advocates posited that a well-funded opposition could show up in 2016 ringing their "reefer madness" bells. Possible sources of opposition fund- ing were the drug-treatment industry, which currently obtains over 60 percent of its cannabis treatment population from the criminal justice system, and phar- maceutical and alcohol companies, which stand to lose revenue if more people have access to cannabis. Other sources of opposition include the prison industrial complex, law enforcement, and groups that oppose legalization on moral grounds (SAMHSA 2001; Ross 2014). Worrying activists too were the intense debates over regulations that would dictate the rules for the cultivation, manufacturing, test- ing, and distribution of cannabis; they feared that these squabbles would deflect attention from the role that legalization could play in unraveling the criminality that has resulted in thousands of Californians (disproportionally young people of color) being charged with cannabis-related felonies every year.

TAKING IT OVER THE FINISH LINE AND INTO UNCERTAINTY

As the initiative camps geared up for the 2016 election, many of the usual suspects were working assiduously to obtain their preferred outcome. California Cannabis Hemp Initiative, also known as the Jack Herer initiative, had collected signatures nearly every two years in an attempt to make the ballot and had yet to be success- ful. The initiative vowed to try again for 2016. The Marijuana Control, Legaliza- tion, and Revenue Act, a competing initiative, also planned to go for the ballot.

Activists, including many who had initiated and managed the Proposition 19 campaign, formed the Coalition for Cannabis Policy Reform and also drafted an initiative for the 2016 ballot (Warner 2015). What had plagued these efforts in the past was the lack of sufficient funding. Running a successful ballot initiative in a state as large as California can cost upwards of $20 million. There was also a concern that having more than one initiative on the ballot could spell trouble for legalization. Key to resolving these pressing financial issues was Sean Parker, Napster founder and tech billionaire, who showed a sustained interested in supporting a marijuana legalization initiative. To some, this was welcome news. Others worried that Parker's involvement was due to his self-interests and signaled a corporate takeover of cannabis (Roberts 2016). Another major player in the 2016 run for legalization was Lieutenant Governor Gavin Newsom. Previously Newsom had convened a blue-ribbon panel on marijuana legalization made up of experts to develop white papers on cannabis regulation in California (Cadelago 2015). The result of this convening was folded into an initiative draft that the Drug Policy Alliance largely wrote; it was modeled on the 2015 Medical Cannabis Regulation and Safety Act, with feedback and counsel from industry and public health and safety stakeholders. At the end of this process, the Sean Parker Initiative, as it was first called, became the Adult Use of Marijuana Act, which became Proposition 64.

Similar concerns resurfaced during the 2016 campaign for Proposition 64. Those who denounced the initiative claimed that youth access would increase, as would traffic accidents. Some of those who used cannabis claimed that legalization would enable a corporate takeover and that patients would end up disadvantaged. Proponents and the wide array of endorsers explained the impacts of prohibition on vulnerable populations and the importance of removing and reducing criminal penalties for cannabis activities (Reiman 2016). Moreover, and unlike the 2010 campaign, the 2016 campaign for Proposition 64 was well funded and utilized social media to enhance and spread what proved to be the winning message. Proposition 64 won with 57 percent of the vote (Ballotpedia 2016), but the celebration turned to uncertainty as the presidential picture became clear.

President Barack Obama had maintained a mostly hands-off policy when it came to states changing their marijuana laws. The election of Donald Trump, and the confirmation of his nominee for attorney general, Jeff Sessions, changed that dynamic. As of this writing, there has been considerable concern that legalization advocates in California and elsewhere might lose the gains they so recently achieved. Sessions is no fan of marijuana and stated during his confirmation hearing that it is not up to him to change federal law, just enforce it, and right now, marijuana is illegal under federal law (Huddleston 2017). It is clear that Sessions could decide to enforce federal marijuana law throughout the country. What is not yet clear is how states like California will respond to such threats. Looking at how California has responded to Trump's executive orders in the first weeks of his presidency, the Golden State likely will not go down without a fight.

California seems like a bastion of liberal ideals and progressive policies. No one was surprised that the state decriminalized marijuana for medical and then recreational use, yet it has been surprising that the Golden State was not the first state to go fully legal. However, when taking a closer look, it is apparent that California is a state of variable attitudes and morals with a penchant for local control and an ineffective legislature. Add to that an enormous cannabis industry that has been growing in a gray market for nearly two decades and the money and power that comes with the promise of a global market share, and the issue of cannabis legalization in California is exposed for the tangled web it really is.

WORKS CITED

ACLU (American Civil Liberties Union). 2013. "ACLU Announces Blue Ribbon Panel Led by Lt. Gov. Gavin Newsom to Study Cannabis Legalization in California." Press release, October 17. https://www.aclu.org/news/aclu-announces-blue-ribbon-panel-led-lt-gov-gavin-newsom-study-marijuana-legalization (accessed August 2, 2015).

Aldrich, M., and Mikuriya, T. 1988. "Savings in California Cannabis Law Enforcement Costs Attributable to the Moscone Act of 1976: A Summary." *Journal of Psychoactive Drugs* 20, 75–81.

Associated Press. 2013. "LA Voters Back Measure to Cap Number of Pot Shops." May 22, as posted on the *Boston Globe*: http://www.bostonglobe.com/news/nation/2013/05/22/voters-back-measure-cap-number-pot-shops/BGdGHAxD7CJWGSfSAsibCL/story.html (accessed August 2, 2015).

Bailey, E. 1997. "State Plan Urged for Supplying Medicinal Pot." *Los Angeles Times*, February 5. http://articles.latimes.com/1997-02-05/news/mn-25720_1_medical-marijuana (accessed August 1, 2015).

Ballotpedia. 2016. California Proposition 64, Marijuana Legalization. https://ballotpedia.org/California_Proposition_64,_Marijuana_Legalization_(2016) (accessed February 8, 2017).

Cadelago, C. 2015. "Gavin Newsom's Panel: Marijuana Should Not Be California's Next Gold Rush." *Sacramento Bee*, July 21. http://www.sacbee.com/news/politics-government/capitol-alert/article28073746.html (accessed February 8, 2017).

Californians for Compassionate Use. 1991. Press Release on Proposition P. http://www.cannabislibrary.org/Proposition_P_Nov_1991.html (accessed September 21, 2015).

Condon, S. 2010. "Schwarzenegger Reduces Charge for Cannabis Possession." *CBS News*, October 1. http://www.cbsnews.com/news/schwarzenegger-reduces-charge-for-cannabis-possession/.

Downs, D. 2015a. "California Lawmakers Regulate Medical Cannabis: Historic Deal Announced." *East Bay Express*, September 10. http://www.eastbayexpress.com/Legal

izationNation/archives/2015/09/10/california-lawmakers-regulate-medical-canna
bis-historic-deal-announced.

———. 2015b. "California NAACP Files Road Rules for California Cannabis Legalization
in 2016." *East Bay Express*, August 20. http://www.eastbayexpress.com/Legalization
Nation/archives/2015/08/20/california-naacp-files-road-rules-for-california-canna
bis-legalization-in-2016.

Drug Policy Alliance. n.d. "Cannabis and the Golden State." http://www.drugpolicy.org
/about-us/departments-and-state-offices/california/cannabis-and-golden-state.

Economist. 2012. "Burn-out and Battle Fatigue: As Violence Soars, So Do Voices of Dissent
against Drug Prohibition." March 17. http://www.economist.com/node/21550296.

Harkinson, J. 2014. "The Landscape Scarring, Energy Sucking, Wildlife Killing Reality
of Pot Farming." *Mother Jones.* http://www.motherjones.com/environment/2014/03
/cannabis-weed-pot-farming-environmental-impacts.

Hecht, P. 2014. "California Police Have No Interest in Setting Pot Rules." *Sacramento Bee*,
January 26. http://www.sacbee.com/news/state/california/california-weed/article25
89646.html (accessed August 2, 2015).

Hoeffel, J. 2010. "Measure to Legalize Cannabis Will Be on California's Ballot." *Los Angeles
Times*, March 25. http://articles.latimes.com/2010/mar/25/local/la-me-marijuana
-initiative25-2010mar25 (accessed August 17, 2015).

Huddleston, T. 2017. "What Jeff Sessions Said about Marijuana during His Attorney General Hearing." *Fortune*, January 10. http://fortune.com/2017/01/10/jeff-sessions-mar
ijuana-confirmation-hearing/ (accessed February 8, 2017).

International Drug Policy Consortium. n.d. "The UN General Assembly Special Session
on Drugs (UNGASS) 2016." http://idpc.net/policy-advocacy/the-un-general-assem
bly-special-session-on-drugs-ungass-2016.

Katz, M. 1997. "AIDS Epidemic in San Francisco among Men Who Report Sex with Men:
Successes and Challenges of HIV Prevention." *Journal of Acquired Immune Deficiency Syn-
dromes & Human Retrovirology* 14, S38–S46.

Klas, M. E. 2014. "Medical Cannabis Opponents Gain Money and Allies, Including Billionaire Sheldon Adelson." *Tampa Bay (FL) Times*, June 10. http://www.tampabay.com
/news/politics/stateroundup/medical-marijuana-opponents-gain-money-and-allies
-including-billionaire/2183785 (accessed August 1, 2015).

Leff, L. 2015. "California Seeks to Rein in Medical Pot Industry." Associated Press, August 25.
http://www.thecannabist.co/2015/08/24/california-medical-marijuana-legislation
/39789/ (accessed August 25, 2015).

Lopez, G. 2014. "Legal Cannabis Created Thousands of Jobs in Colorado." Vox.com, May 20.
http://www.vox.com/2014/5/20/5734394/legal-cannabis-created-thousands-of-jobs
-in-colorado.

McGreevy, P. 2015. "California Sets New Rules for Medical Pot Industry." *Los Angeles Times*,
October 9. http://www.latimes.com/local/political/la-me-pc-gov-brown-on-medical
-marijuana-regulations-20151009-story.html.

McKinley, J. 2009. "Push to Legalize Cannabis Gains Ground in California." *New York*

Times, October 27. http://www.nytimes.com/2009/10/28/us/28pot.html (accessed August 1, 2015).

Mehta, S. 2015. "Gavin Newsom Takes Risk by Seeking to Legalize Recreational Pot Use." *Los Angeles Times,* April 6. http://www.latimes.com/local/politics/la-me-pol-newsom-marijuana-20150403-story.html.

National Conference of State Legislators. 2015. State Medical Cannabis Laws, August 11. http://www.ncsl.org/research/health/state-medical-marijuana-laws.aspx (accessed August 15, 2015).

Peron, D., and J. Entwistle. 2012. *Memoirs of Dennis Peron: How a Gay Hippy Outlaw Legalized Cannabis in Response to the AIDS Crisis.* San Francisco: Medical Use Publishing House.

Pimsleur, J. L. 1999. "Mary Jane Rathburn, Popularly Known as Brownie Mary." *San Francisco Chronicle,* April 13, A19.

Reiman, A. 2016. "Prop. 64 Redux: How the West Was Won." *Freedom Leaf,* December 30. http://www.freedomleaf.com/west-won-prop-64/ (accessed February 8, 2017).

Reuters. 2014. "US States' Pot Legalization Not in Line with International Law: UN Agency." November 12. http://www.reuters.com/article/2014/11/12/us-usa-drugs-un-idUSKCN0IW1GV20141112.

Roberts, C. 2016. "Sean Parker Doubles Down on Marijuana Legalization: Still Won't Say Why." *SF Weekly,* February 16. http://archives.sfweekly.com/thesnitch/2016/02/16/sean-parker-doubles-down-on-marijuana-legalization-still-wont-say-why (accessed Feb-ruary 8, 2017).

Ross, P. 2014. "Cannabis Legalization: Pharmaceuticals, Alcohol Industry among Biggest Opponents of Legal Weed." *International Business Times,* August 6. http://www.ibtimes.com/cannabis-legalization-pharmaceuticals-alcohol-industry-among-biggest-opponents-legal-weed-1651166.

Ruke, K. 2014. "Medical Cannabis Users in Wash. Voice Concern over Legalization of Recreational Pot." *Mint Press News,* March 6. Retrieved: http://www.mintpressnews.com/medical-cannabis-users-in-wash-voice-concern-over-legalization-of-recreational-pot/185819.

SAMHSA (Substance Abuse and Mental Health Services Administration). 2001. "Admissions by Primary Substance of Abuse, According to Type of Service, Source of Referral to Treatment, and Planned Use of Methadone: TEDS 2001, Percent Distribution." http://wwwdasis.samhsa.gov/teds01/3_4.htm (accessed August 15, 2015).

State of California. 2003. "An Act to Add Article 2.5 (Commencing with Section 11362.7) to Chapter 6 of Division 10 of the Health and Safety Code, Relating to Controlled Substances." October 12. http://info.sen.ca.gov/pub/03-04/bill/sen/sb_0401-0450/sb_420_bill_20031012_chaptered.html (accessed August 15, 2015).

US Department of Justice. n.d. Justice Assistance Grant Program. https://www.bja.gov/ProgramDetails.aspx?Program_ID=59.

Warner, J. 2015. "California Marijuana Legalization 2016: With 10 Legalization Efforts Afoot in the Golden State, Which Is Most Likely to Pass?" *International Business Times,* November 4. http://www.ibtimes.com/california-marijuana-legalization-2016-10-legalization-efforts-afoot-golden-state-2166983 (accessed February 8, 2017).

Reading the Tea Leaves

Char Miller and Anthony Silvaggio

"To the red-and-blue map of American politics," the *New York Times* asserted in the run-up to the November 2016 elections, "it may be time to add green." That chromatic adjustment was in reference to the number of states that had already legalized recreational use of marijuana (four, plus the District of Columbia); that had legalized the medical use of the drug (twenty-five); and, more compellingly, the large number of states whose 2016 ballots included initiatives to allow either recreational or medical use (eight). Anticipating the potential outcomes of these elections, the newspaper drew two long-term conclusions. The first involved the possible challenge a series of statewide victories for marijuana reform might pose to the one-time national policy of prohibition: "The map of where pot is legal could include the entire West Coast and a block of states reaching from the Pacific to Colorado, raising a stronger challenge to the federal government's ban on the drug." The second ramification, it suggested, was more about economics than politics: the "passage of recreational marijuana laws in Alaska, Colorado, Oregon and Washington over the past four years may have unlocked the door to eventual federal legalization. But a yes vote in California, which has an economy the size of a large industrial country's, could blow the door open." Gavin Newson, lieutenant governor of California and a strong proponent of legalization, agreed that the Golden State's immense impact had domestic implications: "If we're successful, it's the beginning of the end of the war on marijuana." Yet he also suggested that there could be an equally powerful (and felicitous) international reaction: "If California moves, it will put more pressure on Mexico and Latin America writ large to reignite a debate on legalization there" (Fuller 2016).

The predicted short-term results came true, or at least largely so. California's Proposition 64 passed with 64 percent of the vote; Maine's Question 1 squeaked by with 50.3 percent; Question 4 in Massachusetts garnered 53.5 percent; and Nevada's Marijuana Legalization Initiative (Question 2) secured 54.5 percent of the vote. Only Arizona's initiative, which would have legalized recreational use, went down to defeat, losing 47.8 to 52.2 percent. As for the legalization of medical marijuana, voters in Arkansas, Florida, Montana, and North Dakota lined up in support of the relevant ballot measure, with the Sunshine State's Amendment 2 sailing through with an astonishing 71.3 percent. At one level, the November 2016 results were indeed what the *New York Times* and a number of other media outlets had suggested—a turning point in public discourse and policymaking about marijuana (Fuller 2016).

What is the electorate turning toward, though? This is an important query, given that marijuana legalization has demonstrated its capacity to fire up voters, drawing them into a cause that a decade ago seemed moribund; in 2006, 60 percent of Americans opposed legalization, but by 2016 that same percentage was in favor of it (Ingraham 2016). The question is also pressing for another reason: marijuana reformers and sympathetic legislators in other states, having witnessed the recently successful campaigns, almost immediately began mapping out ways that they too might promote legalization—recreational and/or medical. Within three months of the November 2016 election results, for example, upwards of seventeen additional states indicated serious interest in following the lead of Oregon, Colorado, and California. Among those that began debating legislative action were Connecticut, Hawaii, Maryland, Minnesota, New York, and Rhode Island. There and elsewhere, some state legislators, sensing that legalization had become a foregone conclusion, tried to get ahead of the curve by crafting initiatives that would enhance state control over the production, distribution, and sale of marijuana and its by-products. One of those "cannabis crusaders," Rhode Island state senator Josh Miller, told the *Los Angeles Times* in February 2017 that the moment Massachusetts voted for legalization, his legislative colleagues, who in the past had killed pro-pot laws in committee, started to change their minds (Lee, 2017). They were reacting as much to a February 2017 state poll indicating that nearly 60 percent of Rhode Islanders favored legalization as a political calculation of how much tax revenue the Ocean State might lose to its neighbor to the north. "We see legalization moving into the New England area and out here it's a very regional economy," Rhode Island House Representative Scott Slater, a cosponsor of Miller's legalization initiative, argued. "Why give Massachusetts all the benefit?"—a strategy masked as a question that may well account for why other New England and mid-Atlantic states moved so quickly to reconsider their formerly staunch opposition to the drug (Lee 2017). The future seems bright for those states eager to enjoy the benefits of becoming a "green light" district.

That optimism comes with some necessary caveats. States that have legalized recreational marijuana and raked in substantial financial windfalls—in 2016, Oregon earned $200 million from regulated marijuana sales and Washington pulled in more than $250 million; California anticipates an annual take of $1 billion—remain cautious about potential social costs and public health concerns. Every one of these states has voiced anxiety about shielding youth from too-easy access to marijuana (a rhetorical acknowledgment of that worry was evident in the short title to California's Proposition 64: The Adult Use of Marijuana Act). Every one of them has sought the counsel of Colorado governor John Hickenlooper, who opposed his state's successful legal-pot measure; because "we didn't regulate edibles strongly enough at first," Hickenlooper has noted, he has made it a point to urge public officials elsewhere to tightly control the sale of marijuana-infused lollipops, brownies, and gummy candies (Lee 2016). Moreover, every state that has legalized recreational and/or medical marijuana has run into the heavy burden that federal banking regulations impose: financial institutions face stiff penalties for doing business with any grower or dispensary of pot, creating an all-cash industry that limits its capacity to grow (and, not incidentally, generate tax revenues). Hickenlooper knows that the "old system, the War on Drugs, was a train wreck," yet has continued to be wary of assuming that its replacement is flawless: "It remains to be seen whether the new system is actually going to be better" (Lee 2016).

Washington State appears to have learned from some of Colorado's initial missteps. Local banks and insurance companies there have gambled that federal regulators "will leave the state-licensed production process alone or eventually move to incorporate it. Industry actors are advised to keep every scrap of state-generated official paper, under the theory that if culpability becomes a legal issue, it is somewhat diminished if companies were following state directives" (Jensen and Roussell 2016). Political scientists E. L. Jensen and A. Roussell observe that cannabis consumption in Washington is "certainly safer than it has ever been and an entire stream of criminal cases has been preempted", and they cite the ACLU's upbeat analyses revealing "a substantial drop in the number of cannabis-related misdemeanor court filings against adults." This set of achievements, however, does not represent a "panacea for racial disparity in the criminal justice system" (ibid.). Moreover, they conclude, the state's success is predicated on a particular set of calculations about who bears the burden of legalization:

The political compromise taking place in Washington State makes room for commodification and profit maximization while placing the onus on the individual to self-regulate. The taxation shifts have been largely in the service of profit redistribution, while the license-granting schema has benefitted venture capitalists unafraid of federal repercussions. Their gamble so far is paying off. State regulatory efforts are mainly geared toward preventing illegal diversion and thus the maintenance of profits in a manner that is politically supportable and minimizes state liability. Those adjudicated under the previous prohibition regime have not been addressed by this empowerment of capital interests. Producers, on the other hand, although considered "drug traffickers" at the federal level, are accumulating stakes in economic conformity as they build relationships with the federally insured banking system and carve out new niches within the national insurance sector.

Whether other states will adopt Washington's calibrated strategy remains an open question.

Uncertain, too, is how California's experiment with legalization will unfold and how influential its decisions will be during a post-prohibition era. Policymakers had heralded Proposition 64 (2016), which legalized recreational use of cannabis, as the environmental gold standard of cannabis legalization; and it is unique, in that it provides funding for conservation, restoration, and enforcement of environmental laws. Proposition 64 requires that cultivators prove they are in compliance with a variety of state and local environmental regulations, such as the California Environmental Quality Act, the California Endangered Species Act, and the Clean Water Act. While the proposition's passage creates a tax-and-regulatory framework estimated to generate billions in revenue, the chief challenge the state must surmount is how to develop and enforce a regulatory regime that will bring cultivators into compliance and protect the environment.

One fundamental problem of the current tax-and-regulate scheme is the regressive tax on cultivation. Cultivators, regardless of size, must pay an excise tax of 15 percent, as well as state cultivation taxes of $9.25 per ounce of flower and $2.75 per ounce of leaves they sell. Counties have also levied an additional square-footage tax that can range from $1 to $25 per square foot of cultivation on all legal cannabis cultivators. This is a unique levy: no other agricultural crop in California, such as grapes, almonds, or apples, is subject to a special square-foot tax. As a result, the cultivation and square-footage taxes will encourage cultivators to expand their operations to achieve more harvests annually through outdoor, indoor, and mixed light methods, thus increasing their demands on the environment and its resources and the energy grid (Smith 2016; Mohan 2016). County and city licensing and compliance fees are further barriers to entry for small sustainable cultivators, leaving only those with the financial resources (who in the past have been some of the most egregious violators of environmental laws) access to the regulated market.

An even more troubling environmental dimension of Proposition 64 is evident in what is categorized as a Type 5 license or permit; it removes the previous acreage-size limits set under the state's Medical Cannabis Regulation and Safety Act (2015) and allows for unlimited cannabis cultivation. Although this expansion can only occur after a five-year moratorium, this section of Proposition 64 sanctions the subsequent development of large-scale cannabis agriculture, which runs counter to the environmental directives embedded in other sections of the initiative. This is particularly unsettling because Californians have long experienced the serious environmental effects that come with expanded cultivation, nowhere more so than in the Emerald Triangle. Indeed, Humboldt County was one of the first jurisdictions to enact cannabis-cultivation regulations, but local critics alleged that its new land ordinance did not properly address the environmental impacts of large-scale cannabis cultivation, and promptly sued; "as part of the settlement agreement, the county agreed to conduct full environmental reviews for any changes to the ordinance" (Houston 2016).

This tension between environmental protection and revenue generation is complicated further by a lack of regulation to reduce energy consumption in the industry. With cannabis cultivation already accounting for at least 3 percent of the state's electricity usage (and 1 percent nationally), Pacific Gas & Electric's decision in the aftermath of Proposition 64 to extend its agricultural energy rate to commercial cannabis businesses will certainly intensify demand and increase carbon emissions (Arthur 2017; Mills 2012). As the leading supplier of cannabis in the nation, is it safe to assume that the postlegalization carbon footprint of the cannabis industry will become a bigger problem in the coming years.

As discussed throughout this volume, the reasons for environmental problems in cannabis agriculture and the solutions to them are not nearly as cut and dry as policy makers might lead us to believe. With the "green rush" in full swing (Mohan 2016), for Proposition 64's commitment to protecting the environment to have a chance of succeeding, California will need to do a better job incentivizing compliance with environmental regulations. The regressive tax, for example, should be replaced with a tiered progressive tax that would encourage compliance and level the playing field so small sustainable growers can compete in the market. In addition, cultivators who obtain the appropriate licenses and permits and reduce their ecological footprint should be given sizable state and county tax credits. To address the carbon footprint of the industry and encourage sustainable practices, a progressive carbon tax should be implemented to incentivize energy conservation and reduce waste. Finally, a moratorium on all Type 5 permits (unlimited size) should be put in place until federal prohibition is lifted.

Figure 13.1. Artist Mike Flugennock produced this poster for the DC Cannabis Coalition, January 2017, www.sinkers.org.

Lifting that prohibition became considerably more complicated on the same November day that Proposition 64 secured a healthy majority in California. Donald J. Trump's election as president offers a sharp reminder that however powerful the drive has been to enact legalization at the state level, these initiatives' success ultimately depends on who occupies the White House. In 2013 the Obama administration had relaxed enforcement of the Controlled Substances Act (21 USC § 811), which classifies marijuana as a Schedule 1 drug—signaling that it is highly addictive, on par with cocaine and heroin. That year, the Department of Justice (DOJ) released a memo that took into account the number of states that had legalized medical and recreational marijuana and indicated that it would not directly challenge these state actions, providing that they met the following guidelines (*New York Times*, August 30, 2013):

1. Preventing of distribution of marijuana to minors
2. Preventing revenue from the sale of marijuana from going to criminal enterprises, gangs, or cartels
3. Preventing the diversion of marijuana from states where it is legal under state law in some form to other states
4. Preventing state-authorized marijuana activity from being used as a cover or a pretext to traffic other illegal drugs or other illegal activity
5. Preventing violence or the use of firearms in cultivation and distribution of marijuana
6. Preventing drugged driving and the exacerbation of other adverse public health consequences associated with marijuana use
7. Preventing the growing of marijuana on public lands and the attendant public safety and environment dangers posed by marijuana production on public lands
8. Preventing marijuana possession or use on federal property

Any state that had passed legalization measures or was contemplating doing so has had little problem crafting legislation that would abide by these guidelines, allowing DOJ prosecutors to steer clear of differences in state and federal law.

Yet no sooner had Donald Trump been sworn in as president than officials in his administration signaled their intention to reverse the Obama administration's more laissez-faire approach to enforcement of federal antimarijuana law in those states that had legalized the drug. As of February 2017, the Trump administration seemed bent on reviving federal legal challenges to state authority. At his confirmation hearings, for example, Attorney General Jeff Sessions, a states' rights advocate when it comes to voter-suppression laws, among other racially charged legislation, adopted a prohibitionist stance consistent with his earlier assertions that "Good people don't smoke marijuana." His position was also in line with his claim in 2016 that "we need grown-ups in charge in Washington to say marijuana is not the kind of thing that ought to be legalized . . . that it is, in fact, a very real danger" (Huddlestone 2017). He made his case clear in his response to a question from Senator Mike Lee (R-UT) about whether as attorney general he would prosecute marijuana growers: "It is not the Attorney General's job to decide what laws to enforce" (ibid.). One month later, with Sessions confirmed, the White House issued a kind of split decision about its approach to the enforcement of federal marijuana laws. Trump administration officials conceded it would act in accordance with congressional legislation in 2014 and 2015 that prohibited the DOJ from using funds to prosecute medical users of marijuana. Prosecuting recreational use was another matter. White House press secretary Sean Spicer asserted that "there is still a federal law that we need to abide by in terms of recreational marijuana and other drugs of that nature" and promised that "you'll see greater enforcement" (Hughes 2017). If the promised federal crackdown occurs, then the $7 billion marijuana industry, along with the states that have legalized recreational marijuana, will defend their related interests in federal court. The outcome of any such set of legal skirmishes will go a long way to determining whether the public's substantial support for legalizing marijuana secures ongoing federal sanction, and whether the nation's electoral map continues to go green.

WORKS CITED

Arthur, D. 2017. "PG&E Gives Marijuana Growers Ag Electricity Rates." *Redding Record*, March 1. http://www.redding.com/story/news/2017/03/01/pge-gives-marijuana -growers-break/98611352.

Fuller, T. 2016. "Election May Be a Turning Point for Marijuana." *New York Times*, October 24. https://www.nytimes.com/2016/10/25/us/marijuana-legalization-ballot-measures .html?_r=1.

Houston, W. 2016. "HUMMAP: Humboldt County Violated Its Own Marijuana Rules." *Redwood Times News*, October 3. http://www.redwoodtimes.com/article/NK /20161003/NEWS/161009986.

Huddlestone, T., Jr. 2017. "What Jeff Sessions Said about Marijuana in His Attorney Hearings." *Forbes*, January 10. http://fortune.com/2017/01/10/jeff-sessions-marijuana -confirmation-hearing.

Hughes, T. 2017. "Cannabis Industry Roiled by White House Comments on Enforcement." *USA Today*, February 23. http://www.usatoday.com/story/news/nation/2017/02/23 /cannabis-industry-roiled-white-house-comments-enforcement/98323774.

Ingraham, C. 2016. "Support for Marijuana Legalization Surges to New High." *Washington Post*, October 19. https://www.washingtonpost.com/news/wonk/wp/2016/10/19/gallup -support-for-marijuana-legalization-surges-to-new-highs/?utm_term=.35a7537ec718.

Jensen, E. L., and A. Roussell. 2016. "Field Observations of the Developing Recreational Cannabis Economy in Washington State." *International Journal of Drug Policy* 33, July: 96–101. http://dx.doi.org/10.1016/j.drugpo.2016.02.023.

Lee, K. 2016. "Here's What Colorado's Governor Has to Tell Other States about Legalizing Marijuana." *Los Angeles Times*, December 16. http://www.latimes.com/politics/la-na-colorado-governor-marijuana-2016-story.html.

———. 2017. "Here's What's Driving Lawmakers Working to Legalize Recreational Pot in 17 More States." *Los Angeles Times*, February 21. http://www.latimes.com/nation/la-na-legal-marijuana-legislation-2017-story.html.

Mills, Evan. 2012. "The Carbon Footprint of Indoor Cannabis Production." *Energy Policy* 46: 58–67.

Mohan, G. 2016. "Here's Why Pot Growers Are Paying Millions for Old Greenhouses in the Salinas Valley." *Los Angeles Times*, November 7. http://www.latimes.com/business/la-fi-marijuana-salinas-snap-20161107-story.html.

New York Times. 2013. "Document: Justice Department Memo on Marijuana Enforcement." August 30. http://www.nytimes.com/interactive/2013/08/30/us/politics/30justice-marijuana-memo.html?_r=0.

Smith, P. 2016. "A Marijuana Land Rush Is Underway in Northern California." Alternet, June 4. http://www.alternet.org/drugs/marijuana-land-rush-northern-california.

About the Contributors

Karen D. August teaches courses in environmental sociology, social research methods, and criminology at Humboldt State University. Her master's thesis focused on marijuana growers in Northern California.

Dawn M. Blake is a wildlife biologist for the Hoopa Valley Tribe and is working toward an MS in wildlife biology at Humboldt State University.

Kelly S. Bricker is a professor and director of the Department of Parks, Recreation, and Tourism at the University of Utah. She has research and teaching interests in ecotourism, sense of place, community development, natural resource management, value of nature-based experiences, and the impacts of tourism. She has authored and edited books on sustainability that highlight case studies in tourism meeting environmental and societal issues.

Matthew T. J. Brownlee is an assistant professor in the Department of Parks, Recreation, and Tourism at the University of Utah and is coordinator of the natural resources recreation planning and management emphasis at the university.

Courtenay W. Daum is an associate professor of political science at Colorado State University and coeditor of *State of Change: Colorado Politics in the Twenty-First Century*.

Mourad W. Gabriel is executive director and senior ecologist at the Integral Ecology Research Center in Blue Lake, California; he studied wildlife ecology at Humboldt State University and the University of California, Davis.

J. Mark Higley is a wildlife biologist with Hoopa Valley Tribal Forestry.

Jared Huffman represents the North Coast of California in Congress, including the Emerald Triangle of Mendocino, Humboldt, and Trinity Counties. He served six years in the California State Assembly and was a senior attorney for the Natural Resources Defense Council.

Amos Irwin is the program director for the Law Enforcement Action Partnership. He served previously as chief of staff at the Criminal Justice Policy Foundation.

Anthony Johnson is the director of New Approach Oregon and was the chief petitioner of Measure 91, the Oregon Legalized Marijuana Initiative. He received his law degree from the University of Missouri–Columbia.

Char Miller is the W. M. Keck Professor of Environmental Analysis at Pomona College and the author of *America's Great National Forests, Wildernesses, and Grasslands*; *Not So Golden State: Sustainability vs. the California Dream*; *Seeking the Greatest Good: The Conservation Legacy of Gifford Pinchot*; and *Public Lands, Public Debates: A Century of Controversy*.

John Nores Jr., author of *War in the Woods: Combating the Marijuana Cartels on America's Public Lands*, is a California Department of Fish and Wildlife patrol lieutenant and has been a game warden for twenty-three years.

Amanda Reiman, PhD, MSW, has served as the policy manager for the Marijuana Law and Policy unit at the Drug Policy Alliance and conducted research on medical marijuana dispensaries and the use of marijuana as a substitute for alcohol and other drugs. She is a lecturer at the University of California, Berkeley in the Social Welfare Program.

Jeff Rose is an assistant professor-lecturer in the Department of Parks, Recreation, and Tourism and an affiliate faculty with the Global Change and Sustainability Center at the University of Utah.

Anthony Silvaggio is a lecturer in sociology at Humboldt State University and is on the faculty of the Humboldt Interdisciplinary Institute for Marijuana Research.

Hawes Spencer is an investigative reporter and editor living in Charlottesville, Virginia. As the founding editor of *The Hook*, he and his staff have earned 149 awards from the Virginia Press Association, including the association's top honor, the Journalistic Integrity and Community Service Award, three times.

Craig Thompson is a wildlife research ecologist with the US Forest Service, Pacific Southwest Research Station. His work focuses on sensitive species, the wildlife communities they exist within, and how these communities are impacted by human activities.

Greta M. Wengert is assistant director and senior ecologist at the Integral Ecology Research Center; she earned degrees in ecology at Cornell University and the University of California, Davis.

Index

Numbers in italics refer to tables and figures.